COSMOLOGY AND ESCHATOLOGY IN HEBREWS

Scholars argue over where Hebrews fits in the first-century world. Kenneth L. Schenck works towards resolving this question by approaching Hebrews' cosmology and eschatology from a text-orientated perspective. After observing that the key passages in the background debate mostly relate to the 'settings' of the story of salvation history evoked by Hebrews, Schenck attempts to delineate those settings by asking how the 'rhetorical world' of Hebrews engages that underlying narrative. Hebrews largely argues from an eschatology of two ages, which correspond to two covenants. The new age has come despite the continuance of some old-age elements. The most characteristic elements of Hebrews' settings, however, are its spatial settings, where we find an underlying metaphysical dualism between the highest heaven, which is the domain of spirit, and the created realm, including the created heavens. This creation will be removed at the eschaton, leaving only the unshakeable heaven.

KENNETH L. SCHENCK is Professor of Religion and Philosophy at Indiana Wesleyan University.

SOCIETY FOR NEW TESTAMENT STUDIES

MONOGRAPH SERIES

General Editor: John M. Court

143

COSMOLOGY AND ESCHATOLOGY IN HEBREWS

SOCIETY FOR NEW TESTAMENT STUDIES

MONOGRAPH SERIES

Recent titles in the series

Cosmology and Eschatology in Hebrews

The Settings of the Sacrifice

KENNETH L. SCHENCK

CAMBRIDGE
UNIVERSITY PRESS

CAMBRIDGE UNIVERSITY PRESS
Cambridge, New York, Melbourne, Madrid, Cape Town, Singapore, São Paulo, Delhi

Cambridge University Press
The Edinburgh Building, Cambridge CB2 8RU, UK

Published in the United States of America by Cambridge University Press, New York

www.cambridge.org
Information on this title: www.cambridge.org/9780521883238

© Kenneth L. Schenck 2007

First published 2007

Printed in the United Kingdom at the University Press, Cambridge

A catalogue record for this publication is available from the British Library

ISBN 978-0-521-88323-8 hardback

To Jimmy Dunn, Loren Stuckenbruck
and Hermann Lichtenberger, who started me on
this journey . . .

CONTENTS

ABBREVIATIONS

ALGHJ	Arbeiten zur Literatur und Geschichte des hellenistischen Judentums
AUSS	*Andrews University Seminary Studies*
BFCT	Beiträge zur Förderung christlicher Theologie
BGBE	Beiträge zur Geschichte der biblischen Exegese
Bib	*Biblica*
BZ	*Biblische Zeitschrift*
BZNW	Beihefte zur Zeitschrift für die neutestamentliche Wissenschaft
CBQMS	*Catholic Biblical Quarterly*, Monograph Series
CJT	*Canadian Journal of Theology*
ConBNT	Coniectanea biblica: New Testament Series
CRINT	Compendia rerum iudaicarum ad Novum Testamentum
CTM	*Concordia Theological Monthly*
EBib	*Etudes bibliques*
ExpTim	*Expository Times*
HNT	Handbuch zum Neuen Testament
HSNT	Die Heilige Schrift des Neuen Testaments
HTR	*Harvard Theological Review*
Int	*Interpretation*
JBL	*Journal of Biblical Literature*
JJS	*Journal of Jewish Studies*
JNES	*Journal of Near Eastern Studies*
JSNT	*Journal for the Study of the New Testament*
JSNTSS	Journal for the Study of the New Testament Supplement Series
JTS	*Journal of Theological Studies*
LQ	*Lutheran Quarterly*
NovT	*Novum Testamentum*
NovTSup	Novum Testamentum Supplements
NTS	*New Testament Studies*

PhRev	*Philosophical Review*
PTMS	Pittsburgh Theological Monograph Series
PTR	*Princeton Theological Review*
RB	*Revue biblique*
RBén	*Revue bénédictine*
RevQ	*Revue de Qumran*
SBLDS	Society of Biblical Literature Dissertation Series
SBLMS	Society of Biblical Literature Monograph Series
SBLSP	*Society of Biblical Literature Seminar Papers*
ScrHier	Scripta hierosolymitana
SNTSMS	Society for New Testament Studies Monograph Series
SPhA	*Studia Philonica Annual*
StudNeot	Studia neotestamentica
TLZ	*Theologische Literaturzeitung*
TRu	*Theologische Rundschau*
TSK	*Theologische Studien und Kritiken*
TTZ	*Trierer theologische Zeitschrift*
TU	*Texte und Untersuchungen*
WMANT	Wissenschaftliche Monographien zum Alten und Neuen Testament
WTJ	*Westminster Theological Journal*
WUNT	Wissenschaftliche Untersuchungen zum Neuen Testament
ZNW	*Zeitschrift für dir neutestamentliche Wissenschaft und die Kunde der älteren Kirche*
ZST	*Zeitschrift für systematische Theologie*

1

THE QUEST FOR THE
HISTORICAL HEBREWS

Introduction

The main challenge for anyone wishing to use historical-critical methods to interpret the Epistle to the Hebrews is our almost complete lack of knowledge of its original context. Since the meaning of words is a function of their use in particular 'language games', biblical scholarship faces an uphill battle when attempting to interpret texts whose original 'forms of life' are so far removed from us in time and culture.[1] The case becomes acute with regard to Hebrews, whose origins are so uncertain. We ultimately must consign ourselves to a certain amount of agnosticism as far as the original meaning is concerned.[2] While we may create plausible hypotheses, we may never be able to speak definitively on even the most basic issues.

It is therefore no surprise that the 'riddles' relating to Hebrews' origin have given rise to an immense body of literature, as countless individuals

---

[1] Wittgenstein's well known turns of phrase. See in particular *Philosophical Investigations* (New York: Doubleday Anchor, 1966 [1953]) 23. Wittgenstein refers to the way in which certain contexts (i.e. 'forms of life') give rise to 'rules' for understanding words. If I say 'Break a leg' to someone before going on stage, the 'language game' of drama indicates that I wish him or her to have a good performance.
   In New Testament studies, social-scientific criticism embodies on a macro-level some of Wittgenstein's insights into language. When Bruce Malina writes that the 'meanings realized in texts inevitably derive from some social system' (*The Social World of Jesus* (New York: Routledge, 1996) 13), he indicates that the meaning of words in a text at any point in time is a function of all the ways in which people are using words at that time (language games) in all the various social situations that exist (forms of life).
[2] Even the phrase 'original meaning' is ambiguous. Is it something that the author intended or that the recipients understood? How does one define 'author' if there is more than one source behind a composition, if a text went through various stages of development, or if multiple variations of a tradition existed contemporaneously? Is intention cognitive, emotional, social, or a combination of these? What if the actual words an author produces work at cross purposes to his or her intention?

have attempted to fill in the epistle's glaring gaps in context.[3] Indeed, in addition to the identity of the author and point of origin, the recipients and destination of the epistle are also unidentified, together constituting its 'four great unknowns'.[4] The matter of background in particular remains one of the most important issues on which no decisive consensus exists. Significant disagreement persists concerning what first-century milieu(s) might best explain the epistle's thought and imagery.

This area of Hebrews' research has passed through various phases, and a number of possible options have been proposed at one time or another. Lincoln Hurst's 1990 monograph on the issue surveyed five non-Christian backgrounds that various scholars have suggested as the key to the epistle's meaning (as well as three biblical traditions).[5] As much as any other, this uncertainty has led to a myriad of widely contrasting interpretations of Hebrews and the situation of its origin.

Yet despite the immense quantity of literature, scholarly discussion has failed to yield a definitive consensus on most issues. Indeed, it is judicious to avoid drawing conclusions on many of these questions (e.g. the question of authorship). On the other hand, we cannot avoid the matter of Hebrews' 'background of thought' in interpretation. Words do not have meaning independent of their use in some socio-conceptual framework. One cannot make a judgement on any text's meaning without either intentionally or accidentally investing its words with meanings from some cultural dictionary.

Even if no definitive consensus exists as yet on the background issue, some advances in the discussion have materialized, particularly some methodological advances. For example, scholars now more often than not take seriously the possibility that Hebrews reflects a creative mixture of ideologies. In contrast, many studies from the past assumed that the epistle's conceptual framework largely derived from some monolithic system of thought. We now see that categories like 'Greek thought', 'Hebrew thought', 'Platonic', and 'apocalyptic' were overly simplistic in

---

[3] Reference to these ambiguities as 'riddles' goes back at least as far as J. Biesenthal, *Der Trostschreiben des Apostels Paulus an die Hebräer* (Leipzig: Fernau, 1878) 1. See also W. Übelacker, *Der Hebräerbrief als Appell: Untersuchungen zu* exordium, narratio, *und* postscriptum *(Hebr 1–2 und 13,22–25)* (ConBNT 21; Lund: Almquist & Wiksell, 1989) 11 n.1.

[4] So Übelacker, *Des Hebräerbrief* 12, following O. Kuss, 'Der Verfasser des Hebräerbriefes als Seelsorger', *TTZ* 67 (1958) 1.

[5] *The Epistle to the Hebrews: Its Background of Thought* (SNTSMS 65; Cambridge: Cambridge University, 1990). Hurst's discussion of 'Philo, Alexandria, and Platonism' sneaks in a sixth potentially 'non-Christian' background (revealingly the one Hurst favours): 'apocalyptic'.

the way scholars referred to them as mutually exclusive and self-contained ideologies. In reality these categories could interpenetrate and intermingle extensively with one another.

The possibility that Hebrews might reflect a mixture or merging of thought traditions heralds the need for a shift in approach to the question of Hebrews' thought world. Most notably, it argues strongly against an approach that moves primarily from background to text. An approach to the thought of Hebrews should move more intentionally than ever from text to background*s*, constructing a world of thought on the basis of Hebrews itself vis-à-vis background traditions. It is no longer feasible to import wholesale some self-contained background ideology into the interpretation of Hebrews.

Two central methodological problems

Presumption of a single ideological background

One of the main problems with previous research on Hebrews has been a tendency to pigeonhole the epistle into a *single* ideological background such as Platonism or apocalypticism. For example, L. K. K. Dey interpreted Hebrews almost exclusively against the backdrop of Middle Platonism. His approach was indicative of the *religionsgeschichtliche Schule*: 'It is only when we are able to place Hebrews in its particular religious context that the significance of any concept or idea, the motivation behind it, the purpose of the writing and its literary character can be defined.'[6]

There is, of course, a fundamental truthfulness to these words. Nevertheless, Dey largely presumed that such a 'religious context' would turn out to be a distinct and isolated entity, which in his case turned out to be Middle Platonism.[7] His work then proceeded to force the words of Hebrews into a mould fashioned by parallels from Philo, the Wisdom of Solomon, and other Alexandrian texts. Any Middle Platonic aspect to the epistle was taken so far beyond its original scope that more fundamental aspects of Hebrews' message were lost.

Scholars have often conducted the search for Hebrews' background in such a way that they inevitably 'find what they are looking for'.[8] That is

---

[6] *The Intermediary World and Patterns of Perfection in Philo and Hebrews* (SBLDS 25; Missoula, MT: Scholars Press, 1975) 3.

[7] In reality, even 'Middle Platonism' itself was not a monolithic system of thought. A great deal of diversity existed among the group of philosophers usually included in this category.

[8] M. Isaacs, *Sacred Space: An Approach to the Theology of the Epistle to the Hebrews* (JSNTSS 73; Sheffield: JSOT Press, 1992) 51.

to say, it is not difficult to find parallel passages in the corpus of ancient literature that, with a bit of effort, can be made to bear at least a superficial resemblance to Hebrews. At its worst, this practice places Hebrews into whatever Procrustean bed the scholar has in mind, altering the epistle's form in favour of the background of choice.

In a sense, Hurst's monograph represents the culmination of this kind of approach to the background question, an approach that was typical of the older History of Religions school.[9] His treatment of Hebrews' 'background of thought'[10] follows the contours of previous scholarship as it discusses distinct ideological backgrounds one by one. While he eliminates most of these from consideration, it is significant (1) that his conclusions argue for a mixture of influences on Hebrews' thought and (2) that they are seen more in terms of *traditionsgeschichtlich* than *religionsgeschichtlich* forces.

We now commonly read of multiple influences on the epistle's thought world rather than of solitary conceptual frameworks. On the one hand, Hebrews is of course most fundamentally a document of early Christianity. We would therefore expect *prima facie* that early Christian traditions played the most central role in the background of its thought. Even Dey admits that there is 'in Hebrews both the eschatological language of primitive Christianity as well as the language of Hellenistic Judaism'.[11] Most scholars would agree that Hebrews *at least* mixes a basic Christian perspective with whatever other background tradition(s) it may reflect.

On the other hand, since C. K. Barrett's article 'The Eschatology of the Epistle to the Hebrews', it has become common to suggest a mixture of *non*-Christian traditions beyond the presence of traditional material.[12]

---

[9] *Background*. The so called 'new' *religionsgeschichtliche Schule*, which seeks the appropriate background to early Christianity in terms of Jewish traditions, can learn from the mistakes of the earlier History of Religions school (for the notion of a new History of Religions School, see C. Fletcher-Louis, *Luke–Acts: Angels, Christology and Soteriology* (WUNT 94; Tübingen: Mohr/Siebeck, 1997) 1). It is all too easy to fall into a kind of 'parallelomania' that moves primarily from background to text in interpretation rather than from text to background.

[10] The subtitle to his monograph.

[11] *Intermediary World* 1. So also J. W. Thompson, who also reads Hebrews Platonically: 'An analysis of the intellectual presuppositions of the author necessitates that one distinguish between tradition and redaction more carefully than has been done in previous scholarship. It is likely that the author of Hebrews employed various traditions that he reshaped for the needs of his audience' (*The Beginnings of Christian Philosophy: The Epistle to the Hebrews* (CBQMS 13; Washington, DC: Catholic Biblical Association, 1981) 12). In my opinion, however, Thompson does not fully heed his own advice.

[12] 'The Eschatology of the Epistle to the Hebrews', *The Background of the New Testament and its Eschatology: Studies in Honour of C. H. Dodd*, W. D. Davies and D. Daube, eds. (Cambridge: Cambridge University Press, 1954) 385: 'The heavenly tabernacle and its ministrations are from one point of view eternal archetypes, from another, they are eschatological events.'

Barrett himself suggested that the epistle combined Platonic language with a more fundamental eschatology such as one might find in Jewish apocalyptic literature.[13] James D. G. Dunn has written that Hebrews is 'a fascinating combination of the Platonic world view and Jewish eschatology'.[14] One can count a number of other scholars up to the present who believe Hebrews to be a mixture of Platonic and 'apocalyptic' imagery.[15] The very possibility that Hebrews might blend elements from differing backgrounds reorients our approach to the text. Language reminiscent of one milieu might not carry the precise meaning and implications it had in its background setting. Indeed, a number of scholars believe that Hebrews uses Platonic *language* without that language contributing to the author's thought in any significant way.[16] And we will have to define the word *apocalyptic* very carefully if it is to be a useful category. We will have to be clear whether we are referring to a distinct and coherent movement or to specific imagery that occurs in a number of writings that may in fact be unrelated to one another. Aside from one or two key interpretive decisions in Hebrews, it is not entirely clear to me how we

---

[13] One should keep in mind here that the idea of 'non-Christian' background – when we are referring to Jewish backgrounds – is somewhat of an anachronism. Jewish background is in fact Christian background.

[14] *The Partings of the Ways: Between Christianity and Judaism and their Significance for the Character of Christianity* (London: SCM Press, 1991) 88. Dunn's second edition will likely indicate a few shifts in his understanding of Hebrews.

[15] Some of those who have held to some such mixture include G. Vos, *The Teaching of the Epistle to the Hebrews*, J. Vos, ed. (Grand Rapids, MI: Eerdmans, 1956) 56; H. Braun, 'Die Gewinnung der Gewißheit in dem Hebräerbrief', *TLZ* 96 (1971) 330: 'Metaphysik'; G. MacRae, 'Heavenly Temple and Eschatology in the Letter to the Hebrews', *Semeia* 12 (1978) 179: apocalyptic and Platonic imagery both present; H. Attridge, *The Epistle to the Hebrews* (Philadelphia: Fortress Press, 1989) 223–4: earthly-heavenly intersects with new-old; S. Lehne, *The New Covenant in Hebrews* (JSNTSS 44; Sheffield: JSOT Press, 1990) 96 and 149, n.17: 'blended in a creative way'; H.-F. Weiss, *Der Brief an die Hebräer* (Göttingen: Vandenhoeck & Ruprecht, 1991) 114: it is in a 'Mittelstellung' between apocalyptic and Hellenism; Isaacs, *Space* 50–6: more nuanced than 'a simple "yes" or "no" answer' (56).

[16] E.g. O. Michel, *Der Brief an die Hebräer*, 13th edn. (Göttingen: Vandenhoeck & Ruprecht, 1984 (1936)) 289: one cannot 'von einer Einordnung des Hebr in die philonische Konzeption sprechen'; S. Nomoto, 'Herkunft und Struktur der Hohenpriestervorstellung im Hebräerbrief', *NovT* 10 (1968) 18–19: while the terms are Alexandrian in origin, their content is no longer in a special relationship to its metaphysic or exegesis; R. Williamson, *Philo and the Epistle to the Hebrews* (ALGHJ 4; Leiden: E. J. Brill, 1970) 557; D. Peterson, *Hebrews and Perfection: An Examination of the Concept of Perfection in the Epistle to the Hebrews* (SNTSMS 47; Cambridge: Cambridge University Press, 1982) 131; J. Dunnill, *Covenant and Sacrifice in the Letter to the Hebrews* (SNTSMS 75; Cambridge: Cambridge University Press, 1992), 46: 'Philonic influence is relatively superficial'; G. E. Sterling ('Ontology versus Eschatology: Tensions between Author and Community', *SPhA* 13 (2001) 208–10) believes that the quasi-Platonic imagery comes more from the audience than the author, who used the language rather superficially.

might distinguish 'apocalyptic' as a background for Hebrews from early Christian tradition in general.[17] The realization that the ancient world and ancient Judaism were not neatly partitioned off into distinct and unrelated ideologies argues for a text-oriented approach that allows for a combination of sources and a creative synthesis on the part of an individual author.[18] Hebrews may not be as out of place in the New Testament as some scholars have assumed. Even if it has motifs reminiscent of certain background traditions, the author surely was capable of putting such imagery to new and unique uses in the light of his own particular situation and theology.[19] The identification of a general background and common language does not necessarily imply how an individual author has used that imagery in a specific context.

The interpretation of Hebrews thus requires a rigorous focus on its text if it is to have integrity. The gaps in our knowledge of the epistle's original context can lead all too easily to guessing games for the mystery author, readers, destination, origin, background and occasion, not to mention for the keys to a myriad of interpretive conundrums. While a complete interpretation will often require us to engage in speculation, the starting point must always be the apparent trajectory of the text rather than distinct ideological systems attested in the background literature.

As in all historical interpretation, individual texts are the delimiting factors in the hermeneutical circle. The totality of background information at our disposal provides us with a domain of possible meanings for ancient words, but individual texts themselves delimit these to specific meanings that (ideally) cohere. The text must always have the upper hand in interpretation. The frequently opposite focus of the earlier *religionsgeschichtliche Schule* was its most fundamental weakness.

---

[17] For a discussion of what John Collins calls 'the apocalyptic worldview', see 'Genre, Ideology and Social Movements in Jewish Apocalypticism', *Mysteries and Revelations: Apocalyptic Studies since the Upsala Colloquium*, J. J. Collins and J. H. Charlesworth, eds. (Sheffield: JSOT Press, 1991) 11–32). Early Christianity in general seems to participate in this 'world-view'. See also C. Rowland's, *The Open Heaven: A Study of Apocalyptic in Judaism and Early Christianity* (London: SCM Press, 1982), which denies that eschatology is even an essential element of an apocalypse.

[18] M. Hengel's decisive study, *Judaism and Hellenism* (Minneapolis: Fortress Press, 1974) should be mentioned here along with its sequel, *The 'Hellenization' of Judaea in the First Century after Christ* (Philadelphia: Trinity Press, 1989). See also J. J. Collins and G. E. Sterling, *Hellenism in the Land of Israel* (Notre Dame, IN: University of Notre Dame Press, 2001).

[19] I use the masculine pronoun advisedly in the light of the masculine singular participle in Heb. 11:32.

Lack of attention to rhetorical elements

George MacRae was one of the first to suggest that Hebrews might reflect a mixture of distinct background traditions, particularly in its use of tabernacle imagery. What made his proposal interesting was that he saw this mixture primarily in terms of a distinction between author and audience, whom he believed came from differing ideological perspectives. To use his words, '[I]n his effort to strengthen the hope of his hearers, the homilist mingles his own Alexandrian imagery with their apocalyptic presuppositions'.[20] While we may not agree with his particular reconstruction of Hebrews' situation, MacRae insightfully drew our attention to an easily overlooked, yet crucial factor in the interpretation of Hebrews: the matter of rhetoric.[21]

New Testament scholarship has often overemphasized the *logical* (*logos*) element of argumentation to the exclusion of other ancient forms of proof like *pathos* and *ethos*.[22] George A. Kennedy as much as anyone else has pointed out that ancient rhetoric did not function exclusively on the basis of straightforward reasoning, the favourite of post-Enlightenment Western culture.[23] Equally important were the 'emotional' (*pathos*) and 'personal' (*ethos*) modes, which respectively played on an audience's emotions or confirmed the trustworthiness of a speaker. Because interpreters have not always recognized the varying levels of logical investment an author might have in the particular argument he or she is using, they have sometimes missed points of subtlety, irony or indirectness.

MacRae's suggestion raises the possibility that the author of Hebrews had varying levels of 'logical' investment in his imagery. For example, David A. deSilva has recently drawn our attention to the prevalence of

---

[20] 'Heavenly Temple' 179.

[21] G. E. Sterling has recently reversed the hypothesis, suggesting that the audience utilized certain Platonizing exegetical traditions – traditions with which the more eschatologically orientated author interacted on a somewhat superficial level ('Ontology Versus Eschatology').

[22] Pauline scholarship has made definite improvements in recent years in appreciating the non-conceptual features of Paul's rhetoric. Few now would view Romans as a straightforward 'compendium of his theology', recognizing the centrality of the letter's rhetorical situation for understanding its argument (even if that situation is appraised differently by different scholars, see K. P. Donfried, ed., *The Romans Debate* (rev. and enlarged edn; Peabody, MA: Hendrickson, 1991)). M. M. Mitchell's *Paul and the Rhetoric of Reconciliation: An Exegetical Investigation of the Language and Composition of 1 Corinthians* (Louisville, KY: Westminster/John Knox, 1991) shows a similar sensitivity with regard to 1 Corinthians.

[23] *New Testament Interpretation through Rhetorical Criticism* (Chapel Hill: University of North Carolina Press, 1984).

honour/shame language in the epistle.[24] Such imagery functions primarily on the level of *pathos* rather than *logos*. We must at least consider the question of whether the audience was in as grave a danger of 'falling away' as Heb. 5:11–6:8 seems to indicate, or whether this language was meant to shame the audience into a stronger commitment to values they were not really in danger of losing.[25] While an earlier generation of scholars did not adequately address these possibilities, more recent interpretations of Hebrews have.[26]

Hebrews' extensive use of metaphor further complicates its interpretation. Even when the argument functions primarily in a logical mode, it can be difficult to know how literal its imagery is. Nowhere have such decisions proven more difficult than in the matter of the heavenly tabernacle, arguably the focal point of debate over the epistle's background of thought. Thus while some have considered the heavenly tabernacle to be a Platonic model of some sort (cf. Heb. 8:5), others have seen it as a free-standing structure, more like the 'apocalyptic' structures that were arguably a part of the future Jerusalem envisaged by *4 Ezra* and *2 Baruch* (cf. 8:2). Still others suggest it is similar to the cosmological temple of Josephus and Philo (cf. 6:19–20; 7:26; 9:11–12, 24).

Ultimately, the difficulty of interpreting Hebrews at this point derives from the fact that the author has used the heavenly tabernacle in several different metaphorical ways that do not necessarily cohere with one another. I will argue subsequently that heaven itself corresponds most closely to what the author pictured when he referred to this tabernacle (cf. Heb. 9:24). However, the author also used tabernacle imagery in ways that defy any simple, literal referent in heaven. For example, the cleansing of the heavenly tabernacle in Heb. 9:23 presents a difficult conundrum for interpreters. How could something in heaven need cleansed? I will argue that the author is largely playing out a metaphor and thus that, as with so many metaphors, we run into difficulties if we press them too far. In my opinion, the author was not actually picturing the cleansing of a literal structure in heaven.

The key to assessing how much the author of Hebrews has invested in each particular argument and image does not come from background literature or from the interpretation of individual verses in isolation.

---

[24] E.g. *Despising Shame: Honor Discourse and Community Maintenance in the Epistle to the Hebrews* (SBLDS 152; Atlanta: Scholars Press, 1995); *Perseverance in Gratitude: A Socio-Rhetorical Commentary on the Epistle 'to the Hebrews'* (Grand Rapids, MI: Eerdmans, 2000). Another element in this discussion is the question of genre and the 'species' of rhetoric in view in a particular passage (i.e. judicial, deliberative or epideictic).

[25] DeSilva writes of the 'trap of regarding the passage as a precise diagnosis of the actual state of the hearers' (*Perseverance* 211, n.1).

[26] E.g. B. Lindars, 'The Rhetorical Structure of Hebrews', *NTS* 35 (1989) 382–406.

Rather, it comes from a proper understanding of the author's *overall rhetorical agenda*. Barnabas Lindars' examination of the 'theology' of Hebrews is a good example of a holistic rhetorical approach that takes such factors into consideration.[27] Rather than let traditional questions of author, recipients, destination and point of origin dominate his introduction, he rightfully places the situation of the 'readers' at the forefront, that is, the *rhetorical situation* behind the epistle.[28] Commentaries have intuitively moved toward the same approach as they have taken on board the reality of Hebrews' incurable uncertainties.[29]

Holistic treatments of the epistle's 'thought' also avoid the problem addressed by William G. Johnsson in his article 'The Cultus of Hebrews in Twentieth-Century Scholarship'.[30] In the late seventies he noted that there was a tendency among Protestant scholars to neglect the subject of the cultus in Hebrews, while Roman Catholic scholars often did not integrate their interest in the cultus with a consideration of Hebrews' paraenetic material. Consequently, those who emphasized the cultus tended to downplay futurist aspects of the epistle's eschatology, while those who focused on paraenesis tended to miss the current, vertical aspects of the author's thought. It is thus predictable that Roman Catholic scholars have more often seen Platonic influence in the epistle while Protestants have more typically looked to 'apocalyptic' to explain the epistle's thought. Johnsson's conclusion is still apt: 'the solution to these problems will lie in a holistic view of the book of Hebrews'.[31]

Methodological conclusions

We have identified two central methodological problems in the recent history of Hebrews' interpretation vis-à-vis its world of thought: (1) the

---

[27] *The Theology of the Letter to the Hebrews* (Cambridge: Cambridge University Press, 1991) 4–15. Lindars' use of the term 'theology', a term he of course inherited from the series of which his book is a part, is another indication of how deeply New Testament interpretation is focused on the *cognitive* dimension of the New Testament writings over and against the *emotive* and *personal*.

[28] We should refer to the *audience* of Hebrews rather than its *readers*. The overwhelming majority of the ancients were illiterate, and we should picture the recipients of New Testament documents as hearers rather than readers. This is particularly the case for Hebrews, which styles itself a 'word of exhortation' (Heb. 13:22), a phrase Acts 13:15 associates with a homily given in synagogue worship. Hebrews was likely a short sermon sent to be read at some location the author soon hoped to visit.

[29] DeSilva's treatment (*Perseverance*) is an excellent example of a recent commentary that consciously adopts such priorities in interpretation, styling itself a 'socio-rhetorical' commentary.

[30] *ExpTim* 89 (1977–78) 104–5.

[31] 'Cultus' 106. Isaacs also notes of Hebrews, 'its paraenesis and its theology cannot be considered apart from each other' (*Space* 22).

presumption of a single ideological background behind the sermon and (2) a lack of attention to the rhetorical dimension of its argument. As a result of these two basic errors, other problems have resulted. At times scholars have focused on certain passages to the exclusion of others. We have often failed to recognize the author's level of 'logical' investment in his arguments and imagery. In general, we have failed to let the text speak on its own terms.

We can see Hurst's monograph as the culmination of an era of Hebrews' interpretation. The possibility that Hebrews is a unique synthesis of thought traditions indicates that we can no longer look for the key to its meaning in any one background. Dey's claim that we must 'describe the total framework of its [Hebrews'] religious thought' remains in force, but we cannot (as he) find such a total framework in any particular *religions-geschichtlich* background.[32] We should rather seek out an appropriate text-oriented approach to construct the 'thought world' – or better, the *rhetorical world* – of this ancient homily.

From our discussion thus far, we can see that such an approach should have two primary characteristics: (1) it should let the text generate its own world of thought in terms appropriate to its own categories, and (2) it should take the rhetorical agenda of the whole text of Hebrews into account rather than a particular literary section or specific topical theme. A number of late twentieth-century developments in hermeneutics provide us with new possibilities and caveats for such a text-orientated approach to the meaning of Hebrews. Chiefly, the recognition that most New Testament thought is fundamentally *narrative* in orientation opens the possibility of constructing the world of Hebrews' thought using its 'narrative world' as a starting point.[33] In developing a rhetorico-narrative approach to Hebrews, we can allow the text to generate a world of thought in a category endemic to its own nature (criterion 1), doing so from a consideration of the text as a whole (criterion 2).

Hebrews' world of thought

The model of story and discourse

The category of narrative is by now no stranger to New Testament studies. Structuralism in the 1970s and narrative criticism in the 1980s and 1990s

---

[32] *Intermediary World* 3.

[33] The groundwork for seeing a narrative substructure underlying the rhetorical arguments of a New Testament letter was laid by R. B. Hays in his *The Faith of Jesus Christ: An Investigation of the Narrative Substructure of Galatians 3:1–4:11* (SBLDS 56; Chico, CA: Scholars Press, 1983), especially 21–9.

relied heavily on the distinction between story and discourse to analyse the 'narrative worlds' of the Gospels and Acts. This distinction in narrative relates closely to the notion that there are at least two aspects to the meaning of a text, namely, a sense and a reference. Gottlieb Frege originated this terminology in the late nineteenth century, and Paul Ricoeur adopted it in the late twentieth in his approach to interpretation.[34]

Ricoeur speaks of the 'sense' of a text in terms of its structure, composition, genre and style. On the other hand, the 'reference' is the 'world of the text', that 'reality' to which the sense refers and which is the object of understanding. In this light, interpretation seeks to understand a text by moving from its structure and 'sense' to the world which it creates, that is, its reference.

This scheme is analogous to the theoretical approach of narrative criticism when it treats a narrative in terms of 'story and discourse'. Seymour Chatman provided the foundation for narrative criticism when he wrote,

> Structuralist theory argues that each narrative has two parts: a story (*histoire*), the content or chain of events (actions, happenings), plus what may be called the existents (characters, items of setting); and a discourse (*discours*), that is, the expression, the means by which the content is communicated. In simple terms, the story is the *what* in a narrative that is depicted, discourse the *how*.[35]

In this model, any specific plot is a 'story-as-discoursed' into one of many possible realizations.[36] However, since the same story can be narrated in many different ways, a single story can manifest itself in many different discourses.

Chatman was of course referring strictly to narrative discourses, only one kind of discourse. He has thus provided us with an example of how the broader distinction between sense and reference might play itself out in a specific kind of text. In Chatman's terms, the 'discourse' relates to the sense of Frege and Ricoeur. It is the structure of the text itself. One might

---

[34] For overviews of Ricoeur's interpretation theory, see his own *Interpretation Theory: Discourse and the Surplus of Meaning* (Fort Worth, TX: Christian University Press, 1976), as well as D. Klemm, *The Hermeneutic Theory of Paul Ricoeur: A Constructive Analysis* (London: Associated University Press, 1983) and K. J. Vanhoozer, *Biblical Narrative in the Philosophy of Paul Ricoeur: A Study in Hermeneutics and Theology* (Cambridge: Cambridge University Press, 1990).

[35] *Story and Discourse: Narrative Structure in Fiction and Film* (Ithaca, NY: Cornell University Press, 1978) 19.

[36] *Story and Discourse* 43.

also compare it to surface structure in linguistics, that is, the sentences that actually confront a reader in a text.[37]

On the other hand, the story is what stands behind the text, the principal (though not exclusive) constituent of its 'reference'. In structuralist terms, the story is the 'deep structure' behind any plot, a narrative content that follows the universal pattern pertaining to all stories.[38] Such a story can be subjected to a Greimasian analysis of the sort conducted by Daniel Patte and others who have applied structuralism to the New Testament.

Yet we can analyse the story world behind a narrative discourse in more general terms than structuralist interpretations usually do. As in Chatman's summary above, the key elements to a story world are its events, characters and settings. Theoretically, one can 'project' these from a narrative discourse in a way that anyone who has ever heard a story can follow.[39] In contrast, the structuralist model embeds these three elements in a complex sequence of transactions between both concrete and abstract entities.[40] It is understandable that narrative critics, who use

[37] Cf. P. Cotterell and M. Turner, *Linguistics and Biblical Interpretation* (Downer's Grove, IL: InterVarsity Press, 1989) 228, n.28. I realize that I am running roughshod over a number of distinct theoretical disciplines. However, my aim is only to make broad comparisons, not precise ones.

[38] 'Deep structure' here is not meant in the linguistic sense of that term. Cf. D. Patte, *What is Structural Exegesis?* (Philadelphia: Fortress Press, 1976) 24–5. Again, I do not have a wholesale investment in any one of these particular models, whether that of structuralism, narrative criticism or the interpretation theory of Ricoeur. These are all heuristic constructs that are valuable in so far as they pragmatically 'work' to clarify the process of communication.

[39] S. Moore (*Literary Criticism and the Gospels: The Theoretical Challenge* (New Haven, CT: Yale University Press, 1989) 60–1) has critiqued the whole narrative enterprise, claiming that the level of story actually does not exist. Correctly, Moore notes that *all* narrative discussions of meaning take place on the level of discourse – or more helpfully, the discussions take place as *rhetoric* (cf. D. Rhoads and D. Michie, *Mark as Story: An Introduction to the Narrative of a Gospel* (Philadelphia: Fortress Press, 1982) 35–62). Accordingly, Moore argues that to 'abstract' from a narrative is only to create another discourse (*Literary Criticism* 67). He claims that the distinction between form and content is not viable and therefore that it is impossible to speak of abstracted content (64). While I substantially agree with Moore, I would contend that the re*form*ulation of discourses into such topical headings is a *useful* process and therefore valid as a heuristic tool. Meaning *theories* always deconstruct, but meaning takes place pragmatically – we often at least think we are understanding one another.

[40] In structuralism, events correspond to individual 'syntagms' within 'sequences' that constitute the plot as a whole. Characters correspond to various 'actants' in an 'actantial model'. The settings of a story can correspond to the parameters of the movement of a 'subject' in the acceptance of a 'contract' or can function as 'helpers' or 'opponents' in a given syntagm. For an overview of structural interpretation, see Patte's discussion (*Structural Exegesis*, ch. 3). A much clearer, albeit simplified, version can be found in Hays, *Faith* 92–103.

the less technical approach, have gained a greater audience than the pure structuralists.

In narrative criticism, events, characters and settings form three general headings under which the underlying story of a text can be re-presented. With regard to the discourse, on the other hand, narrative critics discuss the point of view from which the story is told, the relation of discourse time to story time, aspects of the particular narration, and other 'surface' characteristics of the discourse.[41]

The realization that a story world underlies the thought of Hebrews at a fundamental level opens up the possibility of using the narrative-critical model as a starting point for re-presenting its world of thought. While its surface structure, its discourse, is not narrative, Richard Hays and others have used such categories successfully to approach the meaning of non-narrative texts. As we will see subsequently, such an approach to the world of Hebrews is not only possible, it focuses our discussion of Hebrews' meaning in very fruitful ways.

The rhetorical use of a narrative world in a non-narrative text

It should now be beyond question that a narrative world can underlie any discourse, not simply narrative discourses. Further, the notion that New Testament thought is overwhelmingly narrative in orientation is now a well-accepted notion, even though many of the books in the New Testament are not narrative in genre.[42] More than any other work, Richard B. Hays' *The Faith of Jesus Christ* pioneered a narrative approach to a non-narrative text.[43]

Hays had picked up on scattered intimations by Pauline scholars that Paul's letters frequently dialogued with an underlying story.[44] Hays integrated this basic insight with various theoretical currents in literary criticism, particularly those of Northrop Frye and Paul Ricoeur.[45] The result was a study demonstrating that 'Paul's theology must be understood as the explication and defence of a *story*'.[46] Even if one does not agree

---

[41] Cf. M. A. Powell, *What is Narrative Criticism?* (Minneapolis: Fortress Press, 1990) chs. 3–6. Moore, *Literary Criticism* 60–1, again claims by way of critique that the whole narrative enterprise works on the level of discourse. See n. 39 above.

[42] A concept N. T. Wright has especially championed in his *The New Testament and the People of God* (Minneapolis: Fortress Press, 1992) 38–44, 122–37.

[43] See n. 33 above.　　[44] *Faith* 9–14, 52–70.　　[45] *Faith* 21–9.

[46] As Hays put it over ten years later in his article, 'Πίστις and Pauline Christology: What is at Stake?', in *Pauline Theology, Volume IV: Looking Back, Pressing On*. Ed. by E. E. Johnson and D. M. Hays (Minneapolis: Fortress Press, 1997) 37.

with Hays' solution to the πίστις Χριστοῦ issue, at least this point seems established.[47]

To provide a theoretical basis for his study, Hays first utilized Northrop Frye's expanded Aristotelian distinction between *mythos* and *dianoia*. In this approach *mythos* refers to the plot of a story and *dianoia* to the 'total design' of a narrative, a 'sense of simultaneity' caught by a reader participating in the continuity of a narrative.[48] Hays suggested that in Galatians we find Paul's 'critical representation of the *dianoia* of the story of Jesus Christ'.[49]

In a similar vein, Paul Ricoeur has distinguished between a narrative's 'episodic dimension' and what he called its 'configurational dimension'. This latter dimension arises as one attempts to 'grasp together' the significance of the events that appear one after the other as episodes.[50] Once again, Hays concludes that a Pauline letter can be understood 'as a new "speech act" that attempts to rearticulate in discursive language the configurational dimension of the gospel story'.[51]

When a story is 'discoursed' into a narrative, that narrative can take on rhetorical force in a number of ways. For example, individual narratives frequently do not present a story in the order in which the events 'chronologically' occurred. The author can begin a story *in medias res* and utilize flashbacks to highlight key events, or an author can flash forward in anticipation of what is to come. Similarly, an event that may have taken only a minute portion of the story's overall time (story time) may dominate a narrative in terms of the 'discourse time'. Such is the case with the Gospels – about a third of Mark is dedicated to the final week of Jesus' life. Further, an author can present a story from a number of different points of view, each leaving a unique impact on a narrative discourse.

---

[47] In 'Πίστις and Pauline Christology', which Hays originally read at the 1991 Pauline Epistles Group of the Society of Biblical Literature, Hays rightly expressed puzzlement that the narrative orientation of Paul's thought could even be regarded as controversial (38).

[48] *Faith* 23. Hays drew the reference to *dianoia* as a narrative's 'total design' from N. Frye's *The Stubborn Structure: Essays on Criticism and Society* (Ithaca, NY: Cornell University Press, 1970) 164. He drew the reference to *dianoia* as a 'sense of simultaneity caught by the eye' from N. Frye, *The Anatomy of Criticism* (Princeton, NJ: Princeton University Press, 1957) 77. Frye's emphasis on participation in the narrative and Hays' concern to demonstrate that the *dianoia* is not 'something abstracted from the narrative but as an organic property of the narrative' (*Faith* 23) relates to some of the criticisms of narrative criticism proffered by S. Moore (see n. 39 above). Since I am using this model heuristically and pragmatically, this distinction is less important for my purposes. I am comfortable with the idea that my approach is a re-presentation from a particular perspective. Also, I *am* attempting to analyse abstracted components of the underlying story.

[49] *Faith* 24.   [50] P. Ricoeur, 'The Narrative Function', *Semeia* 13 (1978) 184.

[51] *Faith* 25.

The situation is somewhat different when a discourse is arguing from a story in a non-narrative medium. It is possible to lose to varying degrees the overall flow and context of the story, forcing one to engage in some speculative reconstruction. Certain key elements in the story's overall structure may be lost completely.[52] In other ways, the rhetorical force of the story is more explicit at points, especially when an author makes arguments directly from the story. The potential distinction between author and narrator largely collapses and the author's 'point of view' on the story usually becomes more explicit.[53]

In this whole discussion, it is important to note that we are not speaking of stories strictly as 'art for art's sake'. The story worlds of the New Testament are rhetorical worlds. Its narratives, in keeping with other ancient *bioi* and histories, wished to move and convince their audiences on various points and courses of actions. This orientation is even more obvious when it comes to the New Testament letters. When we analyse the events, characters and settings presupposed by a work like Hebrews, we are engaging in events, characters and settings set to a purpose, set to make arguments. Especially when such writings are judicial or deliberative in nature, we must consider the strong likelihood that they are offering competing interpretations to stories held in common to some degree with those they oppose. Indeed, Hays rightly recognizes that 'Paul's letters may be read as running arguments with opponents who draw different inferences from the same story'.[54] In this comment alone we probably find one of the most generative ideas in Hays' entire study.

For a narrative world to have rhetorical force, an audience must of course find the story in question relevant. Neither Paul nor the author of Hebrews could convince their audiences to a particular course of action if those audiences did not see the story as *their* story in some way. In this regard it is significant that both Paul and Hebrews place both themselves

---

[52] E.g. the opening 'sequence' in which the conflict giving rise to the story takes place. Of course narratives do not always present the opening sequence either. The Cinderella story is usually a bit sketchy over the details of how Cinderella came to find herself in such a dismal state in the first place.

[53] For the potential distinction between author and narrator, see Powell, *Narrative* 27. I say 'usually' because a master of persuasion will adopt to varying degrees the perspective of the opposing position in order to deconstruct it or better persuade the audience to a certain course of action. These aspects of a writing like 1 Corinthians make it very difficult to ascertain the level of Paul's commitment to some of the positions he takes (e.g. on meat sacrificed to idols). The hypotheses of MacRae and Sterling mentioned above (nn. 20–1) would urge similar caution in accessing the logical investment of the author of Hebrews in some of his arguments.

[54] *Faith* 7.

and their audiences *within* the story as characters in the overall plot.[55] Unfortunately, we are severely hampered by our inability to know with certainty the audience's investment in the story. The author of Hebrews apparently thought that his audience still saw itself in the story to some degree or he would not have argued in the way he did.

The need to take the rhetorical use of a story into full consideration drives us to make an important categorical distinction. The term *narrative world* commonly has come to refer to the events, characters and settings presupposed by a particular discourse as these elements interrelate and function together in such a way as to constitute a plot. As we have already seen, such a discourse need not be a narrative discourse. A non-narrative discourse can draw upon or argue from a story as well.[56]

Accordingly, I offer the phrase *rhetorical world* in reference to the total rhetorical force of a discourse. In a case such as that of Hebrews, its 'rhetorical world' draws significantly upon the narrative world that stands at its centre. To a large degree (although not totally), the rhetorical world of Hebrews is the use of its narrative world as a tool of persuasion. On the other hand, Hebrews does not use every aspect of its presupposed narrative world in its rhetoric – the audience did not need to be persuaded on every aspect of the story. It is at the points of disagreement and emphasis that the narrative substratum of Hebrews became a part of its rhetorical world. We can thus see the two worlds as two overlapping circles. The rhetorical world of Hebrews is overwhelmingly preoccupied with its narrative world, yet it does not subsume the narrative world in its totality. Similarly, there are aspects of Hebrews' rhetoric that do not draw on its narrative world.

The rhetorical use of a narrative world thus focuses heavily on those aspects of the story that are a matter of contention or whose implications are perceived differently between author and audience. In Galatians, the implications of the death of Christ, particularly as they relate to non-Jews, constitute the point of the story most in question. The situation is analogous in Hebrews, although the rhetorical strategies and ultimate conclusions of its author differed somewhat from those of Paul.

For the moment I will simply suggest some of the ways in which two parties might argue differently from the same basic story. From a

---

[55] N. R. Petersen's *Rediscovering Paul: Philemon and the Sociology of Paul's Narrative World* (Philadelphia: Fortress Press, 1985) in fact approached the situation of Philemon from such a perspective, focusing on the writing of this letter as part of a segment in the story of Paul's ministry. The story world with which we are concerned, however, is much broader – cosmic and eternal in scope.

[56] In this study I will use the terms *story world* and *narrative world* interchangeably, although I will use the term *narrative* strictly to refer to a particular genre of discourse.

structuralist perspective, every story begins with some unattained goal. Although some stories do not end with this goal fulfilled, the stereotypical story does end with the initial goal finally accomplished. Between this 'initial' and 'final' sequence is a sequence in which whatever obstacle that stood in the way of the plot's proper fulfilment is removed, often called the 'topical' sequence. Along the way there are those elements of the story that would 'help' the plot along and those that hinder its progress. A. J. Greimas termed these 'helpers' and 'opponents'.[57]

Two parties may agree on the basic events, characters and settings of a story yet still disagree on how these relate to one another in the sequences I have just mentioned. For example, they may disagree on what the ultimate goal of the plot is. They may disagree on what the proper resolution of the story might be. Perhaps even more commonly they may disagree on whether specific characters in the plot (which may or may not be humans) are helpers or opponents to the plot's progress. I will have recourse to expand on these rhetorical dynamics in the course of this study.

Hermeneutical concerns

The majority of biblical scholars still see relevance in the attempt to recover the 'original meaning' of an ancient text and still speak of 'authorial intention'. This fact alone validates a study such as this one. Even if one believes these are fallacious constructs, surely we can affirm the 'original meaning community' as one group among many groups of readers who read the text similarly.[58] Even if one places them on the same plane as other reader-response groups, they deserve a space. For this reason I will not provide an extensive hermeneutical defence of this project. I should, nevertheless, mention some related hermeneutical issues.

First of all, many of the arguments related to the so called 'intentional fallacy' are valid caveats. Yet I ultimately reject the notion as overly extreme.[59] I accept, on the one hand, many of the claims of Paul Ricoeur that, once a text has issued from an author, it becomes autonomous.[60]

---

[57] His discussion of this so-called 'actantial' model appears in *Sémantique structurale* (Paris: Librairie Larousse, 1966) 173–82.

[58] For this approach to reader-response criticism, see S. Fish, *Is there a Text in this Class? The Authority of Interpretive Communities* (Cambridge, MA: Harvard University Press, 1980).

[59] This phrase was coined by W. K. Wimsatt and M. C. Beardsley in their classic essay, 'The Intentional Fallacy', *On Literary Intention*, D. Newton-deMolina, ed. (Edinburgh: Edinburgh University Press, 1976) 1–13.

[60] I.e. 'the semantic autonomy of the text'. See *Interpretation Theory: Discourse and the Surplus of Meaning* (Fort Worth, TX: Christian University Press, 1976) 25.

I accept that an author does not retain control over a text once s/he has created it. I also accept that a 'speech utterance' can draw an audience, reader or observer into its 'world' and critique its 'receivers'.[61]

On the other hand, from a practical perspective a text tends to take on as many different readings as there are readers. Whether we like it or not, Ricoeur's 'world of the text' is ultimately a slave to the whims of its readers. Some readers in practice assign almost no value or 'rights' to the text as an entity to be heard.[62] Some do this intentionally while others are unaware of their 'violent' tendencies.[63] Ricoeur envisages the perfect audience, the 'implied' audience of the text, if you would.

However, even with Ricoeur we see that the notion of the 'intentional fallacy' is overly extreme. Certainly texts have a polyvalence that exceeds any conscious intention an author might have had. Certainly Ricoeur's world of the text implies meanings completely unforeseen by the original author. Certainly there are countless gaps in our knowledge of the original contexts that make even the original 'world of the text' somewhat inaccessible to us, let alone the conscious intended meanings of the original author. Nevertheless, from a pragmatic perspective, individuals regularly *think* that communication and understanding is taking place. While we cannot speak of certitude in understanding, we can quite reasonably speak of varying degrees of probability in 'correct' understanding.[64]

I accept as foundational Ludwig Wittgenstein's recognition that the meaning of a word is to be found in the way the word is *used* and that meanings do not inhere within words themselves. The meaning of a word comes from its context – or as Wittgenstein put it, from the *language game* in which it is used in a particular *form of life*.[65] We might reconceptualize Wittgenstein's programme in terms of practical situations such as

---

[61] By 'receiver' we refer to the 'addressees' of speech-act theory, the person on the receiving end of communication. The pioneering work on speech-act theory was Roman Jakobson, 'Closing Statement: Linguistics and Poetics', in *Style in Language*, T. A. Sebeok, ed. (Cambridge, MA: MIT Press, 1960) 350–77.

[62] Ironically, fundamentalist interpretations at times share with deconstruction and some reader-response readings of the Bible an almost complete disregard for the text in itself, placing the meaning of the text almost completely in the domain of the reader. Deconstructionists and the relevant reader-response approaches do so intentionally, while fundamentalists may not even realize they are reading their own traditional interpretations and concerns into the text.

[63] For the importance of reading Scripture in community because of the way in which the Bible so easily becomes a tool of violence and oppression, see S. E. Fowl and L. G. Jones, *Reading in Communion: Scripture and Ethics in Christian Life* (Grand Rapids, MI: Eerdmans, 1991).

[64] See R. Firth, 'The Anatomy of Certainty', *PhRev* (1967) 3–27 and J. L. Pollock, 'Criteria and our Knowledge of the Material World', *PhRev* (1967) 55–60.

[65] See n. 1 above.

the act of 'speech' creation by an author/'sender' or the act of 'speech' recognition by an audience, reader or observer.[66] From this perspective, there is no world of the text, only the world of persons perceiving them.[67] While we understand and agree with how Ricoeur is 'using' his words when he speaks of the 'world of the text', more fundamentally and pragmatically a text is a collection of squiggles on a page, 'signs' that only come to have 'signification' when a mind ascribes meaning to them.[68]

In the first instance, therefore, what we mean by the term 'original meaning' is a function of the way people were using words at the time when the document in question was created. Recognition of this fact brings relative certainty about a vast host of things that the text does *not* mean, namely, anachronistic interpretations whose aspects simply do not pertain to the time in question. The 'original meaning', whatever it might have been, was certainly a function of the ways in which words were being used in the ancient world, not the way we use them today.[69]

Once we agree, however, on the ancient domain of meanings as the appropriate context against which to seek the original meaning, we are immediately beset upon by immense gaps in our knowledge. Not only is our knowledge of the ancient world limited to the coincidences of archaeological and literary survival, domains in which we cannot at all be certain that the most typical 'artefacts' have survived, but we are also faced with varying levels of incomplete knowledge in relation to the specific contexts of individual documents. As I mentioned at the beginning of this chapter, the case is particularly acute with regard to Hebrews. The matter of genre can also present difficulties with regard to a text's interpretation. If we think we are reading a history when in fact we are reading a novel, this 'gap' in our knowledge will significantly alter our understanding of the original meaning.

---

[66] By 'sender' I refer to the 'addresser' of speech-act theory, the 'author' of a speech utterance. See n. 61 above.

[67] While Jacques Derrida phrased his approach in the opposite direction – there is *only* writing – I perceive my comments here to get at a similar 'phenomenon'. See Derrida's *Of Grammatology* (Baltimore, MD: Johns Hopkins University Press, 1974 (1967)).

[68] A philosophically inclined reader should take my language here as non-technical – I am using the 'mythical' language of modern parlance because it works: signs and signifieds (without engaging issues of signs as signifiers *and* signifieds), minds (without engaging issues of subject and object).

[69] Some readers of the biblical text would of course like to remove it from the human plane altogether and ascribe its meaning to a divine 'language game' in which the meaning of the text is a function of the meaning God thinks as God perceives the text. The difficulty with this perspective lies not only in the fact that the meaning of the biblical text consistently coheres well with the domain of ancient meanings, but also the fact that if its words were to be defined strictly on the basis of some divine 'dictionary', humans would not be capable of understanding it.

A second factor is the almost inevitable polyvalence of words and texts. Even within the domain of ancient meanings, a single text could foster multiple readings and interpretations. The meaning in the author's mind likely differed to some degree from the meaning understood by those in the ancient audience, which also probably differed somewhat from individual to individual. Ricoeur's 'world of the text' probably differs somewhat from all of these, a world we might define as the symbolic universe a text 'projects' on the basis of the domain of possible meanings in its original context. We might liken this world to the world of the 'implied reader', a term used by narrative critics in reference to the ideal reader of a narrative.

An author might actually agree with some elements in this hypothetical 'world of the text' that he or she did not consciously 'send' in the act of utterance. On the other hand, we – the ones constructing this implied world of the text – will no doubt 'infect' the process with our own reading of it. Ricoeur's world is a theoretical world, a useful construct that does clarify the meaning of texts, but such theoretical constructs regarding the text-in-itself tend to deconstruct when we bring them down to the sphere of human understanding. In practice there are no texts-in-themselves, only texts beset upon by human minds.

A final complication I should mention is the disunity of texts. Deconstruction has capitalized on the almost inevitable cracks and fissures that a text will have if one looks hard enough. The situation often becomes acute with regard to biblical documents due to their frequent redaction of sources and the incorporation of earlier traditions.[70] The situation is particularly acute when it comes to the Gospels, which have incorporated not only literary but oral sources as well.

James Dawsey's narrative-critical analysis of Luke, for example, led him to conclude that the 'implied narrator' of the text was unreliable.[71] This conclusion was the logical result of 'bracketing' authorial intent and not considering Luke's use of sources. Because Dawsey's narrative-critical method required him to analyse the text as it stands, such unintended disunity had to be incorporated into his interpretation of the text's inherent meaning. Similarly, Luke transposed the mockery of the Roman soldiers from the morning before the crucifixion, as in Mark 15:16–20, to the time of the crucifixion itself (Luke 23:36–8). Raymond Brown noted

---

[70] I mentioned earlier in the chapter the disunity that can result from the use of language that functions on more than one level, whether it be variation between literal and metaphorical or language used on the level of *ethos* and *pathos* in contrast to *logos*.

[71] *The Lukan Voice: Confusion and Irony in the Gospel of Luke* (Macon, GA: Mercer University Press, 1986) 110.

that this transposition created an awkwardness in the reading of the text of Luke 23:26. Now Pilate appears to hand Jesus over to the Jewish authorities and people to be crucified, rather than to the soldiers as in Mark.[72] Brown contends that the 'awkward' situation is an oversight on Luke's part, rather than an intended meaning.

Disunities such as this one impinge most upon the study of Hebrews in those instances where Hebrews has incorporated Old Testament citations or utilized traditional material. Hebrews' incorporation of Jer. 31 (38 LXX) into the argument of Heb. 8 creates some apparent disunity within the text. In the Jeremiah material, the need for a new covenant lies in the fact that Israel did not remain faithful to the first covenant. On the whole, however, Hebrews implies that God had always planned to reveal himself in a new covenant, even before the failure of Israel.[73] The incorporation of 'foreign' material into the text results in a tension that obscures the author's broader intent.

A second example of this type of disunity appears in its imagery of Christ's intercession (e.g. Heb. 7:25). David Hay has suggested that the author may have taken over this idea from Christian tradition associated with the session of Christ at God's right hand (cf. Rom. 8:34).[74] However, he notes that 'this idea of eternal intercession is something of a "foreign body" in the epistle's theology', not least because it stands in some tension with the finality of Christ's high-priestly work. The author's primary use of the session theme is to show that Christ *completed* his sacrificial, high-priestly function with one offering and then sat down, only 'waiting that his enemies be placed under his feet' (Heb. 10:12–13). These examples illustrate the caution we must take when traditional material has been incorporated into the text.

We see, therefore, that quite significant obstacles stand in the way not only of finding a domain of likely original meanings, but even more so in terms of what a specific author might have understood his or her text to mean. Nevertheless, as one who writes this chapter with intended meanings, I recognize the existence of such intentions. It would border on lunacy to deny that the authors of ancient books did not also have such intentions. To point out the immense difficulties of the task at hand is not

---

[72] *The Death of the Messiah: From Gethsemane to the Grave*, vol. 1 (London: Geoffrey Chapman, 1994) 71 n.82.

[73] Since Hebrews uses the masculine pronoun to refer to God (e.g. 2:10) and for the sake of convenience, this study will also use the masculine pronoun of God. Of course no orthodox Jewish or Christian consideration of God holds God to be literally male.

[74] *Glory and the Right Hand: Psalm 110 in Early Christianity* (SBLMS 18; Nashville: Abingdon Press, 1973) 132.

to deny that the goal exists and is attainable to some degree. At times the difficulties will prove insurmountable, and we must always present conclusions with some degree of tentativity, but we need not give up until we have at least tried the climb.

The key is to speak of varying degrees of probability rather than of certitude. It is overwhelmingly likely, for example, that the author of Hebrews believed Jesus was a historical individual who died upon a cross in such a way as to have positive benefits for himself and his audience. He *intended* his discourse to convey at least some of those positive benefits in some way to his audience. Such broad, original, intended meanings are overwhelmingly probable. On the other hand, we must speak with much less certainty about the specifics of what those positive benefits were and how they related to the specific context of the audience.

This study proceeds with such hermeneutical concerns in mind. It operates under the assumption that the historical author of Hebrews 'uttered' this discourse with intended meanings that largely related to an underlying narrative world. It assumes that the audience shared this narrative world to at least some degree. The author no doubt both reinforced beliefs and values the audience still shared and wished to persuade them at other points. The domain of these meanings lies in the ancient world, a world to which we have only limited access. We must be careful to speak in terms of varying degrees of probability rather than certitude.

The scope and purpose of this study

One could launch any number of investigations on the basis of the theoretical foundations we have discussed in the preceding pages. We could launch into a treatment of the author's narrative world in and of itself without extensive reference to the rhetorical use to which he has put it. On the other hand, we might launch an investigation meant to describe the total rhetorical framework of Hebrews, a study that would require extensive discussion of its literary-rhetorical structure. Both of these enterprises would be worthwhile, although the former does not greatly advance our understanding of Hebrews as a 'word' meant to persuade and the latter might become compendious in scope.

At this point I return to where this chapter began, namely, the ongoing debate over the background of Hebrews. As I mentioned at the beginning of this chapter, much of this debate has centred on the question of whether apocalyptic or Platonism provides the greatest key to the epistle's meaning. To reorient the debate in terms of Hebrews' own categories, the debate has largely focused on the nature of Hebrews' eschatology and cosmology. From a narrative perspective, we can identify these components of Hebrews' thought world as the 'settings' of the narrative. The eschatology of Hebrews relates to the *temporal* settings of the plot, the temporal movement of the story through time. On the other hand, the cosmology of Hebrews relates to the *spatial* settings of the plot, the locations in space where the plot takes place. A study that elucidated the settings of the story would thus focus on exactly the dimensions of Hebrews that seem most crucial at this point in history in order to unlock its meaning.

This study purports to pursue exactly this goal. Since Christ's death is arguably the focal event of Hebrews' narrative world, I will analyse the settings of this event, the 'settings of the sacrifice', if you will. Throughout we will have in view not just a description of the function of these settings in the narrative world of Hebrews, but also their function in Hebrews' rhetoric and rhetorical world. Chapter 2 will provide a synopsis of Hebrews' overall rhetorical strategy by a broad consideration of the epistle's rhetorical situation and the way Hebrews addresses it by way of its underlying narrative world. Chapters 3 and 4 will then explore the temporal settings of the narrative world. Chapter 3 will show how this event enables the eschatological fulfilment of the plot's overall goal. Then chapter 4 will focus on Christ's sacrifice as the transitional, topical sequence in the plot that enables the plot's successful completion.

Chapters 5 and 6 then turn to the spatial settings of the plot, which arguably stand at the very heart of the background question. Chapter 5 will treat the epistle's dualism both in terms of the universe and in terms of human nature. Chapter 6 will focus on the heavenly tabernacle, its nature and function in Hebrews' rhetorical world. The conclusion will then synthesize various aspects of this study. It will present the narrative world of Hebrews in story form. It seems appropriate thereafter to return briefly to the question of Hebrews' background. The conclusion thus ends with some speculation about the details of Hebrews' rhetorical situation in retrospect. I wonder if Hebrews, rather than being a polemic against the Levitical sacrificial system, is in fact a consolation in the wake of its destruction. In such a situation, the author powerfully implies that the temple's destruction need not call into question the fundamentals of Christian Judaism. In the consummation of the ages, Christ has made reality what the Levitical system was never actually designed to accomplish.

2

THE RHETORICAL STRATEGY
OF HEBREWS

The 'rhetorical situation' of Hebrews

We might define the rhetorical situation behind a speech or writing as
the complex of persons, settings and events that results in the creation
of that piece of rhetoric. In this definition I am building on the work of
Lloyd Bitzer.[1] We can identify three basic factors in such a situation: (1)
the particulars of the audience, (2) the particulars of the rhetor, and (3)
what Bitzer calls the 'exigence', the efficient cause behind the creation of
the rhetorical piece.[2] While we can induce some basics from the text of
Hebrews about the author and audience, the focus of our interest should
be the so-called exigence. The exigence is what actually leads to the
creation of a discourse, that which culminates in speech or writing. Bitzer
defined it as 'an imperfection marked by urgency . . . a defect, an obstacle,
something waiting to be done, a thing which is other than it should be'.[3]
This exigence corresponds closely to what George Kennedy has called
the central 'rhetorical problem' that an author addresses.[4]

The purpose of this chapter is to understand the overall rhetorical strategy of Hebrews enough to interpret individual passages relating to its
eschatology and cosmology appropriately. The first chapter identified the
failure to consider this overall strategy as a key methodological pitfall
in prior studies of specific topics in the book. To delineate the rhetorical

---

[1] He defined a rhetorical situation as 'a complex of persons, events, objects, and relations
presenting an actual or potential exigence which can be completely or partially removed
if discourse, introduced into the situation, can so constrain human decision or action as
to bring about the significant modification of the exigence' ('The Rhetorical Situation',
Philosophy and Rhetoric 1 (1968) 6).

[2] Here I am also modifying in particular D. F. Watson's delineation of Bitzer's definition. Watson identified the three components as (1) the exigence, (2) the audience and (3)
the constraints brought to the situation by the rhetor (*Invention, Arrangement, and Style:
Rhetorical Criticism of Jude and 2 Peter* (SBLDS 104; Atlanta: Scholars Press, 1988) 9).

[3] 'Situation', 6.

[4] G. A. Kennedy, *New Testament Interpretation through Rhetorical Criticism* (Chapel
Hill: University of North Carolina Press, 1984) 36.

strategy of Hebrews first requires us to infer the basic rhetorical situation it addresses and thus the rhetorical problem that gave rise to it. To get at this rhetorical problem, we must first consider Hebrews' fascinating alternation between exposition and exhortation.[5] The paraenetic material of Hebrews tends to repeat exhortations with similar content, a key datum in ascertaining its rhetorical problem and exigence.[6] Its expositional material, on the other hand, tends to build an argument.[7] The exhortations often interrupt this argument as a strategy to retain the audience's attention and reinforce the rhetorical point of the sermon, but the train of thought often resumes where it left off after the exhortation ends.

The recurring exhortations of the author provide more or less direct information on the rhetorical problem and exigence behind the sermon's creation. We must of course take care in assessing the degree of 'logical' (*logos*) investment the author truly has in each warning. Yet he has left us enough information to make some general inferences about what he saw as the central need of the audience. The exposition, while less direct in its evidence, also reflects the exigence behind the sermon by way of its focus and emphasis. Those elements of the story that the author does not mention or mentions in passing apparently did not constitute a major point of disagreement in his mind. In contrast, those points that preoccupy the discourse are either main points of disagreement or at least points in the story wherein the author saw solutions to the rhetorical problem. Hebrews 8:1 is particularly helpful in this regard as it indicates the 'main point' (κεφάλαιον) of the exposition, which presumably corresponds in some way to the main point of Hebrews' exhortations.

Once we have a basic grasp of the central problems the author was attempting to address, we can see more clearly how his interpretations of the underlying story contributed to his solutions. In other words, his rhetorical strategy will become more apparent. At this point what Duane Watson has called 'the constraints brought to the situation by the rhetor' come more forcibly into play.[8] For example, we can detect in Hebrews a number of points at which the author was building upon traditional motifs from early Christianity or using common interpretations of the Greek Old Testament. It will become clear that the underlying narrative from which Hebrews argues is basically the same narrative world as that of Paul and other early Christians. To be sure, Hebrews has its own perspectives on certain aspects of the story, but the overall plot remains quite similar.

---

[5] Very helpful in this regard is G. H. Guthrie's study *The Structure of Hebrews: A Text-Linguistic Analysis* (NovTSup 73; Leiden: E. J. Brill, 1994).
[6] *Structure* 127.   [7] *Structure* 121–7.   [8] *Invention* 9.

We will find that the most unique differences between Hebrews and earlier Christian tradition lie in the significance of the settings of the story. The nature of the author's contrast between old and new, heaven and earth effected in practice a greater discontinuity between the old and new covenants than earlier Christian writings had envisaged. Yet by relating the two to one another in the relationship of literal to metaphorical, the author was able to retain a significant verisimilitude of continuity.

The rhetorical problem of Hebrews

The exhortations of Hebrews

Numerous proposals exist for the literary structure of Hebrews.[9] For our purposes it is not necessary to enter into such discussions in detail. Nevertheless, George H. Guthrie's observations concerning Hebrews' alternation of exhortation and exposition are very suggestive from a heuristic standpoint. Guthrie sees the author's exposition from Heb. 1:5 to 10:18 more or less as a single argument punctuated by occasional interruptions with hortatory material. He also understands this argument in narrative terms, beginning with the pre-existent Christ and ending with the exalted Christ at God's right hand.[10]

While I disagree with Guthrie at some points on the progress of the argument in the exposition of Hebrews, his overall thesis seems generally valid.[11] In particular, Guthrie is correct that the exhortations of Hebrews largely repeat the same basic point in various ways. Rhetorically, they functioned both to make the relevance of the exposition clear, as well as to maintain the audience's attention. The author's direct and indirect exhortations all pushed the audience to the same course of action, namely, continuation in Christian Jewish faith as the author understood it.[12] In this regard some admonitions functioned positively by way of encouragement and command. Others functioned negatively in the way they discouraged

---

[9] For an excellent presentation of the issue and for very helpful suggestions, see Guthrie, *Structure*.

[10] *Structure* 121–4, 142.

[11] It is not clear, for example, that Heb. 1:5–14 has Christ's literal pre-existence in view. In general we would see greater disjunction than Guthrie in the progress of Hebrews' exposition. Guthrie is nevertheless correct that, in various sections, the removal of the exhortations yields a continuous argument.

[12] Because reference to 'Christian' faith runs the risk of importing false assumptions regarding how the author might have viewed his relationship to Judaism, I will frequently refer to the author's faith as 'Christian Jewish' faith, making it clear that the author may not have seen his Christian faith as a departure from Jewish faith.

failure to persist. These negative exhortations utilized prohibition and dissuasion.

Positive exhortations

At least since the time of Wolfgang Nauck, scholars have noticed the quasi-inclusio created in Hebrews by 4:14–16 and 10:19–23.[13] Not only do these verses have a high degree of overlap in content, but they arguably frame the central theological exposition of Hebrews on the topic of Christ's high priesthood. They thus hold a very prominent place in the rhetorical structure of Hebrews' argument. Because of their close relationship to this sermon's exposition, they also highlight the principal inference the author drew from his theological argument. The core positive exhortations these two passages make is (1) to hold fast the confession (Heb. 4:14; 10:23) and (2) to approach God confidently for grace and help (4:16; 10:22). Both passages give the certainty of Christ's atonement as the basis for such positive action. The 'confession' relates, on the one hand, to the sonship and high priesthood of Christ (4:14; 10:19–21). To a high degree these 'offices' in Hebrews correlate functionally to the atonement provided through Christ. In this sense, the author did not view such ideas as abstract theological constructs. Rather, the affirmation of such beliefs entailed the Christian hope for ultimate salvation (10:23).

The other positive exhortations of Hebrews reiterate the basic substance of these two core admonitions. Hebrews 4:11 encourages the audience to strive to enter into God's rest, a metaphor that probably entailed both a daily recommitment of faith to the Christian hope (e.g. 4:7) and an endurance until the day of salvation (e.g. 4:1, 9).[14] Hebrews 6:11 exhorts the audience to demonstrate diligence in their affirmation of hope until the end, a diligence the author insists they have shown in the past (cf. 10:32–5). He identifies their core need as one of endurance (10:36) and thereafter launches an encomium on faith (fulness) in ch. 11. When the author finishes praising faithful figures from the Jewish Scriptures, his conclusion reiterates the theme that launched the encomium: run with

---

[13] 'Zum Aufbau des Hebräerbriefes', *Judentum, Urchristentum, Kirche: Festschrift für Joachim Jeremias*, W. Eltester, ed. (Berlin: Alfred Töpelmann, 1960) 200–3. I say 'quasi' because 10:19 probably begins a new literary unit, rather than ending the previous one. The literary device of inclusio requires the common words or themes to lie within the unit they bind together.

[14] So also C. K. Barrett, 'The Eschatology of the Epistle to the Hebrews', *The Background of the New Testament and Its Eschatology*, W. D. Davies and D. Daube, eds. (Cambridge: Cambridge University Press, 1964 (1954)) 372: 'The "rest", precisely because it is God's, is both present and future; men enter it, and must strive to enter it.'

patience the race set before us (12:1). While we will need to consider the degree of logical investment the author had in these admonitions, the exigence behind the creation of this sermon seems clear enough. The author perceived that, on some level, the audience needed encouragement to endure in their commitment to the Christian Jewish confession of hope. He punctuated this basic message a number of times by comparing the audience's situation to that of individuals in the Jewish Scriptures who were faced with analogous choices.

Abraham, for example, functions positively as an example of someone who persisted in faith throughout his earthly pilgrimage. The author surely intended his comments about Abraham and the patriarchs in Heb. 11 to parallel the audience's situation:

> In faith these all died, although they had not received the promises. But they saw and greeted them from afar, and they confessed that they were strangers and refugees on the earth. For those who say such things make it known that they are seeking a homeland. And if they still had regard for the one from which they departed, they could still return. But now they desire a better one, that is, a heavenly one. Therefore, God is not ashamed to be called their God: he prepared a city for them.[15]
>
> (11:13–16)

In this passage we see the same dynamics at play that I have already mentioned. The author encourages the audience to make the same *confession* as Abraham and the patriarchs, namely, that they are seeking a heavenly rather than an earthly homeland. They are to continue in faith (fulness) until the end, as Abraham did – even if they do not receive their promised hope before they die.

It would not be appropriate to speculate much further about the hortatory implications of this passage at this point. Nevertheless, it seems reasonable to think that the *exempla fidei* in Heb. 11 probably served as indirect exhortations addressing the perceived situation of the audience.[16] For example, this passage suggests that the audience may die before they see the promised hope arrive. Various elements of the chapter anticipate possible persecution or exile (e.g. 11:24–7, 35b–38), although it also presents the possibility of escape and vindication (e.g. 11:5, 29–35a). Finally, the passage may imply that the audience was conflicted

---

[15] All translations are the author's, unless otherwise noted.

[16] See ch. 7 of my book, *Understanding the Book of Hebrews: The Story behind the Sermon* (Louisville, KY: Westminster/John Knox, 2003).

over some 'homeland' that held a competing claim on their loyalty. But I will resist the urge to speculate at this point of the study.

Negative exhortations

If the narrative of Abraham's faithful pilgrimage provided a positive example of endurance until the end, the wilderness generation provided a negative one. Hebrews 3:7–4:13 excellently illustrates how the author can interrupt the flow of his argument to reiterate his basic hortatory point. As in other cases, he makes this point in a way relevant to the exposition he is interrupting. Since the immediate context of the exhortation is a contrast between Moses and Christ (3:1–6), the author turns to the example of the wilderness generation to reiterate his basic admonition to endure.

Hebrews 3:7–19 draws on Ps. 95 (94 LXX) to illustrate that faith is necessary *until the very end* in order to enter into God's rest. Like the wilderness generation, the audience had 'left Egypt' (3:16) when they were enlightened as Christians, when they 'tasted of the heavenly gift and became partakers of Holy Spirit' (6:4). They had appropriated the sacrifice of Christ for their sins (e.g. 6:6; 10:26). But like the wilderness generation, it is not enough simply to leave Egypt. After all, the corpses of those who left Egypt fell in the desert (3:17) because of their unbelief or lack of faith (3:19). The author thus used this story to show that it is only those who 'hold firm the first substance until the end' (3:14) who will prove to 'have become partakers of the Christ'. His conclusions are familiar: do not fall short of the promise (4:1); let us be diligent to enter into that rest (4:11); do not have an 'evil heart of disbelief' that turns away from the living God (3:12).

Hebrews 12:16–17 uses the story of Esau to make the same point in even starker terms. Esau gave away the rights of a firstborn son in exchange for one meal.[17] Then he was rejected afterward when he wished to inherit the blessing. In some of the most frightening rhetoric in the New Testament, Hebrews warns that 'he did not find a place of repentance although he sought for it with tears' (12:17).[18] In the light of the parallelism between this exhortation and the other admonitions we have been examining, it is clear that the author meant this story as yet another warning to the

---

[17] The parallel between this statement regarding Esau and the similar exhortations regarding food in Heb. 13:9–11 is enticing.

[18] It is of course grammatically possible that Hebrews refers to the blessing rather than repentance as that which Esau sought with tears (e.g. C. R. Koester, *Hebrews* (New York: Doubleday, 2001) 531). In either case the basic point remains – 'selling your birthright' entails a failure to inherit the 'blessing'.

audience: do not turn away from the living God; do not abandon your 'sonship'. If you do, you will never be able to get it back.

In both instances, after the author used the wilderness generation and Esau as examples, he punctuated his message with reference to the fearsome judgement of God. In the case of the wilderness generation, he ended his digression with almost hymnic language on the discerning power of God's *logos*, before which 'everything is naked and exposed' (4:13). The author no doubt meant this imagery of the *logos* as a sword (cf. Wis. 18:15) to have the force of a deterrent: watch out, for the *logos* can 'cut' between the thoughts and intents of your heart. In 12:18–29 the author evokes even more explicit images of judgement. Here he pictures the end of the age when God will shake the entire created realm. That discussion ends with reference to the fact that 'our God is a consuming fire' (12:29).

The author's most direct exhortation, however, the central exhortation of Hebrews, takes place in yet another digression: Heb. 5:11–6:20. Within this exhortation, 5:11–6:8 addresses the deficiencies and dangers facing the audience, while 6:9–20 expresses the author's encouragement and conviction that they will in fact make it till the end. This latter unit reveals a confidence on the author's part that the audience will heed his warnings and that they will remain consistent with their past acts of faithfulness (6:9–12). Hebrews 5:11–14 indicates the author's sense that the audience has not matured appropriately in their ability to discern good from evil (e.g. 5:14). The author uses well-known educational and athletic imagery to shame the audience for their failure to move to the level of 'teacher'. A number of commentators have rightly noted that the situation was not likely as dire as the author makes it sound. David deSilva notes that '[t]he goal of this section is to provoke the addressees to acquit themselves of the charge that they are not ready for mature instruction'.[19] Jean Héring notes further that the author actually goes on to give them the strong 'meat' that they supposedly were not yet mature enough to eat, namely, Christ's role as a high priest after the order of Melchizedek (5:11–12).[20]

Nevertheless, while these rhetorical considerations soften the force of these statements, they do not negate the clear direction in which they are moving. While the audience is redeemable and not in as dire a faith crisis as these words might initially suggest, the author believes they have a genuine need for encouragement and dissuasion so that their commitment remains intact. I could mention any number of scholarly speculations

---

[19] *Perseverance in Gratitude: A Socio-Rhetorical Commentary on the Epistle 'to the Hebrews'* (Grand Rapids, MI: Eerdmans, 2000) 213.

[20] *The Epistle to the Hebrews* (London: Epworth, 1970) 43.

about what the 'detractors' might be in relation to who the audience might be. I will resist filling in the gaps in our knowledge at this point, however, so that I do not prejudice my inquiry before it even gets underway.

Conclusion from exhortations

I conclude in broad terms that the fundamental 'exigent' in the rhetorical situation behind Hebrews is the perception of the author that the audience needs to be encouraged to continue in their commitment to the Christian Jewish confession. The author also dissuades them from giving up in their pilgrimage, but it is not entirely clear that this outcome is a real danger at this point. Throughout the sermon he punctuates his message with positive encouragement to endure, as well as with negative statements of the consequences of not enduring. To substantiate these exhortations, he provides examples of both faith and disbelief. Meanwhile, he also substantiates his exhortations with arguments from the narrative of salvation history. This latter point brings us to the exposition of Hebrews. It is natural to presume a close relationship between the exposition and exhortation of Hebrews, to see the author's interpretations of salvation history as material to the circumstances of the audience. While in theory the two could be only superficially related, such does not seem to be the case.

The exposition of Hebrews

My purpose at this time is to suggest in very broad terms how Hebrews' exposition might contribute to a basic understanding of its exigent circumstances. If the exposition of Hebrews substantiates its exhortations, then we would expect its *topoi* to relate to those factors the author perceives to endanger the audience's continued commitment to their Christian Jewish confession. It is of course possible theoretically that Hebrews' arguments are simply epideictic affirmations amounting to 'what great things we believe'. But the actual logic of these passages, along with the fact that Hebrews' argument pushes us toward consistent themes, suggests that these arguments relate directly in some way to the exigent circumstances behind the sermon.

Hebrews 1:5–2:18

These verses arguably constitute a coherent section of expositional discourse interrupted by a brief exhortation in 2:1–4. The first half contrasts the greatness of Christ with the angels (1:5–14), while the second half expands on the relationship between Christ and 'those about to inherit salvation' (1:14).[21] The exhortation to 'hold fast' in 2:1 is predicated on the contrast that precedes (thus, διὰ τοῦτο), and 2:5–18 then further substantiates this exhortation (thus, γάρ in 2:5). While it is not wise to speculate at this point what role angels might have played in the thought of the audience, note in particular their association with the Jewish law in 2:2. Because ὁ δι' ἀγγέλων λαληθεὶς λόγος (2:2) is inferior to the salvation spoken through Christ, an even greater attention is necessary to the message of Christ than was necessary to the law under the old covenant. Hebrews 2:5–18 then expands on the greatness of Christ's word of salvation. It gives in a nutshell the benefits of Christ's atonement for believers (e.g., 2:9, 17–18), including the fact that he makes it possible to attain the glory originally intended for humanity (2:8, 10). The exposition of 1:5–2:18 thus seems to substantiate the exhortation to hold fast in 2:1–4 by way of (1) the superiority of Christ to the old covenant and (2) the incredible benefits of Christ's atonement.

Before I leave this section, I should not neglect to mention 2:17–18, which some have identified as the *propositio* of Hebrews.[22] These verses give us the first mention of Christ as a 'high priest with regard to things in relation to God in order to atone for the sins of the people' (2:17). In these verses we have a hint that the part of the old covenant about which the audience was waning the most in confidence related in some way to atonement.[23] My consideration of the remaining exposition will powerfully confirm this first impression.

Hebrews 3:1–4:13

The precise contours of this section are not essential to my argument. I simply note that, once again, an exposition in 3:1–6 is interrupted by the exhortation of 3:7–4:13.[24] The relationship between this short exposition

---

[21] For my understanding of the Christ–angels contrast as eschatological in nature, see ch. 4, as well as my 'A Celebration of the Enthroned Son: The Catena of Hebrews 1', *JBL* 120 (2001) 469–85.

[22] W. G. Übelacker, *Der Hebräerbrief als Appell: Untersuchungen zu exordium, narration, und postscriptum (Hebr 1–2 und 13,22–25)* (CB 21; Stockholm: Almquist & Wiksell, 1989). Vanhoye's breakdown of the letter's literary structure nearly implies the same, *La structure littéraire de l'épître aux Hébreux*, 2nd edn (StudNeot 1; Paris: Desclée de Brouwer, 1976).

[23] As B. Lindars argued, perhaps to an extreme, *The Theology of the Letter to the Hebrews* (Cambridge: Cambridge University Press, 1991).

[24] To be sure, this exhortation has its own exposition within it. We can, however, distinguish in Hebrews between exposition that is incorporated within its exhortation and is 'local' and exposition that is sustained and builds.

and the more extended exhortation that follows is one of logical cause
and effect. Given the argument of 3:1–6, the exhortation of 3:7–4:13 is
a logical conclusion (cf. διό in 3:7). The exhortation warns the audience
not to harden their hearts (3:8) or have an evil heart of unbelief that turns
away from the living God (3:12). The basis for these imperatives in 3:1–6
is the superiority of Christ as son over Moses as servant.

Here is Hebrews' standard *qal wahomer* argument. The audience was
apparently inclined to believe that Moses was important to salvation history. Similarly, they were apparently inclined to accept the authority of
Scripture as well, given the author's use of it to substantiate his claims.
Without denying that Moses is a significant figure in the story of salvation, the author asserts that Christ is even more important. The point is
much like the argument in 2:1–4, where the author uses the superiority
of Christ to the angels to argue that it is even more important to heed
Christ's message than that of the angels. In 3:1–6, the author apparently
uses the superiority of Christ to Moses to argue the same conclusion.
Moses' message was important, but Christ's is even more important.

Hebrews argues for the superiority of Christ to Moses in two ways.
First, 3:3 uses the analogy of the superiority of a house builder to a house,
with Christ as the builder and Moses as the house. Hebrews 3:5 then shifts
the metaphor slightly: Moses is a servant in a house where Christ is the
son. Hebrews 3:4 subordinates both of these individuals to God as the
one who builds everything and who is ultimately the house owner (3:6).
Hebrews thus places both Christ and Moses in the same story of salvation,
but with Christ as the superior. The logical conclusion the author wished
the audience to draw from this superiority is that to reject Christ or the
Christian Jewish hope (3:6) would be to reject God's workings in the same
way the wilderness generation did. Indeed, Hebrews insists on more than
mere assent to such beliefs. It admonishes the audience to hold fast in
'boldness' and 'boasting' about this hope (3:6).

Does any connection exist between the rhetorical purpose of the exposition in 1:5–2:18 and its purpose in this section? Indeed, they do serve
quite similar rhetorical purposes. At the very least, in both passages Christ
is an even more important part of salvation than the respective agent in
the mainstream Jewish story, whether angels or Moses. If Christ presents
a more crucial revelation than the angels did, so Christ is more significant
in God's plan than Moses was. All these characters are part of the same
story, but Christ plays a more important role than either angels or Moses.

The author must also have linked both Moses and the angels (cf. 2:2) to
the Law and thus to the old covenant. To contrast Christ with these figures
was thus to contrast the new covenant with the old covenant. Further, we

find in 3:1–6 evidence for something the rest of Hebrews will confirm, namely, that the author focused primarily on the cultic and atoning significance of the Law when he wrote of the old covenant. Hebrews 3:5 tells us that Moses was a witness τῶν λαληθησομένων (3:5). What are these things? The use of λαλέω here connects 3:1–6 to the events to which Heb. 1:1–2 allude. In many and various ways, God formerly 'spoke' to the fathers by the prophets (1:1). It seems all too likely that the author included Moses as one of these prophets, especially given the prophetic sense of Moses as a witness of 'things that will be spoken'.[25] In contrast, Jesus is the son through whom God has recently spoken at the beginning of the eschaton, in 'these last days', an allusion to the eschatological phrase used so frequently in Jeremiah.[26]

What is the speaking of Jesus to which Heb. 1:2 refers and thus that to which Moses gave witness? Hebrews 1:1–4 only mentions two tasks that Jesus performed at the turn of the ages: (1) he made a cleansing of sins (1:3), and (2) he sat on the right hand of majesty in the heights. Since 2:3 refers to Christ's speaking as a 'word of salvation', we can reasonably infer that the atoning work of Christ, confirmed by his session at God's right hand, is the principal 'speaking' Hebrews has in mind. I thus conclude that the exposition of 3:1–6 serves some of the same basic rhetorical purposes as 1:5–2:18 did. In particular, these verses reflect (1) the superiority of Christ to the old covenant and (2) the incredible benefits of Christ's atonement, particularly in relation to the Mosaic Law.

Hebrews 4:14–16

I have already mentioned these verses briefly in our consideration of the exhortations of Hebrews. Structurally, they serve as a kind of introduction to the next six chapters or so of Hebrews (5:1–10:18) and thus to the extended exposition that follows them. Prior to these verses, Hebrews has affirmed Christ's high priesthood in 2:17–18 and has indicated the author's intention to consider it in 3:1. With 4:14, the author begins to address Christ's priesthood directly. Notice this thread that connects the exposition thus far. It reinforces our increasing sense that the author connected the need of the audience for continued confidence with the reality of Christ's high priesthood and, thus, with his atoning intercession.

---

[25] For a systematic treatment of Moses in Hebrews, see M. R. D'Angelo's, *Moses in the Epistle to the Hebrews* (SBLDS 42; Missoula, MT: Scholars Press, 1979).
[26] E.g. Jer. 7:32; 9:25 (24 LXX); 16:14; 19:6; 23:5, 7; 30 (37 LXX):3; 31 (38 LXX):27, 31, 38; 48 (31 LXX):12; 49 (30 LXX):2; 51 (28 LXX):52

Because the audience has such a great high priest who has passed through the heavens, they should hold fast to their confession.

I mentioned earlier two key points that 4:14–16 makes as exhortation, points that it shares with 10:19–23: (1) to hold fast the confession (Heb. 4:14; 10:23) and (2) to approach God confidently for grace and help (4:16; 10:22). Yet these verses also partake of exposition. The audience is urged to hold fast its confession because of the greatness of Jesus as a high priest who has passed through the heavens (4:14). And the author singles out Christ's ability to sympathize with human weakness in temptation while at the same time being victorious over it (4:15). In consequence, the audience is urged to approach the throne of grace with boldness when help is needed (4:16).

What might these allusions to the Christian story say about the rhetorical situation and problem behind Hebrews? A number of conclusions seem immediately apparent. For one, Hebrews reinforces confidence by way of Christ's role as intercessor, someone able to help in a time of temptation. This fact suggests that the audience may be facing some crisis or potential crisis in its environment, indeed that they may already stand in need of some forgiveness for failure. Further, the consistent connection in Hebrews between the need for endurance and Christ's atoning priesthood increasingly points us to see the audience's lack of confidence in relation to the ability of the Christian Jewish confession to provide an adequate atonement for sins.

Hebrews 5:1–7:28

Continuing the pattern we have already seen twice in Hebrews, the author begins a train of thought in 5:1–10 only to interrupt it with the exhortation of 5:11–6:20. The author then resumes this train of thought in Heb. 7 in greater particularity. The dominant question addressed by the exposition both in 5:1–10 and 7:1–28 is how we might consider Christ a high priest. The relevance of this theological exposition to the situation of the audience is reflected most clearly by the point which sparks the author's shift to exhortation. This shift occurs after the author first mentions that Christ's sufferings made him an αἴτιον σωτηρίας αἰωνίου and constituted his appointment as a 'high priest after the order of Melchizedek'.

It is surely significant that the most intense exhortation of the entire book occurs at this point and resumes from this point after it has finished. The digression of 5:11–6:20 begins with the author's regret that the dullness of the audience's hearing hinders his ability to proceed with a discussion of Christ's high-priestly role (5:11). The significance of Christ as high priest is 'strong food' they should be able to eat but are not eating (5:12). Of course, much of this shaming language is rhetorical and aimed at moving the audience. The author *does* go on to discuss Christ as a Melchizedekian priest and thus does not consider them as deft as he makes them sound.[27]

If all we had was this particular section of the sermon, we would already have strong evidence that some aspect of Christ's high-priestly role stood at the centre of the audience's need for renewed commitment to the Christian confession. Yet this conclusion is also supported soundly by the other expositional units we have examined thus far. Again and again, the argument resurfaces with a twofold conclusion: (1) the superiority of the new covenant to the old and (2) the superior adequacy of Christ's salvation/atonement/high priestly intercession. The exposition of 5:1–7:28 continues this line of argument in much greater detail than we have seen heretofore. Hebrews 5:1–10 sets out the qualifications for a priest. A priest cannot appoint himself – so also Christ did not appoint himself (5:4–10). The degree of substantiation involved in this argument suggests that the audience may have doubts about Christ's 'high priesthood', whatever it might mean for them. Hebrews 5:7–10 provides a glimpse of that process of appointment.

In Heb. 7, the author goes to great lengths to unfold what Ps. 110:4 might mean when it refers to the Christ as a 'priest after the order of Melchizedek'. This chapter pits the Levitical and Melchizedekian priesthoods in contrast to each other. That of Melchizedek is superior to that of Levi for Melchizedek was superior to Abraham (7:4–10). Similarly, the Levitical priesthood on which the Law was instituted was not sufficient to bring about perfection or atonement for those who worshipped through them (7:11). The change of priesthood reflected in the arrival of Christ as a Melchizedekian priest signifies a change of law (7:12). The earthly priests died continually, but Christ's eternity implies a finality of priesthood (7:15, 27–28).

We thus see in this argument (1) substantiation that Christ was in fact a priest, (2) that his Melchizedekian high priesthood was superior to the Levitical priesthood because (3) the Levitical system of atonement did not actually perfect those who approached God by way of it, and (4) it was not permanent in its salvific effect, as Christ's service is. If these points relate to the waning confidence of the audience – and we should suppose they do – they provide significant insight into the rhetorical situation/problem behind the letter. Believers who formerly demonstrated

[27] See n. 19.

valiant faithfulness (6:10; 10:32–4) now waver in boldness. The reasons for their wavering seem wrapped up in the significance of Christ's atoning work vis-à-vis the Levitical cultus. In response, the author substantiates the validity and superiority of Christ as high priest and as one who brings salvation.

As a final note, I should mention the supporting arguments of 6:13–20 and 7:20–25, both of which urge endurance on the basis of God's faithfulness to his promises and oaths. Hebrews 6:13–20 uses the example of God's faithfulness to keep his promises to Abraham as an example of how God follows through with his will. Hebrews 7:20–5 makes the same point from the oath of Ps. 110:4 relating to Christ as a Melchizedekian priest. These passages suggest that the audience, once convinced of what God's will was, were now wondering if he had changed it, perhaps if they had even understood it correctly in the first place. Any number of exigents could be involved in such questioning, and scholars have suggested all of them: questions arising from the destruction of the Jerusalem temple, questions arising from the deaths of the apostles, questions arising from the delay of Christ's return, questions arising from a time of persecution.

I will not speculate further on such potential exigents at this time. My concern is more broadly to identify the connection between Hebrews' exhortation and exposition. Here we have repeatedly seen (1) a desire on the part of the author to show the superiority of the dispensation signified by Christ to that of what the author will refer to as an 'old' covenant and (2) more specifically, the superiority of Christ and his atonement/salvation to anything provided by the Levitical system or the old covenant. With the argument of Heb. 7, I may now indicate a third point, namely, (3) that this superiority indicates a definite shift in the means of approach to God. Not only is Christ superior to the old covenant, but he replaces it as a means of access to God and to salvation from God's judgement.

Hebrews 8:1–10:18

Hebrews 8:1 confirms that the high priesthood of Christ is indeed the κεφάλαιον of the author's exposition. We can thus presume that whatever Christ's high priesthood entailed for the author, it provided the perceived solution to the audience's problem of waning confidence. The significance of Christ's high priesthood is the focal expositional point that substantiates the author's exhortations to hold fast in faithfulness. Thus far we have seen the significance of that high priesthood in terms of (1) the superiority of a new covenant to the previous one, largely entailing (2) a superior atonement and priestly intercession on the part of Christ vis-à-vis the

Levitical cultus, and further (3) that in fact the author believed the new covenant with its atonement displaced and replaced the old covenant and its atonement.

If we had any lingering doubts about these three points, the central exposition of the sermon removes them. First, the author now explicitly presents the contrast between the old and new covenants (e.g. 8:6). Hebrews 8:1–13 provides these overarching categories in order to describe and conceptualize the change in God's dispensation signified by Christ. Secondly, the superiority of Christ's atonement and priesthood is presented throughout this section by way of two related contrasts: the superiority of Christ's sacrifice to previous Levitical sacrifices and the superiority of Christ's sanctuary to the wilderness tabernacle. Hebrews 9:1–10 lays out the contrasting sanctuaries in detail, and 9:11–28 contrasts the sacerdotal roles performed in the two contrasting 'holies'. Hebrews 10:1–8 continues and reiterates these themes in a somewhat generalizing way that gives us the climactic big picture of the entire exposition thus far.

Thirdly, 8:13 presents the decisive shift represented by the change of covenants in perhaps the starkest form in the whole sermon: 'when he says "new", he has declared the first covenant "old". And what is old and infirm is near its disappearance.' The author expends a good deal of exegetical energy not only to show that Christ's priestly service is superior to that of any earthly Levitical priest, but that it *replaces* the Levitical cultus and displaces the law on which it was based (cf. 7:12; 10:9). We should carefully consider the way in which the author presents this decisive change and the superiority of the new over the old. Despite strong rhetoric, the author never directly tells the audience not to rely on the Levitical cultus. While such non-reliance is *an implication* of his argument, his point seems more positive than negative: *rely* on Christ's atonement rather than *do not rely* on the Levitical cultus. We should pay close attention to this distinction when we explore what exigent circumstances might have inspired such an intense argument.

Miscellaneous exposition

With the author's primary expositional point made, 10:19 and the verses that follow reiterate in full force exhortations appropriate to the truths the author has been setting forth. We have already discussed briefly some of those exhortations to endure in faithfulness and to hold fast to the confession. The author asserts that he and the audience are not people who shrink back and are destroyed. They are people of faithfulness who preserve their soul (10:39). It is worthwhile to mention a few other expositional elements scattered in the remaining chapters of Hebrews that are consistent with the author's main exposition of Christ's high priesthood. While these interpretive items are 'embedded' in hortatory material, they testify to the author's use of the story of salvation history in relation to the audience's situation.

First, note the allusion to sacrifice in Heb. 11:4, where the author mentions Abel's superior sacrifice to that of Cain. The perfect tense of προσήνεγκεν is noteworthy in the author's statement, for it seems to imply that Abel's sacrifice *remains* offered or, better, that the truth of the biblical text remains in force for the audience. Indeed, although Abel has died, he still speaks through his sacrifice. It is certainly possible that this exemplum means to encourage the audience to endure whatever persecution or suffering they might face. In the context of contrasting sacrifices, however, this verse also evokes images of the contrast between Christ's sacrifice and that of Levitical priests. It is at least possible that we see in Abel and Cain an allegory of reliance on Christ's sacrifice and reliance on the Levitical cultus.

We might further notice the parallel between Esau in Heb. 12:16 and the mention of food in 13:9. In the former passage, the author uses Esau as a negative example to avoid. He serves as such an example because he was a πόρνος and βέβηλος man. He sold his birthright ἀντὶ βρώσεως μιᾶς. The imagery seems to imply that the audience would not want to exchange its 'sonship' for whatever is symbolized by Esau's meal. When we couple this with the reference to βρώματα in 13:9 and place it in a cultic context, our suspicions increase that at least some derivative of the Levitical cultus was in view in relation to this difficult verse.

Hebrews 13:9 is an ambiguous verse from our current perspective. It has brought its own fair share of speculation. I offer the barest of observations simply to bolster and refine my conclusions thus far. First, the allusive nature of the comment implies that its referent was well enough known to the audience. It cannot be merely a reference to the Jerusalem cultus, for the author refers to something that fits under the heading 'strange teaching'. The author further contrasts 'those who serve the tent' with the altar from which the audience can eat. In keeping with the earlier imagery of the sermon, Christ's sacrificial 'meat' would appear to be the altar appropriate to the audience, probably at least a metaphor for Christ's atoning death. It seems impossible to know exactly what 'foods' in the audience's environment might relate to some 'strange teaching' with a relation to the 'tent'. Nevertheless, the comment implies that the author's contrast of Christ's atonement with the Levitical cultus is at this point something more than a mere epideictic reinforcement of things the audience already believes. At least some of the rhetoric must relate to some real Levitical alternative to Christ in the audience's environment, likely one involving food.[28] I will suggest further possibilities at the end of this study.

Conclusion on the rhetorical problem

Hebrews repeats the same basic exhortation throughout its whole, namely, that the audience must remain confident and bold in their commitment to the Christian confession. They need to 'pay attention' (2:1), 'hold fast' (3:6, 14), 'hold to the confession' (4:14; 10:23), 'bring to completion' (6:1), 'approach God with boldness for help' (4:16; 10:22), not shrink to destruction but persist in faith (10:39; ch. 11), and many other images of endurance. It is more difficult to ascertain the reasons for their waning confidence, although a number of statements imply that persecution or hardship of some sort may be involved. However, the 'main point' is that Christ is an effective high priest (8:1). This focal point leads us to believe that the atoning efficacy of Christ bore directly on their waning confidence in some way.

The author of Hebrews went to great lengths to show Christ as superior to the atoning and intercessory efficacy of the Levitical cultus, as well as the covenant and law of which it was a part. While the author does not explicitly tell the audience *not* to rely on the Levitical cultus, his exposition of Scripture repeatedly and emphatically implies that to rely on it would be inappropriate and contrary to God's purposes in history. He places any atoning or conciliatory function of the Levitical cultus squarely within the now obsolete old covenant, a shadowy system that Christ removed when he offered his body in performance of God's will (e.g. 10:5–10). We can only speculate about what situation or situations might have made this message bolster confidence in the audience, but they clearly bore directly on the exigent circumstances of this sermon.

The rhetorical problem, the exigence that gave rise to Hebrews, was thus at least twofold. First, the author perceived the audience to be waning or drifting to some degree in its commitment to the Christian Jewish confession as he understood it. Further, the author believed he could best address this waning confidence by unfolding the full, covenant-changing, atoning significance of Christ to them. It thus seems likely that the author

---

[28] Cf. especially the work of J. Thyrén, *Das Lobopfer der Hebräer: Studien zum Aufbau und Anliegen von Hebräerbrief 13* (Åbo: Åbo Akademi, 1973).

also perceived a second 'problem', namely, a need to appreciate the full significance of Christ vis-à-vis the Levitical cultus. At this point we must tread very carefully with our presuppositions. We should not assume, for example, that the author's tone here is primarily *polemical*. In other words, the dynamics of the situation change significantly if the author's main argument is not made in relation to an *existing* Levitical alternative. I have just argued that 13:9 likely referred to an existing 'Levitical' option, but this verse might very well relate to a more tangential issue. It is not at all clear that the heart of Hebrews' exposition on the Levitical cultus is aimed directly at whatever that verse addressed.

We must be careful not to assume one or the other at this point of the study. We should, however, leave open the largely unconsidered possibility that Hebrews' main argument is more apologetic than polemic. If the temple had already been destroyed, it is possible that the primary thrust of the exposition was to console or even defend Christian Judaism in the absence of a temple. Whatever the specifics of these two 'problems', the rhetorical situation of Hebrews was the combination of the author's identity and background brought to bear on the particulars of the audience in the light of them. The author sought to bolster their waning confidence by convincing them of the superior and definitive 'sacrifice' of Christ.

The rhetorical strategy of Hebrews

Points of continuity between author and audience

A good rhetorician finds points of common ground between his or her perspective and that of the target audience. Accordingly, we might call the rhetorical strategy of a rhetor the way in which she joins her particulars to the particulars of an audience in the light of certain exigent circumstances. In the remainder of this chapter, I want to unfold in very broad terms the rhetorical strategy of Hebrews in the light of the rhetorical problem I have identified. In particular, I identified the perceived rhetorical problem of Hebrews as (1) a waning confidence and commitment to the Christian Jewish confession as the author understood it and (2) a related need for confidence or understanding in relation to the atoning efficacy of Christ vis-à-vis Levitical means of atonement, at least in the author's mind.

If the author's argument was in any way appropriate and effective, we can discern a number of elements in it that the author must at least have thought were persuasive to the audience. For example, the pervasive use of Scripture and the author's continual recourse to the narrative of salvation history imply that the audience had significant knowledge of that story and was inclined to accept its authority over them in a significant way. It would hardly make sense to contrast Christ with angels, Moses, Levitical priests, and other elements of the 'old' covenant repeatedly if the audience was not inclined to consider the Jewish story valid in the first place. Of course, this observation need not imply that the audience was ethnically Jewish any more than such a sermon would in a modern Gentile church. While most commentators conclude that the audience was primarily Jewish, the list of 'first word of Christ' teachings in Heb. 6:1–2 does not read entirely like things a group of Jews who had accepted the Christian message would need to learn at their point of entry into the Christian community.[29] In any case, the specific ethnicity of the audience is not material to our current line of inquiry.

We can presume that this list of beginning instruction in 6:1–2 was also common ground between author and audience, even if the author shamed the audience by suggesting they might need to relearn *even* such basics. The list includes 'repentance from dead works and faith toward God, teaching about baptisms and laying on hands, the resurrection of the dead and eternal judgement'. If repentance from dead works and faith toward God relate to conversion from pagan gods to the true God, then we can indeed presume that the audience is primarily Gentile. David deSilva suggests that the baptisms, plural, here relate to something like we find in 10:22, where we find both a washing of the body and a sprinkling of the heart.[30] We might also note the New Testament connection elsewhere between Spirit baptism and laying on hands (e.g. Acts 8:17; cf. 2 Tim. 1:6–7).

But the point of contact between author and audience in which I have greatest interest is surely the matter of Christ and atonement. To what extent did the audience believe Christ's death to have atoning efficacy? Here we should acknowledge that the books of the New Testament themselves probably vary somewhat in their perspectives on Christ's atonement, particularly in terms of the scope of its coverage. We additionally lack enough evidence to reconstruct the perspective of the audience in detail, except to note that at some point they must have confessed Jesus as the Son of God (cf. 3:1) and accepted some basic message of salvation associated with Christ (e.g. 2:3) and relating to the world to come (e.g. 2:5).

I propose to approximate their view by two observations about the nature of Hebrews' argument. First, we can discern a certain soteriological

[29] Cf. H. W. Attridge, *The Epistle to the Hebrews* (Philadelphia: Fortress Press, 1989) 163–4; deSilva, *Perseverance* 216–17.
[30] Cf. *Perseverance* 217–18.

substratum to Hebrews' argument that parallels soteriological images in Paul's writings.[31] While we cannot be certain that the audience stood within the Pauline tradition, this substratum at least reflects an earlier *traditionsgeschichtlich* 'layer' *prior* to any expansion on the part of the author. Second, we note that the author's main expositional point relates to the effective high priesthood of Christ (8:1) and further that the most pointed exhortation occurs at the mention of Christ's Melchizedekian priesthood. We can conclude with reasonable certainty that the 'point of extension', the point where the author wishes to extend the audience's perspective on Christ's atonement, departs from the author's claim that Christ is a priest after the order of Melchizedek.

When we apply these two observations to Hebrews, we can identify several points where the author seems to build on prior Christian traditions. The audience may have known and/or assented to such traditions at some point in their pilgrimage. Hebrews clearly draws, for example, on prior early Christian interpretations of Ps. 110:1 in reference to Christ's exaltation and enthronement as Lord at God's right hand.[32] References and allusions to this verse abound in the New Testament, ranging from Paul's writings to Acts and the Gospels.[33] From these references we can conclude that the early Christians took this verse to be a prophecy about the Messiah, the Lord, whom the early Christians could distinguish from *the* LORD. The citations and allusions in Acts and Hebrews point us toward seeing Ps. 110:1 primarily in relation to Christ's exaltation to God's right hand, which we can associate with the time of his 'ascension' and resurrection in Acts. Thus Acts cites Ps. 110:1 and then interprets it to mean that καὶ κύριον αὐτὸν καὶ χριστὸν ἐποίησεν ὁ θεός, τοῦτον τὸν ησοῦν ὃν ὑμεῖς ἐσταυρώσατε (Acts 2:36). All the New Testament citations and allusions to Ps. 110:1 thus see the post-resurrection period as the time when Jesus is most literally acclaimed 'Lord'.

Indeed, Ps. 110:1 may actually have catalysed the early Christian affirmation of Jesus as Lord, an affirmation that Christian tradition associated with the time after Christ's resurrection (e.g. Rom. 10:9; Phil. 2:9–11). This psalm, in the light of resurrection belief, likely served as the principal biblical basis for the epithet of 'Lord' in reference to Jesus, along

---

[31] Note further the mention of a 'Timothy' in 13:23, quite possibly indicating some connection between the author and the Pauline circle.

[32] See D. M. Hay, *Glory at the Right Hand: Psalm 110:1 in Early Christianity* (SBLMS 18; Nashville: Abingdon Press, 1973).

[33] E.g. Pauline epistles: 1 Cor. 15:25; Rom. 8:34; Eph. 1:20; Gospels: Matt. 22:41–5; Mark 12:35–7; Luke 20:41–4; Acts: 2:34–6. In Hebrews itself we have 1:3, 13; 5:6; 8:1; 10:12; 12:2.

with the fact that Christian Jews could easily link the title to Messianic expectations as well.[34] Accordingly, it is not difficult to imagine that the audience of Hebrews was well acquainted with traditions relating to Ps. 110:1. At the very least, such traditions stood close at hand for the author to be able to incorporate them into his argument and extend them. Pauline tradition linked Ps. 110:1 to Ps. 8. The association is easily made on the basis of the catchword 'feet' in the phrases 'enemies as a footstool of your *feet*' (Ps. 110:1) and 'all things under his *feet*' (Ps. 8:7). Indeed, Paul himself glides smoothly from one to the other in 1 Cor. 15:25–7. He even conflates the two in 15:25, speaking of how Christ must reign ἄχρι οὗ θῇ πάντας τοὺς ἐχθροὺς ὑπὸ τοὺς πόδας αὐτοῦ. In this verse, 'until', 'put' and 'enemies' are unique to Ps. 110:1, but the 'all' and 'under' come from Ps. 8:6. A *gezerah shewa* argument based on the common term 'feet' links the two.

Hebrews clearly draws on this same early Christian association. Hebrews 1 ends with a reference to Ps. 110:1 (Heb. 1:13), only to resume its exposition with Ps. 8 (Heb. 2:6–8). I will argue in the following chapter that this association allowed the author to consider Christ the resolution of the plot of salvation history. Christ is the one who makes it finally possible for humanity to attain the glory God had originally intended for it. In the thought of Paul and the author of Hebrews, linking these two Scriptures in effect linked the beginning and ending of the plot of salvation. The one indicates God's unfulfilled intention at the beginning of the story (Ps. 8), and the second refers to the inauguration of its fulfilment at the commencement of the end of history (Ps. 110:1). If the audience stands in the Pauline tradition, I can presume they were aware of such traditions.[35]

Finally, we should note that at least some early Christians understood Christ's death in sacrificial terms. Romans 3:25, usually taken as a traditional datum, makes this fact clear regardless of how one interprets ἱλαστήριον. The fact that Paul does not primarily operate with cultic imagery, yet can use it without explanation to a community he has never visited, implies that these metaphors for Christ's death were widely familiar among early Christians in his day.[36] For our purposes, it is not necessary to explore various suggestions for how and when such metaphors

---

[34] Psalms of Solomon 17, for example, refers to a coming military messiah as 'Lord Messiah', opening the possibility that Ps. 110:1 was already used in Jewish circles as an expression of Messianic expectation. Cf. also 1 Cor. 16:22 and Rev. 22:20.

[35] Again, the mention of Timothy in 13:23, along with the incorporation of such traditions, could indicate a familiarity with Pauline categories.

[36] Thus J. D. G. Dunn, *Romans 1–8* (Dallas: Word Books, 1988) 164: 'The fact that Paul can put this forward as a bare assertion, without substantive supporting argument, confirms

came to be used of Jesus' death. But we can assume that the audience of Hebrews was aware of such claims and probably assented to them at some point in their journey.

We can confidently say, therefore, that the traditions I have mentioned above pre-existed the composition of Hebrews. The author no doubt knew of early Christian traditions about Ps. 110 in relation to Ps. 2, as well as traditions that considered Christ's death to be an atoning sacrifice in some way. It is reasonable to think that the audience was also aware of such traditions, although we have no way of knowing to what degree they might have affirmed or questioned them. Nevertheless, the author of Hebrews clearly pushes the audience to extend the significance of these traditions for their religious perspective.

The high priestly metaphor

We cannot know for certain whether it was the author of Hebrews himself or some other early Christian who first extended the metaphors and traditions I mentioned in the previous section. But his use of these extensions constitutes his rhetorical strategy in Hebrews to address the perceived situation of its audience. We remind ourselves that it was the mention of Christ as 'a priest after the order of Melchizedek' that sparked the most pointed exhortation in the letter. It was the mention of this concept that launched the author's central admonition toward the audience's endurance and progress (cf. 5:10–11). Similarly, the author identifies his 'main point' as Christ's priesthood with its concomitant efficacy (cf. 8:1). The 'high-priestly metaphor' is thus the author's rhetorical strategy, his development of earlier tradition or his use of such developments, in order to address the rhetorical problem he perceives in the audience.[37]

The rhetorical problem is that the author perceives the audience to be waning in its commitment to the Christian confession as he understands it. This waning confidence connects further to a need to see the full significance of Christ's atoning efficacy (in the author's view), whatever its specific cause. In this light, the author formulates a rhetorical strategy that starts with certain Christian traditions, particularly those relating to

that the pre-Pauline formula expressed a fundamental element of the confession of the first Christian churches.' Cf. also Rom. 8:3.

[37] E. W. Stegemann and W. Stegemann ('Does the Cultic Language in Hebrews Represent Sacrificial Metaphors?: Reflections on Some Basic Problems', *Hebrews: Contemporary Methods – New Insights*, G. Gelardini, ed. [Leiden: E. J. Brill, 2005] 13–23) seem to misconstrue what many mean when referring to Christ's death or priesthood as 'metaphorical'. I use the term only in reference to a particular mode of speaking that is not literal, implying nothing about the truth or reality of the referent thereby.

the atoning efficacy of Christ's death and Christ's session at God's right hand. He – or less likely some other Christian before him – synthesizes these traditions into an all encompassing metaphor that allows him to contrast Christ with the entirety of the Levitical cultus and its system of atonement. Herein lies the metaphor of Christ's high priesthood in Hebrews.

Whereas previous Christian tradition understood Christ's death on the cross as an atoning *sacrifice* offered by God, Hebrews now understands Christ himself to be a *high priest* who offers himself in heaven (cf. 8:4). While earlier Christian tradition pictured God seating Christ at his right hand, Hebrews pictures Christ's passage through the heavens as the entrance of a heavenly high priest into a heavenly sanctuary (cf. 4:14; 7:26; 9:24).[38] To tie these metaphorical extensions together, Hebrews builds on Ps. 110:4 to see Christ as a priest from a different order than Levi, namely, the order of Melchizedek. Now the author can pit the entirety of two priesthoods and two cultic systems against each other and, with Christ's sacrifice, declare the end of the Levitical system of atonement.

The traditional building blocks of this strategy are thus (1) the sacrificial death of Christ and (2) the session and perhaps the ascension of Christ to heaven. It is also possible, perhaps even likely, that (3) Christians already thought of Christ in priestly terms as an intercessor at God's right hand (cf. Rom. 8:34). If so, such overtones seem rather undeveloped prior to Hebrews. Hebrews synthesizes and extends these components into a high-priestly metaphor in which Christ (1) is a high priest after the order of Melchizedek who (2) offers a spiritual sacrifice (3) in a heavenly tabernacle. We have the rest of this study to explore how this strategy plays itself out with regard to the 'settings of the sacrifice', particularly how the spatial dimensions of this metaphor make their way into the epistle's rhetoric and the surface structure of its discourse.

Conclusion

The primary focus of this study is on the 'settings' of the sacrifice of Christ in time and space and their significance for the argument of Hebrews. These settings pertain of course to the narrative world of Hebrews, the

---

[38] Since it is difficult to date Luke–Acts and Hebrews in relation to each other with certainty, we must remain somewhat tentative about whether the idea of Christ's ascension was already traditional by the time the concept appears in Hebrews. It is, of course, a logical consequence of the idea of Christ's session, which no doubt developed very early, coupled with the cosmology of the day.

story by which the author identified himself and in which he placed himself and his audience. Nevertheless, if we are to understand these settings for their rhetorical significance, we need to locate the overall story within the overall rhetorical purposes of the author. Accordingly, this chapter has attempted to sketch the general contours of the rhetorical problem Hebrews addresses along with the rhetorical strategy the author employed to address that problem. By examining both the exhortations and exposition of Hebrews, we determined that the rhetorical problem of Hebrews was at least twofold: (1) the author perceived the audience to be waning or drifting to some degree in its commitment to the Christian confession as he understood it and (2) this drifting related in some direct way to a need (in the author's mind) for the audience to appreciate the full significance of Christ's atonement vis-à-vis the Levitical cultus. The exhortations of Hebrews address the first problem by way of both positive and negative examples and admonitions. The audience is repeatedly told to hold fast and not to drift away. The exposition of Hebrews supports these exhortations by demonstrating the final superiority of Christ to every aspect of the old covenant, particularly its system of atonement.

Herein we see the rhetorical strategy of Hebrews. The author builds both on earlier Christian tradition and on areas where the author perceives the beliefs of the audience to be in less jeopardy. He inundates the audience with examples and supporting texts from Scripture. He reminds them of earlier Christian leaders (cf. 13:7) and builds on the kinds of traditions those leaders likely taught. In particular, the author builds on prior Christian traditions that considered (1) Christ's death as an atoning sacrifice, (2) Christ's victorious session at God's right hand after his resurrection, and perhaps (3) some sense of Christ in a priestly, intercessory role. In his hands, Christ becomes (1) a heavenly priest after the order of Melchizedek who (2) offers himself as a once and for all spiritual sacrifice in (3) a heavenly tabernacle. This imagery allows the author to pit Christ and his atonement against the *entirety* of the Levitical cultus in the relation of new covenant to old (whether as a polemic, apologetic or consolation). Because the new covenant replaces the old covenant, the audience need no longer rely on – or perhaps be concerned with the absence of – Levitical means of atonement. They can be fully confident in the Christian confession of faith.

The Settings of the Story in Time

3

THE DESTINY OF HUMANITY

An overall sense of the story

Richard Hays' *The Faith of Jesus Christ* is not only significant for the way in which it marks a major turning point in scholarly discussion on the interpretation of πίστις Χριστοῦ.[1] The first chapter also noted how seminal this work is for its use of narrative categories to analyse a non-narrative document. To be sure, many readers find structuralist analyses a bit cumbersome and unnecessarily technical. Yet Hays' presentation of the theory, given as background to his work, must rank as one of the clearest and simplest explanations of the Greimasian model in existence.[2] Despite its occasional complexity, the overall concept of narrative sequence is sound and potentially helpful, at least for heuristic purposes.[3]

For our purposes it seems unnecessary to present a full analysis of Hebrews' plot from the perspective of Greimas' system, although it could easily be done. Those who wish to play out the next two chapters in the precise categories of that model need simply to read the analysis in light of the categories Hays presents in his third chapter. My goal is much less extensive and more general, namely, to analyse the way Hebrews structures time as it argues from the story of salvation. Accordingly, this chapter and the next only engage with Greimasian categories as they seem to clarify the nature of Hebrews' narrative world and the settings of the story in time in particular. What follows is thus meant to equip the reader on a minimal level for that engagement.

On the whole, Greimas suggested that we could break down any plot into three basic phases or sequences: (1) an initial sequence that initiates the plot, (2) any number of middle or 'topical' sequences that generally

[1] *The Faith of Jesus Christ: The Narrative Substructure of Galatians 3:1–4:11*, 2nd edn (Grand Rapids, MI: Eerdmans, 2002).

[2] Ibid, esp. 84–95.

[3] N. T. Wright used the model fruitfully in *The New Testament and the People of God* (Minneapolis: Fortress Press, 1992), esp. 71–7, 221–3, 382–3, 389–90.

dominate the actual time of the narrative, and (3) a final sequence in which the unfulfilled goals of the initial sequence reach fulfilment.[4] To put things in more straightforward terms, some unfulfilled goal or deficiency stands behind the typical plot.[5] Greimas would relate the origins of this situation to what he calls the initial sequence. Accordingly, the final sequence of the plot is the sequence of events that fulfils that goal. Topical sequences are then the events in the meantime that, in the end, make the final sequence possible. From the standpoint of the plot's movement, the key topical sequences are those that move the plot along toward its goal. It is not necessary for us to prove these claims in relation to broader literature. What is important for our purposes is the fact that this pattern plays itself out in relation to the story behind the book of Hebrews.

In this chapter I will show how Hebrews' use of Ps. 8 provides us with a clear sense of the initial – and thus the final – sequence in the story that stands in the background of Hebrews' argument. God created humanity with the intention that we would have glory and honour in the creation. Hebrews points to death under the power of the Devil as a major culprit in humanity's failure to achieve this intended glory. Accordingly, the final sequence of Hebrews is when humanity actually attains this glory and honour. As we will see, this fulfilment is made possible through the help of Christ. The following chapter will discuss three key topical sequences in which Christ overcomes death and the Devil to make the final sequence possible.[6]

But before we delve further into the initial and final sequences of Hebrews' story world, I should mention another key feature of Greimas' model, namely, its so called 'actantial model'. This model analyses narrative sequences in terms of the relationships between characters or objects that are involved in a sequence of events. The model deems these agents and objects 'actants'. In general, Greimas expects to find six such actants in any given sequence of events: (1) a 'sender' that initiates the sequence, (2) an 'object' that the sender wishes to relay to (3) a 'receiver' of some kind. A fourth actant, (4) the 'subject', is the character to whom the sender gives the charge to convey the object to the receiver. This subject is the hero or protagonist of the sequence. Finally, we can usually identify both

---

[4] For these comments and the other features of Greimas' system, see especially A. J. Greimas, *Du Sens* (Paris: Seuil, 1970).

[5] Greimas would say it stands behind all plots, but in a post-structuralist world, it seems sufficient to say it stands behind the stereotypical plot.

[6] Hebrews alludes to many topical sequences in the overall story, but these three are especially key.

(5) helpers and (6) opponents, who respectively either help or hinder the conveyance of the object to the receiver.

Greimas diagrams this relationship in the following way:

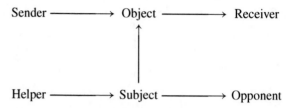

These elements can become quite abstract in the hands of a practised structuralist. Again, it is not my intention to explore or defend the technical details of this rubric. On a basic level, however, this model proves to be valuable in fleshing out the way in which the story world of Hebrews unfolds. Thus if we apply this model to the initial sequence of Hebrews' story world, it plays out in something like the following way:

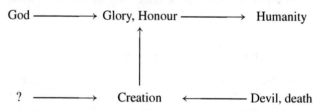

God begins the story with the goal that humanity have glory and honour in the creation. God thus makes a 'contract' with humanity to 'send' them glory and honour by way of the creation. The Devil proves to be the principal opponent to the fulfilment of this contract. Although Hebrews nowhere clarifies for us exactly what this opposition was (or is), Heb. 2:14 makes it clear that the Devil plays this role in the sequence. The Devil has the power of death, which implies that death also stands in some way as a further opponent to the completion of the contract.[7]

---

[7] It is difficult to identify what entities might have been 'helpers' who were foiled in the initial sequence, a testimony to the obtuseness of Greimas' model at times. In a fuller analysis of Hebrews' story world, I have suggested the spirits within human bodies as potential helpers along with the fellow creatures who might have submitted to humanity (*Understanding the Book of Hebrews: The Story behind the Sermon* (Louisville, KY: Westminster/John Knox, 2003) 25–6. We should also, however, note the strong possibility that the author might not have thought through various segments of his theology in great depth. Particularly in relation to the less prominent parts of his theology, the author might have operated simultaneously with elements from conflicting paradigms.

By contrast the final sequence of the story behind Hebrews will see the fulfilment of that which is unfulfilled in the initial sequence. We might diagram the final sequence of Hebrews' plot something like the following:

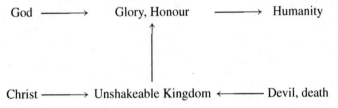

In the final sequence of the plot, a sequence to which Hebrews alludes but does not fully enumerate, humanity finally attains the glory and honour God intended them to have. The helper, Christ, overcomes the opposition of the opponents, death and the Devil. The status of the creation in this sequence is somewhat ambiguous, for it is removed in some way (12:27). Whatever its relationship to the eschaton, Hebrews tells us that humanity will participate in a βασιλεία ἀσάλευτον (12:28).

Psalm 8 and the coming world

Scholars have often understood Hebrews' use of Ps. 8 Christologically (Heb. 2:6–8).[8] This tendency is not surprising for several reasons. For one thing, the rest of the New Testament predominantly understands this passage Christologically. Thus it is often used in conjunction with Ps. 110:1, which is also important for Hebrews.[9] These two psalms were

---

[8] E.g. E. Käsemann, *The Wandering People of God: An Investigation of the Letter to the Hebrews* (Minneapolis: Augsburg, 1984 (1957)) 122f.; O. Michel, *Der Brief an die Hebräer*, 8th edn (KEK; Göttingen: Vandenhoek & Ruprecht, 1984) 138–9; O. Cullmann, *Christology of the New Testament* (London: SCM Press, 1959) 188; S. Kistemaker, *The Psalm Citations in the Epistle to the Hebrews* (Amsterdam: Van Soest, 1961) 29–31; A. T. Hanson, *Jesus Christ in the Old Testament* (London: SPCK, 1965) 163, 166; S. G. Sowers, *The Hermeneutics of Philo and Hebrews* (Zürich: EVZ-Verlag, 1965) 80f.; G. W. Buchanan, *To the Hebrews* (Anchor Bible; Garden City, NY: Doubleday, 1972) 26; P. Giles, 'The Son of Man in Hebrews', *ET* 86 (1975) 328–32; H. Weiss, *Der Brief an die Hebräer* (Göttingen: Vandenhoek & Ruprecht, 1991) 194; to name a few.

[9] In 1:3, 13; 8:1; 10:12; and 12:2. For a discussion of the way in which the author uses Ps. 110:1 in each case, see D. M. Hay's *Glory at the Right Hand: Psalm 110 in Early Christianity* (SBLMS 18; New York: Abingdon Press, 1973) 85–9 and J. D. G. Dunn, *Christology in the Making: An Inquiry into the Origins of the Doctrine of the Incarnation*, 2nd edn (London: SCM Press, 1989) 108–13. H. Weiss writes, 'der Autor des Hebr mit seiner christologischen Deutung von Ps 8 seinerseits bereits in einer urchristlichen Auslegungstradition steht, in der mit der christologischen Deuten von Ps 8 zugleich auch die entsprechende Deutung von Ps 110,1 verbunden war' (*Hebräer* 194).

associated through their common use of the word πούς and their similar statements of subjection. While Ps. 8:7 reads, πάντα ὑπέταξας ὑποκάτω τῶν ποδῶν αὐτοῦ (originally in reference to humanity), Ps. 110:1 (109 LXX) says, κάθου . . . ἕως ἂν θῶ τοὺς ἐχθρούς σου ὑποπόδιον τῶν ποδῶν σου. It is not difficult to see how these two passages came to be interpreted in the light of one another. The earliest association between the two comes in 1 Cor. 15:25–7, where Paul transposes the 'all' of Ps. 8:7 to the 'enemies' of Ps. 110:1. In doing so, Paul is able to claim that the last of the enemies to be put under Christ's feet is death.[10] The author of Ephesians similarly places every ruler, authority, power and lordship under the feet of the already reigning king (1:20–2).[11] The association elsewhere in the New Testament is not definitive, but may be implied in the use of ὑποκάτω rather than ὑποπόδιον in Mark 12:36 and Matt. 22:44,[12] as well as in the standing posture of Stephen in Acts 7:55–6 and the submission of heavenly powers in 1 Pet. 3:21–2.[13] This regular association of Ps. 8 with Ps. 110:1 in early Christian tradition makes it likely that the use in Heb. 2:6–8 should also be understood Christologically.

A second aspect of Ps. 8 which might lend itself to a Christological interpretation is the phrase υἱὸς ἀνθρώπου in Ps. 8:5.[14] Although the author does not make any explicit, Christological use of this expression in his argument, many believe the phrase held such connotations to him. For example, Otto Michel argued '[d]as Geheimnis des Menschensohnes wird vorausgesetzt', although 'wie bei Paulus so auch im Hebr der Begriff des Menschensohnes an sich fehlt'.[15] He believed that the phrase 'son of man' in Heb. 2:6 referred exclusively to Christ.

It is also possible, however, that Hebrews understood the psalm both in relation to Christ *and* humanity in general, implying a radical relationship between Christ and the other 'sons' of God. The psalm would then imply that the sons were destined for glory and honour like Christ, as well as to rule over the All like Christ. Indeed, it becomes possible to see Christ's glory as a solution to the problem of humanity's failed glory. Christ and humanity become identified with each other, as 2:9 now moves from the glory promised to humankind to the glory fulfilled in Jesus as the representative of his 'brothers'. Some years ago, Ernst Käsemann took

---

[10] Again, for further exploration of the way the two are associated with each other here, see Hay, *Glory* 36–7 and Dunn, *Christology* 107–13.
[11] See *Glory* 127.　　[12] *Glory* 35.　　[13] *Glory* 75–6, 127–8.
[14] Those who read Ps. 8 exclusively in terms of Christ would naturally tend to understand this phrase in this way. See n. 8.
[15] *Hebräer* 138.

strong exception to this 'anthropological' reading of the psalm, arguing against Julius Kögel that '[n]owhere in the New Testament is Jesus set on the same level with us in such fashion'.[16] Käsemann's reasons for rejecting the anthropological reading no longer stand – rooted in notions of some Gnostic *Urmensch* – but many scholars nevertheless remain opposed to it. It is clear that the psalm applies to Christ. The question is whether it also pertains to humanity in some way as well.

A first observation is that the Son of Man title is not used in Hebrews. If the author has it in mind, it is implicit in the argument *at best*. It is not even clear that the author's Christological reading of the psalm understood the phrase in this way.[17] Further, the important association of Ps. 110:1 and Ps. 8 in early Christian tradition does not preclude both an anthropological *and* Christological dimension to the argument. Indeed, it is not improbable that the connection of the two *assumed* something like the narrative I am suggesting here. Nevertheless, the immediately preceding context does push us toward Christ as a primary referent of the psalm. Hebrews 2:5 introduces the citation of Ps. 8 with the statement that '[God] has not subjected the coming world to angels'. The implication is that the one(s) to whom God has subordinated that world is the referent of the psalm quotation. When we look to the preceding context, the contrast in Heb. 1 is between Christ and the angels, a contrast which continues in the paraenesis of 2:1–4. In 2:2–3, the angels as the 'speakers' of the Law are contrasted with Christ as the 'speaker' of salvation in the new covenant. Since 2:5 follows directly on this exhortation, it seems likely that the contrast between Christ and the angels is still in view.

We also, however, find a third party in the discussion: those who are 'about to inherit salvation'. In 1:14 Hebrews describes the angels as 'ministering spirits sent to minister because of those about to inherit salvation'. The object of angelic ministry is thus none other than those humans destined for salvation, and a primary function of angelic ministry is to help humanity in its pilgrimage toward that goal.[18] This role is about to change in the coming world, for then humans will have no need for this particular service from the angels. In that sense, the futures of the angels and

---

[16] Kögel preferred this interpretation at the beginning of this century in *Der Sohn und die Söhne: Eine exegetische Studie zu Hebräer 2,5–18* (BFCT 8.5–6; Gütersloh; Bertelsman, 1904) 34. Käsemann argued against Kögel's claim that Jesus was the 'preeminent type of the human race' (*Wandering* 122–6).

[17] And our 'anthropological then Christological' interpretation does not preclude a secondary echo to the phrase in reference to Christ.

[18] The phrase εἰς διακονίαν ἀποστελλόμενα seems best taken in this way, taking the participle with what precedes it rather than with what follows.

humanity also contrast with each other. Humanity's destiny is glory (Heb. 2:10).

The statement that the destiny of humanity is glory, just as Christ's is glory, piques our interest. After all, the original meaning of Ps. 8 referred to humanity in general. Could the author understand the psalm both in relation to Christ and humanity? Indeed, Heb. 2:11–13 implies an amazing solidarity between Christ and humanity that seems exactly the kind of connection Käsemann denied. It would easily fit the train of thought to say that because of Christ, humanity also fulfils the psalm. I add to these observations the fact that the author not only contrasts Christ with the angels but humanity with the angels as well in 2:16: '[Christ] certainly is not taking hold of angels, but he is taking hold of the seed of Abraham'. Presumably we should understand this enigmatic statement in the light of 2:10, where Christ is the 'leader of salvation' who brings 'many sons to glory'. Christ thus takes hold to lead the seed of Abraham to glory. It is thus possible to see humanity as part of the introduction to the psalm: '[God] has not subjected the coming world to angels'. Instead, he has subjected the coming world to Christ and to Christ's brothers, as the psalm indicates.

I should likely equate the future glory of humanity in some way with the salvation mentioned in 1:14 and 2:3. The sons and daughters of God are clearly 'those about to inherit salvation', and the salvation which is 'spoken' by the Lord is addressed to the people of God. When the author goes on to note in 2:5 that he has been speaking about 'the coming world', surely this 'world' is none other than the place of salvation and glory to which Christ is leading the sons. The angels are only servants for the sons until they inherit salvation, for the coming world is not subjected to them, but to Christ and the sons.[19] Christ is not leading the angels to this glory, but he is assisting the seed of Abraham.

Kögel also offered the placement of Jesus' name in 2:9 as an argument for this reading of the psalm: 'Die Nachdrucksvolle, auch durch die Stellung ausgezeichnete Hervorhebung des Namens Jesus bestätigt, daß

---

[19] G. H. Guthrie, *The Structure of Hebrews: A Text-Linguistic Analysis* (SNT 73; Leiden: E. J. Brill, 1994) 115, raises the possibility that 'the author points to some semantic continuation between units of the same genre that is not shared by intervening units of the other genre'. By this he implies that there is a certain continuity of argument between 1:14 and 2:5 which is not destroyed by the intervening paraenesis. Although one should be extremely cautious about this suggestion, it does make excellent sense of the problematic unit 5:11–6:20. If this contention is roughly the case, then my contention that the author has at least the people of God in mind in 2:5 is given very strong support, since they are certainly the ones about to inherit salvation in 1:14.

bisher von ihm nicht die Rede gewesen sein kann.'[20] While not definitive, Kögel certainly makes an 'anthropological' reading of the psalm plausible alongside the Christological one. In this interpretation, the author mentions the psalm at first with reference to humanity in general (the 'seed of Abraham'), but points out that this situation with everything in subjection to a glorified humanity is 'not yet' the case (2:8). Rather, we see another person made lower than the angels for a little while, namely, Jesus, who makes it possible for the sons to come to the glory intended them in God's purposes (2:10).[21] The author, thus, sets up a problem as he presents the psalm, highlighting the fact that humanity's intended glory is presently in a state of unfulfilment. He does this, however, in order to introduce God's solution to the problem, namely, Jesus, who is also made lower than the angels for a little while, until he finds the glory and honour of the psalm through his suffering of death, now only waiting until his enemies might be put under his feet (10:13).

The preceding argues that the author wanted or expected his recipients to think of humanity in general when they first heard the psalm, and thereafter to see Christ as the path to the psalm's fulfilment. Accordingly, the Christological reading does not preclude that the psalm apply to the seed of Abraham as well. Christ came to make it possible for the sons to achieve glory, as in 2:10, and thus read Ps. 8 both in relation to the Son and the sons. The author understood the psalm 'filially', applying to all of God's children, both as fundamentally Christological and anthropological, for the two parties are both ἐξ ἑνός.[22] Such a reading does not contradict the way in which the rest of the New Testament understands the relationship between Ps. 8 and 110:1. Rather, it suggests that early Christianity always understood Ps. 8 to apply to Christ as the Last Adam, the one who fulfils the true destiny of humanity, a destiny they were never able to fulfil on their own.[23] Once the psalm is applied to Christ in this way, it can then be related to Ps. 110:1 of Christ in his exalted state.

Therefore, Ps. 8 in Heb. 2:6–8 presents us with the ultimate goal of the plot. It is the 'object' in the initial sequence and thus the 'object' in

---

[20] *Sohn* 33.

[21] L. D. Hurst writes, 'The author takes βραχί τι not as an expression of degree but as a period of time according to the Jewish two-age theory', 'The Christology of Hebrews 1 and 2', *The Glory of Christ in the New Testament: Studies in Christology in Memory of George Bradford Caird*, L. D. Hurst and N. T. Wright, eds. (Oxford: Clarendon Press, 1987) 154 n.11.

[22] I have discussed the relationship between Sonship and sonship in great detail in 'Keeping his Appointment: Creation and Enthronement in the Epistle to the Hebrews', *JSNT* 66 (1997) 91–117.

[23] Such is Dunn's interpretation of the psalm's use in Hebrews and elsewhere in the New Testament (*Christology* 110–13).

the final sequence of the plot. God initiated movement toward this goal as the story began. But the initial sequence failed, in Hebrews perhaps because of the Devil and death (2:14–15). For Paul, 'all have sinned and are lacking the glory of God' (Rom. 3:23). The final sequence must then be the attainment of this glory, and the topical sequences between must overcome whatever obstacle prevented the initial achievement of glory.

To put these thoughts in exegetical terms, humanity is intended for glory and honour, as well as to rule. But this goal has not yet been attained. The main hindrance, as it appears in the latter part of Heb. 2, would seem to be death, at least at this particular rhetorical moment. Jesus is said to have been crowned with glory and honour 'on account of death', and he is said to do this 'so that he might taste death on behalf of everyone' (2:9). For humanity, a tension exists between their inevitable death and their intended crowning with glory and honour. Whereas for Christ, his victorious death *entails* being crowned with glory, this is not the case for humanity in general. They live in the fear of death all of their lives (2:15) and have not thus far attained to the exalted status of the psalm.[24]

Christ's righteous death, on the other hand, was ordained in the purposes of God (2:10). It destroyed the one holding the power of death, the Devil (2:14), and thus enabled the other sons to pass through the barrier of death into their intended glory. Through the atonement provided by Christ (2:17), the seed of Abraham are thus led to glory in fulfilment of the psalm (2:16). The one for whom the All exists, and through whom it came to be, knew the appropriate means by which he might lead his sons to the glory intended for them (2:10). This interpretation of the psalm thus provides us with a reference point when considering God's continuity of purpose throughout salvation history.

Promise and fulfilment

Psalm 8 in Hebrews gives God's intention to lead humanity to glory and honour through Christ. It is this intention that is unfulfilled in the initial sequence of the plot and fulfilled in the story's final sequence. We know that the author equated this intended glory with salvation (1:14; 2:3) and with the coming world (2:5). We know that this 'glory and honour' involves a superseding of death. Another motif that contributes to a more

---

[24] The basis of this difference between Christ and the other sons in relation to death is not explicitly stated in the epistle, although there are hints of an explanation in the fact that Christ was 'without sin' (4:15) and was saved 'out of death' because of his 'reverent fear' (5:7). For this interpretation of 5:7, see H. Attridge's article '"Heard Because of his Reverence" (Heb 5:7)', *JBL* 98 (1979) 90–3.

specific understanding of this future glory is the sermon's imagery of promise and fulfilment. Since the theme of promise appears in various contexts throughout Hebrews, it allows us to connect several of Hebrews' images together.[25] Although the author does not use promise language in a completely uniform manner, he repeatedly considers the readers the bearers of a promise which God has tendered to them.[26] In particular, Hebrews almost without exception uses the singular of ἐπαγγελία with eschatological overtones, interlocking it with other images to flesh out what is meant by expressions like 'salvation', 'coming world' and 'glory and honour'.

The promised rest

The first occurrence of ἐπαγγελία in the epistle is in 4:1, where the recipients are encouraged to guard against falling short of entering God's rest, in the light of the fact that God has given this promise. The metaphor of entering into rest, therefore, is yet another image of the 'destiny' of humanity. The phrase is drawn from the language of Ps. 95 (94 LXX), where it is said that the Israelites did not enter into God's rest because they had hardened their hearts, referring to God's punishment of the wilderness generation by not allowing them entrance into the promised land. The author uses this example of disobedience as a warning to the hearers of the epistle not to disobey or disbelieve God's promise to them.

The passage in question (3:7–4:13) does not make clear the exact time of entrance into God's rest, resulting in some ambiguity on the exact nature of what the author means by 'rest'. On the one hand, the fact that the author can exhort his audience to encourage one another each day not to harden their hearts implies that they have not yet entered definitively

---

[25] C. Rose has even gone so far as to consider whether promise and fulfilment can be considered 'das *"Basismotiv des Hebräerbriefes"*', 'Verheißung und Erfüllung: Zum Verständnis von ἐπαγγελία im Hebräerbrief', *BZ* 33 (1989) 191. It certainly is one of several central motifs which the author uses to make a connection between salvation history and the author's exhortation.

[26] S. Lehne addresses the possibility that the author is inconsistent in his use of the singular and plural of ἐπαγγελία, *The New Covenant in Hebrews* (JSNTSS 44; Sheffield: JSOT Press, 1990) 20. After attempting to apply the epistle's multiplicity/unity pattern to the use of ἐπαγγελία, Lehne, *Covenant* 20, notes of the word *promise* that, in general, 'singularity denotes the new dispensation and plurality the old'. As Lehne indicates, however, Hebrews does not exhibit this pattern consistently. While God is always the one who gives a promise in Hebrews (God is always the subject of ἐπαγγέλλομαι in Hebrews: 6:13; 10:23; 11:11; 12:26), the author can speak of both promises already received (e.g. 6:15; 11:33) and promises yet to be inherited (e.g. 11:13).

into rest. On the other hand, the author states that εἰσερχόμεθα into rest, using the present tense (4:3) and speaks in terms of doing so 'today' (4:7). This seeming ambiguity has led different scholars to speak of the entrance into rest as occurring either in the present or the future, often in relation to their interpretation of the background of the epistle.

For example, Çeslas Spicq, whose commentary is perhaps the most consistently Philonic in interpretation, predictably holds that εἰσερχόμεθα in 4:3 'n'est pas à prendre au sens du futur (Vulg. *ingrediemur*), ni de "nous sommes sûrs d'entrer" (Lemonnyer, Moffatt, Gayford, Médebielle)'. Rather, 'c'est l'affirmation d'une réalité actuelle envisagée d'une part en fonction du dessein de Dieu (Westcott) qui garantit à la foi l'accès au repos . . . et d'autre part de la conscience chrétienne qui sait que la foi est pleine d'espérance'.[27] In contrast, Otto Michel, who interprets the epistle 'apocalyptically', writes, 'εἰσερχόμεθα tritt für das Futurum ein ("wir werden eingehen . . .")'.[28] Finally, C. K. Barrett, seeking a *via media*, speaks of the rest as 'both present and future; men enter it, and must strive to enter it'.[29]

Barrett has not only found an intermediate position, but seems to capture best the author's intent. On the one hand, Michel correctly observes the inevitably future dimension to the passage. When the author says that a promise remains of entering into rest (4:1), 'die Verheißung steht also noch aus'.[30] The recipients cannot reach a point in their earthly life when they can say that they have conclusively entered God's rest. They will only have such surety when they have held the substance of their faith μέχρι τέλους βεβαίαν (3:14). The imagery of a heavenly homeland which occurs later in the epistle is too similar to this language of entrance for them not to be generally equated. All of these factors inevitably put the principal accent of rest language on the future entrance into the heavenly Jerusalem.

On the other hand, the present dimension of this entrance should not be underplayed. The emphasis which the author places on σήμερον indicates that he sees this 'entrance' as a matter of daily decision to endure. We are to exhort one another ἄχρις οὗ τὸ σήμερον καλεῖται, so that we are not hardened by the deceit of sin (3:13). Each day, therefore, is yet another 'today' in which one must enter into God's rest. In a figure, we enter

---

[27] *L'épître aux Hébreux*, vol. 2, 3rd edn (Paris: Gabalda, 1953) 81–2.
[28] *Hebräer* 194.
[29] 'The Eschatology of the Epistle to the Hebrews', *The Background of the New Testament and Its Eschatology*, W. D. Davies, ed. (Cambridge: Cambridge University Press 1964 (1954),) 372.
[30] *Hebräer* 193.

into God's rest every day that we choose to be faithful and rest from our 'works' (4:10).

The term *today* actually serves an even broader function in the epistle than simply as a reminder of the need for daily endurance. In the larger context of the epistle, 'today' is an eschatological category.[31] It appears, for example, in 1:5 in the citation of Ps. 2. Since the author cites two psalms with this motif and explicitly draws attention to the term in 3:13 and 4:7, it seems logical to conclude that there was a connection in his mind.[32] Since σήμερον appears in the context of Christ's exaltation in 1:5, it seems likely that 'today' is a term strictly appropriate for the new age, when Christ has initiated a new covenant and has sat on the right hand of God. Charles Anderson writes, '[t]oday is identical to the "last days", that relatively brief period between the two appearances of Jesus (9:28) in which the opportunity of salvation is offered'. 'It never existed prior to the age of the new covenant.'[33] When the author concludes the epistle by saying that Jesus Christ is the same 'yesterday, today, and forever' (13:8), 'today' is that period of eschatological fulfilment in which Christ has caused the new age to begin although the old has not yet definitively vanished. It is that 'other day' about which God spoke in Ps. 35 (cf. Heb. 4:8), the ever recurring day in which his people choose to enter rest.

I conclude that the rest of God is primarily future but with an important present dimension. It is primarily future, for those who believe must daily 're-enter' into God's rest, never reaching it definitively in this present in-between time. On the other hand, they do in a sense enter into God's rest daily, especially since Christ has already definitively provided perfection for those who are being sanctified (10:14). The motif of rest, therefore, seems to connect in some way both to the future 'coming world' of 2:5 and to the present cleansing of conscience which Christ has effected (e.g. 9:14).

The image of the heavenly city of the coming world, with all of its connecting pictures and content, pertains to the ultimate meaning of rest, in contrast to any present situation or suffering of the community (e.g.

---

[31] C. P. Anderson speaks of 'today' as an 'apocalyptic category', making the same basic claims as I am, 'The Heirs of the New Age in Hebrews', *Apocalyptic and the New Testament: Essays in Honor of J. Louis Martyn*, J. Marcus and M. L. Soards, eds. (JSNTSS 24; Sheffield: JSOT Press, 1989) 255–7. Given recent debate on the usefulness of the term *apocalyptic* in such contexts when not referring to the genre (e.g. see C. Rowland's *The Open Heaven* [London: SPCK, 1982]), the term *eschatological* seems more appropriate.

[32] The other of course being Ps. 95 (94 LXX) in the context under discussion.

[33] 'Heirs' 256.

12:4).[34] The author holds out the promise that there will be a day when the people of God will not feel like strangers in a foreign land but will find an end to their wandering. On the other hand, the rest also seems to be related to perfection language, which is also related to the motif of promise in Hebrews. These other images further elucidate both what the content of God's promises is and what the author understood by 'the rest of God'.

The land of promise

Later chapters will discuss the cosmological aspects of heaven in relation to the created earthly realm. Nevertheless, I should introduce the heavenly realm as integral to enabling the final sequence of the plot to occur, focusing on heaven as an eschatological destination. More than any other, Heb. 11 utilizes the motif of promise to exhort the recipients of the epistle to endurance. The word first appears in the singular in 11:9, where Abraham is said to have sojourned in the 'land of promise' in tents with Isaac and Jacob, who were 'fellow heirs' of the promise. At first glance, someone might find exception in this verse to the idea that the singular of ἐπαγγελία usually has eschatological overtones in the epistle. Here the word is clearly used of the land of Canaan promised to the patriarchs, and 6:15 even goes so far as to say that Abraham *obtained* the promises, there in reference to the multiplication of his seed.

In the immediate context of Heb. 11:9, however, 11:13 says that the patriarchs and Sarah all died 'not having received the promises'. This verse indicates that the author's purpose in Heb. 11 is somewhat different from his purpose in Heb. 6. In that chapter, the author's purpose was to substantiate the reliability of God's promises in order to bolster the confidence of the hearers in their faith. To this end, his exhortation stays on the level of Old Testament history. He wishes to show that God kept his promise to Abraham because Abraham was patient (6:15). But in Heb. 11 the author's interest is eschatological and aims at the audience which has not yet received God's promise. Thus the 'land of promise' does not simply refer to Canaan, therefore, as can be seen by the remainder of 11:13. The patriarchs died without having received the promises, but they saw them afar off and greeted them and confessed 'that they were strangers and exiles on the earth'. The author now comes to his point.

---

[34] The repeated exhortations to endure, particularly in the midst of discussions of God's 'discipline', make it difficult to deny that the recipients of Hebrews were anticipating or already undergoing some sort of difficult time.

Persons such as the patriarchs are really seeking a 'homeland' (11:14). This country is not earthly, however; it is a 'heavenly' reality (11:16). This heavenly homeland is the 'city' which God has prepared for the people of God (11:16). When the author speaks of the 'land of promise', therefore, he is really alluding to the eschatological destination of those who believe and endure.

The fact that the people of God are 'aliens on the earth' and long for a homeland ties in directly with the motif of rest in 3:7–4:11, for there the people of God are also seeking the promised land of rest. The motif of rest and that of a heavenly city constitute elements of the same promise given to those who believe. The theme is taken up again in Heb. 13, although there without any reference to promise. In 13:13–14, the author's exhortation to go 'outside the camp' to Christ, bearing his reproach, is justified by the fact that 'here we have no lasting [μένουσαν] city'. Rather, 'we are seeking the one to come [μέλλουσαν]'. The idea of a 'coming' city is surely related to the 'coming [μέλλουσαν] world' of 2:5 and the 'ones about [μέλλοντας] to inherit salvation' in 1:14. All of these images are referring to the same thing: the future destination and hope of those who are being saved. It is the rest of God, a heavenly homeland, a city prepared by God. It is the coming world and salvation.

The 'land of promise' thus relates directly to the futurist aspect of the rest motif. It also relates to the author's description of the heavenly Jerusalem and Mt Zion in 12:22, the city of the living God and the ultimate destination of God's people. The purpose of this image is to explain to the audience how it is that they can struggle on earth despite the truth of their confession, while at the same time offering them hope as an incentive to endure. The promise offered by this motif, therefore, is that of a home, a place where they truly belong and will no longer be subject to the troubles of resident aliens. This is an eternal inheritance (9:15), one which they will never have to fear losing as long as they stay faithful till the end.

Perfection and promise

Thus far, we have discussed the motifs of rest and homeland to elucidate the nature of the promise which God has given to his people. These themes, on the one hand, have certain implications for the location where the future promise will be inherited, namely, the heavenly Jerusalem, the city of the living God. This is arguably the ultimate location of promise, both part of the promise and possibly where it will be experienced in its fullness. The promise thus also includes rest from struggle and hope of belonging in a true homeland.

Perfection is another key motif in Hebrews which relates to the idea of promise. I have already mentioned a possible relationship between this theme and the 'present' aspect of entrance into rest. From 11:39 to 11:40 it is clear that perfection is related to the promise, for the author explicitly connects the perfection of believers to the eschatological promise in these verses. After the author has used the cloud of witnesses in Heb. 11 to exhort the recipients to faithfulness, he brings the chain of witnesses to a climax by noting that 'these all . . . did not receive the promise, since God foresaw something better relative to us, that they might not be perfected without us'. The parallelism between promise and perfection demonstrates that the two are closely related. At the very least, these verses imply that perfection is a necessary prerequisite for the reception of the promise, if not a part of the promise. This inference is confirmed in 12:22–4 in the reference to the heavenly city. There it is mentioned that, in addition to the heavenly Jerusalem, the recipients have also come to 'the spirits of righteous ones who have been perfected' (12:23). A close connection thus exists between reception of the promise and perfection. An examination of perfection language in the epistle, therefore, is necessary for a thorough understanding of the promise motif.

The meaning of τελειόω and its derivatives in Hebrews has long been a matter of debate, and a number of possible interpretations have been presented over the years.[35] Alternatives which have been put forward have varied from a 'formal' or 'general' reading of the terms, letting each particular context determine the precise meaning, to 'religious' and 'cultic' interpretations, to readings which associate perfection with death or a rational ascent to the noumenal realm.[36] In general, David G. Peterson

---

[35] For a full discussion of the issues involved, see D. G. Peterson's *Hebrews and Perfection: An Examination of the Concept of Perfection in the Epistle to the Hebrews* (SNTSMS 47; Cambridge: Cambridge University Press, 1982). For a brief, but very helpful summary of the options, see Attridge, *Hebrews* 83–7.

[36] E.g. formal: J. Kögel, 'Der Begriff τελειοῦν im Hebräerbrief im Zusammenhang mit dem neutestamentlichen Sprachgebrauch', *Theologische Studien für M. Kähler*. Ed. by F. Giesebrecht (Leipzig: Deichert, 1905) 37–68. Others who have at least used this as a starting point include Peterson himself, *Perfection* 46f.; M. Rissi, *Die Theologie des Hebräerbriefs* (WUNT 41; Tübingen: Mohr/Siebeck, 1987) 79; J. M. Scholar, *Proleptic Priests: Priesthood in the Epistle to the Hebrews* (JSNTSS 49; Sheffield: JSOT Press, 1991) 195; and M. Isaacs, *Sacred Space: An Approach to the Theology of the Epistle to the Hebrews* (JSNTSS 73; Sheffield: JSOT Press, 1992) 102; religious and cultic: Peterson, *Perfection* 4–5, 25–6, speaks of Michel's 'religious' reading of τελειόω in the light of LXX usage, interpreting perfection as a person's whole position before God (i.e. consecration – 'Die Lehre von der christlichen Vollkommenheit nach der Anschauung des Hebräerbriefes', *TSK*, 106 (1934–5) 337f.; Peterson points out that such a use is actually quite limited in the LXX). T. Häring, 'Über einige Grundgedanken des Hebräerbriefs', *Monatsschrift für Pastoraltheologie* 17 (1920–1) 260–76, on the other hand, was the first proponent of a reading of Hebrews in

and others rightly find that the formal definition of 'to complete'[37] or 'ans Ziel bringen'[38] is the most helpful starting point for understanding perfection language in Hebrews. In practice, of course, the various ways in which a word is used need not have any connection to the other ways it is used. Hebrews itself uses the word group in several different contexts. The author can speak of the perfection of Christ and the perfection of the sons, as well as of the possibility of being τέλειος (seemingly in the sense of maturity – 6:14) and of the heavenly tent being 'more perfect' (9:11). Each of these usages has a different specific nuance when applied to a particular context. In each case, perfection implies something different on the level of specificity. Nevertheless, the key uses of τελειόω in Hebrews all relate in one way or another to the core sense of 'completeness'.

The perfection of Christ seems different in significant ways from that of the other sons. He is perfected through sufferings (2:10; 5:8–9), while the children are perfected through Christ himself (10:14). These different pathways to perfection reflect the seemingly different connotations the word group has in each specific case. Christ's perfection, on the one hand, seems to involve the attainment of suitability for his office as high priest.[39] After he has learned obedience through suffering, he is able to

the light of a cultic reading. Such a reading is often seen in relation to the cultic expression מלא היד, which is sometimes translated with τελειόω in the expression 'to fill the hands' (cf. Exod. 29:9, 29, 33, 35; Lev. 8:33; 16:32; Num. 3:3). Peterson, *Perfection* 26–30, and Attridge, *Hebrews* 85, both point out that it is the phrase *as a whole* which has become a technical term. The single instance where the verb is used by itself with such a consecratory meaning (Lev. 21:10) is meagre evidence on which to base such an interpretation. Scholer, *Priests* 190, also points out that this is only one of the many uses of τελειόω in the LXX and that 'the cultic consecratory character of τελειοῦν is not grounded in the word itself, but in the context in which the word is situated'. Scholer, *Priests* 191, has also argued that 'even the staunchest advocates of "consecration" have had to elaborate their positions, while clinging to the concept itself'. The result, in his opinion, is that they have come closer and closer to the formal usage of the word group without realizing or acknowledging that such was the case; death or rational ascent: although no scholar would place an *exclusive* association of perfection in Hebrews with death, the usage in the background literature (e.g. Wis. 4:13; 4 Macc. 7:15; *Leg.* 3.45) is often considered to be relevant to the discussion (e.g. Attridge, *Hebrews* 85–6 and Peterson, *Perfection* 26, 30). L. K. K. Dey is the name most associated with the philosophical reading of perfection in Hebrews in which even for Christ perfection is access *in this life* to the noumenal world, *The Intermediary World and Patterns of Perfection in Philo and Hebrews* (SBLDS 25; Missoula, MT: Scholars Press, 1975) 219 and *passim*.

[37] *Perfection* 46f.   [38] E.g. Rissi, *Theologie* 79, and Scholer, *Priests* 190–1.

[39] So Attridge, *Hebrews* 86, 'Christ's perfecting, as developed in the text, may be understood as a vocational process by which he is made complete or fit for his office'. So also G. Vos, 'The Priesthood of Christ', *PTR* 5 (1907) 589; Kögel, 'τελειοῦν' 61; J. Moffatt, *A Critical and Exegetical Commentary on the Epistle to the Hebrews* (Edinburgh: T&T Clark, 1924) 31–2; W. Manson, *The Epistle to the Hebrews: An Historical and Theological Reconsideration* (London: Hodder & Stoughton, 1951) 101, 110; P. DuPlessis, ΤΕΛΕΙΟΣ: *The Idea of Perfection in the New Testament* (Kampen: Kok, 1959) 218; F. F. Bruce, *The Epistle to the Hebrews* (Grand Rapids, MI: Eerdmans, 1964) 43–4; Peterson, *Perfection*

become a cause of eternal salvation, since he has been perfected (5:8–9). Associated with this is Christ's exaltation to the right hand of God, the attainment of glory and honour, for this is the context of 2:10.[40] Since Christ is 'without sin' (4:15), this is not a bringing to moral perfection and Christ does not need atonement, although his perfection does involve struggle and development, as 5:7–8 indicates.[41] On the contrary, it is because Christ was definitively without sin at the point of his death and proved to be obedient to God in suffering that he was able to be a priest 'perfected forever' (7:28). His definitive moral uprightness, including his obedient suffering of death, 'completes' his preparation for office and constitutes in part his qualifications as a heavenly high priest.

In contrast, the people of God are not able to access the heavenly realm on the basis of their own lives. The Law and the Levitical priesthood were also inadequate in this regard, for they were not able to 'perfect' those who turned to them for atonement (7:11, 19). They were not able to perfect the worshipper with respect to their sense of having sin (9:9; 10:1).[42] Christ, on the other hand, with one sacrifice perfected forever those who are being sanctified (10:14). Here it is clear that, for believers, perfection involves atonement and cleansing (rather than suffering) at least as a prerequisite and is related in some way to the attainment of acceptability with God and, as a result, legitimate access to his presence.[43]

What begins to emerge as one sifts through the vast literature on perfection language in Hebrews is that, while interpreters differ widely on

66f.; R. McL. Wilson, *Hebrews* (Grand Rapids, MI: Eerdmans, 1987) 56–7; W. L. Lane (although he believes the cultic interpretation forms the background of the usage), *Hebrews 1–8* (Dallas: Word Books, 1991) 57–8; and others.

[40] In the light of the fact that Christ's vocation is as a *heavenly* high priest (8:4), the exaltation is a necessary prerequisite for functioning in this office. Peterson, *Perfection* 104f., agrees that the exaltation is a part of Christ's perfection, as does Rissi, *Theologie* 79: 'Der Christus ist von Gott an das ihm von Gott verordnete Ziel geführt worden, das in seiner Verherrlichung im himmlischen Allerheiligsten besteht.' It should be noted that several of the diverse interpretations of perfection language in Hebrews include Christ's exaltation and glorification in some way as a part of his perfection, as in Kögel, 'τελειοῦν' 67–8; E. Riggenbach, *Der Brief an die Hebräer*, 3rd edn (Leipzig: Deichert, 1922) 47 n.20; Käsemann, *Wandering* 141; Rissi, *Theologie* 79; and Scholer, *Priests* 196. Dey, *Patterns* 219, is one of the few who actually excludes the exaltation from what it means for Christ to be perfected.

[41] So Peterson, *Perfection* 66, 98, who also mentions Riggenbach, *Hebräer* 136, and O. Cullmann, *The Christology of the New Testament* (London: SCM Press, 1959) 97.

[42] See below, n. 53.

[43] Regardless of which interpretation is taken of perfection language in general, virtually all interpreters would agree that access to God's presence is involved in what it means for a believer to be perfected, whether it be actual entry into heaven itself, e.g. Kögel, 'τελειοῦν' 56; Käsemann, *Wandering* 141; W. R. G. Loader, *Sohn und Hoherpriester: Eine traditionsgeschichtliche Untersuchung zur Christologie des Hebräerbriefes* (WMANT 53; Neukirchen: Neukirchener Verlag, 1981) 45; and Isaacs, *Space* 103; or access to heaven while on earth (the majority of scholars).

the precise contours of the definition or overarching nuance of the word group, there is a great deal of agreement on those factors which are at least related to or involved in perfection. In particular, a 'formal' or 'general' sense of 'completion' or of 'bringing to a goal' seems the best way to approach the term in Hebrews. In addition, it is largely agreed that perfection for Christ *involves* suffering, exaltation and vocational qualification.[44] Finally, most scholars would acknowledge that perfection for believers *involves* a cleansing of sins and is related in some way to access into the heavenly realm, whether actual entry into heaven or access while on earth.[45]

However, what is needed is movement toward consensus on how these particulars might relate to the general meaning of completeness or, in the absence of such, an agreement that no overarching pattern exists. On the one hand, it is difficult to conceive that there is not a more general relation between the perfection of Christ and that of believers. Given the pervasive presence of perfection language throughout the epistle, it is unlikely that the author does not connect the main usages together with some more general 'connotation', even if he did so unconsciously. This fact is even more obvious when it is noted that every explicit instance of perfection language applies to some entity within the new covenant. The author does not use perfection language to speak of anything outside the new covenant and the new age.[46]

Such an observation led S. G. Sowers to the conclusion that 'applied perfection means *the bringing to completion in the new covenant of that which was anticipated in the old*'.[47] Similarly, Moses Silva sees the

---

[44] Not all scholars agree on all the elements within such perfection in Hebrews. Suffering, for example, does seem to be the process *through which* Christ is perfected (2:10), a prerequisite for perfection rather than perfection itself. These experiences qualify Christ for high priesthood, both in terms of the ability he gains to sympathize with our weaknesses and in that he undergoes this suffering without sinning (4:15), rather learning obedience (5:8). Most see Christ's perfection proper as including his entrance into the heavenly realm (cf. n. 40) and that a vast number see it as principally involving Christ's attainment of his high priestly office (cf. n. 39).

[45] See above, n. 43.

[46] Although τελειότερος in 9:11 might be taken to imply that the earthly tent was 'perfect' in some way, the word seems to mean little more than 'better', as M. Dibelius, 'Der himmlische Kultus nach dem Hebräerbrief', *Botschaft und Geschichte: Gesammelte Studien*, vol. 2: *Zum Urchristentum und zur hellenistischen Religionsgeschichte*, G. Bornkamm and H. Kraft, eds. (Tübingen: Mohr/Siebeck, 1956), and Scholer, *Priests* 186, have noted. If a general 'connotation' for perfection language can be established, however, then the use of τέλειος here may also be due to the association of the heavenly tent with perfection.

[47] *Hermeneutics* 113 (italics his), mentioning also J. Van der Ploeg as one who takes the same line of interpretation, 'L'exégèse de l'Ancien Testament dans l'épître aux Hébreux', *RB* (1947) 189.

'concrete designation' of the term in Hebrews in reference to Christ as 'the fulfilment of the promise', the eschatological exaltation of Christ.[48] These comments are moving in the right direction because they note generally that perfection really pertains only to entities within the new covenant. If by these statements Sowers and Silva mean to imply that, in general, realities within the new covenant can be said to be perfect in contrast to the 'imperfect' items of the old covenant and that these new age entities are 'complete' in some sense in contrast to the 'incomplete' aspects of the old age, then Sowers and Silva have hit upon an important dimension to perfection language in Hebrews.[49]

The notion that perfection language in Hebrews entails some sort of relationship to heavenly realities also has a strong claim. John M. Scholer has written, 'τελειοῦν serves to describe the "attaining to the goal", which is the direct presence of God'.[50] As such, Scholer sees the perfection of Christ as his entry into the heavenly holy of holies and the perfection of believers as that 'present access to God's heavenly sanctuary which they enjoy already, not at some future point when they die'.[51] Marie Isaacs, similarly viewing perfection as attainment to the heavenly realm, goes so far as to deny perfection to believers until they actually enter into the heavenly city. In the present it can only be experienced by believers 'proleptically'.[52]

Once again, these analyses have much to commend them because they have noted that, whatever perfection might be, it usually implies some change of relation with the heavenly realm. Even if perfection were possible for believers while upon the earth, a relationship with heaven makes sense because they are tying into heavenly realities in some way. Chapter 5 will also make it clear that the realm of spirit is associated far more with heaven than with earth and bodies. There are serious objections, however, to a view which sees perfection exclusively as reaching the presence of God, attaining the 'spatial' goal of heaven. Similarly, perfection does not always involve the heavenly realm. Three instances in Hebrews make this point clear. First, with regard to the perfection of Christ in 7:28, Christ is said to have been perfected forever in contrast to the high priests 'who have weakness'. It is difficult to see how access to the heavenly realm

---

[48] 'Perfection and Eschatology in Hebrews', *WTJ* 39 (1976) 67.

[49] I suspect, however, that they have slightly skewed their interpretations by claiming that in *specific* occurrences of perfection language in Hebrews, the items are considered perfect because they are the complete forms of their old covenant counterparts. Rather, the specific connotations of perfection in Hebrews always relates to what 'completion' would mean for that particular entity, not in terms of its old covenant counterpart.

[50] *Priests* 200, following in general the suggestions of Rissi, *Theologie* 79, 102–3.

[51] *Priests* 196, 200.   [52] *Space* 102–3.

contrasts here with weakness. It is not the location of Christ which is the point of contrast, but rather the fact that he is not weak like the earthly high priests. To restrict the proper meaning of perfection to access seems to miss the real point of the verse.

Another instance where a 'spatial' meaning seems unlikely is in 9:9 and the parallel statement in 10:1. In 9:9 it is stated that the gifts and sacrifices of the earthly tabernacle are not able to 'perfect' the worshipper κατὰ συνείδησιν. Hebrews 10:2 elaborates on this claim by noting that if these sacrifices had been able to 'perfect' those who offered them, such a practice would have stopped, 'since the worshippers would have no longer have had any consciousness of sins'.[53] Rather, they would have been cleansed once (and for all). In these verses, 'to perfect those who approach' (10:1) seems to be parallel to 'the worshippers once having been cleansed' (10:2). On the one hand, the completeness involved in perfection is clear from the fact that if perfection had been possible, they would have been able to stop offering sacrifices. Therefore, perfection in this verse involves the accomplishment of cleansing rather than the reaching of a destination. The parallelism of perfecting with the cleansing of the worshipper is also striking. These verses, while certainly implying access to the heavenly realm in the theology of the epistle, do not in these instances speak of perfection in any such terms.

Probably the clearest use of perfection language which in reality excludes the 'spatial' reading is in 12:2. Here, that which is perfected is 'the faith'. This 'faith' refers to all those elements involved in the author's understanding of God's purposes in salvation history through Christ. Such an entity cannot enter into the heavenly realm, for it is an abstract term rather than a person. In this verse more than any other, the formal definition of perfection asserts itself.

In the end, it seems impossible to generalize the meaning of τελειόω in Hebrews beyond a basic formal sense of completion. Scholer's comment on those who read perfection as 'consecration' eventually applies to his own interpretation as well: to fit all of the occurrences into a certain mould, scholars 'have had to elaborate their positions, while clinging to the concept itself', whatever it might be.[54] In the end, it must simply be admitted that the particular kind of perfection in each instance varies depending on the entity in question. There is always the idea of 'bringing to the appropriate goal' or 'completedness' in mind, but there is not

---

[53] Since συνείδησις is parallel to ἀνάμνησις in 10:3, it must mean something like 'consciousness' rather than 'conscience'.

[54] *Priests* 191.

one specific goal in each case. For each kind of item, there is its own appropriate 'completeness'.

When each particular instance of perfection comes within the purview of the author's theological system, his standard for completeness always turns out to be the purpose which God has intended for that particular item in the plan of salvation history. In Hebrews, something is perfected when it has attained its appropriate status within the purposes of God.[55] Such a state can only be attained within the new covenant and ultimately will involve the heavenly realm, since that realm alone is the *telos* for the people of God in the epistle's eschatology. In every relevant instance in Hebrews, perfection is the attainment of God's intended destiny and is thus to reach true rest and finality. The verb τελειόω or the nouns τελείωσις and τελειοτής, therefore, refer either to bringing some entity into its destined state of completedness or to the attainment of such a state.[56] The relevant connotations of such 'perfection' follow in each particular context.

The preceding indicates both why the author can use perfection language parallel to so many different items and why so many different interpretations of this language have been propounded. In terms of Christ, the goal is high priesthood in heaven and the atonement which follows. In the theology of the author, this requires that Christ die without sin, although having been tempted in every way like those for whom he is atoning. It is thus appropriate for God to bring Christ to this point through suffering (2:10) so that he can become a cause of eternal salvation (5:9). His perfected high priesthood lasts forever because perfection is by definition

---

[55] For the author, this 'appropriate status' would have been obvious. To him, therefore, the meaning of perfection in each case would be fairly self-evident and would not require my more methodical inquiry in each case as to what would be the proper status of each item within God's purposes.

[56] This connotation does not really apply to the two occurrences of τέλειος in the epistle (5:14; 9:11) nor to the one instance of τελειότης in 6:1. These words are used in different senses. For example, τελειότερος in 9:11 means little more than 'better', while the uses of 'perfect' and 'perfection' in 5:14 and 6:1 could just as well be translated 'mature' and 'maturity'. Although in each case these words are indeed associated with the new covenant and the appropriate in God's purposes, the latter two in particular reflect a rather widespread use of paideutic language in the literature of the period. Cf. 1 Cor. 2:6; 3:1; 14:20; Eph. 4:13f.; Phil. 3:15; Col. 1:28; Epictetus *Enchir.* 51; and numerous examples in Philo (e.g. *Agr.* 9; *Cong.* 18f.; *Prob.* 160), although these are developed along quite different lines from Hebrews (see R. Williamson, *Philo and the Epistle to the Hebrews* (ALGHJ 4; Leiden: E. J. Brill, 1970) 277–308). For more general discussions of this type of 'paideutic' language, see Moffatt, *Hebrews* 71, and Attridge, *Hebrews* 161–3. J. W. Thompson's treatment is less helpful in *The Beginnings of Christian Philosophy: The Epistle to the Hebrews* (CBQMS 13; Washington, DC: Catholic Biblical Association, 1982) 17–40.

final, and it attains God's high standard because Christ was without weakness (7:28).

With reference to the sons, the Law (7:19) and Levitical priesthood (7:11) were not able to bring them to the final and appropriate state of cleanness once and for all (9:9; 10:1–2). Under the Levitical system, their consciences always remembered their sins (10:2), and thus could never have any sense of finality about their sanctification. With one sacrifice, however, Christ brought them into this appropriate state in relation to God forever (10:14). Within God's purposes, this cleansing would only take place in the new covenant; therefore, the great cloud of the faithful could not be brought to this state apart from those living in the eschatological age (11:40). All of these spirits who in the new age finally have access to heaven, the place of final rest, have reached their God-destined state of cleanness (and, in the end, glory and honour) and can thus be considered to be 'perfected' (12:23). Since Christ has brought all this about, he can be said to be the 'perfector' of the faith (12:2), for he has brought this same faith to its appropriate and finished state in relation to God, and he now sits at the right hand of God.

This understanding of the perfection motif accounts for all of the relevant occurrences in the epistle, while it also accounts for interpretations of perfection language which have focused on one or another of the many pertinent aspects of God's intended destiny for Christ and his people. It also ties into the images of promise which we have looked at thus far. For example, it is clear that the author's use of perfection language ties in with the notion of entrance into rest. For Christ or believers to reach their completed state is for them to attain a kind of rest and finality of state. The forever perfected Christ sits at the right hand of God. As David M. Hay pointed out, while Ps. 110:1 is cited with different emphases throughout Hebrews, the allusion in 10:12 focuses 'on the fact that he sits'.[57] Christ's perfection, involving his once and for all sacrifice and its strong emphasis on its finality, is clearly reminiscent of attaining rest.[58]

In the same vein, believers are exhorted to 'rest' from their works, as God himself rested from his works (4:10). God is thus also at rest in his 'realm of perfection', and the perfected believer has (ideally) reached a point of final cleansing, and access into the heavenly realm. In a sense, Isaacs is right to say that believers can only be considered perfected on this earth 'proleptically', for while they can be said to have already come

[57] *Glory* 87–8.
[58] Although Christ has completed the sacrifice, he must technically wait for his 'enemies' to be put under his feet until he can be completely at rest (10:13).

to 'the spirits of just ones having been perfected', this state of perfection is provisional upon them holding their faith firm until the end (3:14).[59] On the other hand, the cleansing, which is the most important component of perfection for believers, can be considered as already accomplished (e.g. 10:22), and the author can use the perfect tense in stating that believers have already come to the realm of perfected spirits (12:23), adding a strong present dimension to perfection. Like the rest of God, therefore, perfection is primarily future, while having a strong present aspect and implication.

Perfection language also ties into the promised land motif. As we have noted, the association of access to heaven and perfection has seemed so apparent in the epistle that it has led some to see 'entrance into heaven' as the essence of what it means to be perfected. We can partly sympathize with their perspective because the earthly realm in Hebrews is transitory and will eventually be 'removed'. Thus the heavenly sphere is the only possible realm for the true perfection of a person, for perfection intrinsically implies finality. The perfected Christ, therefore, enters into heaven, while the cleansed spirits of believers have present access to heaven through Christ and will eventually be part of the heavenly assembly in the city of the living God.

There is thus a strong link between promise and perfection in Hebrews. Since perfection is the attainment of God's destined purpose for humanity, it has exactly the same content as that which God has promised. God's promise, in effect, includes all those things which are involved in being perfected. As a result, the content of God's promise to his people includes a final cleansing from sin and definitive access to his presence. This similarity between promise and perfection also explains why the author is not wholly consistent in his use of the singular and plural for promise, for *the* promise, so to speak, involves many promises.[60]

Integrating the motifs

The attainment of glory and honour in victory over death, coming salvation, the rest of God, land of promise, and perfection motifs account for most of the language of promise in the epistle. As I have gone along, I have attempted to integrate them with one another. For example, both the future rest of God and the place of true perfection relate to the heavenly realm. This location embodies a good deal of the promise. The present possibility of cleansing is also an important part of perfection and thus a

[59] *Space* 102–3. [60] Cf. n. 26.

part of the promise as well. These images account for most of what the author includes in the content of the promise.

Such perfection is only possible in the new age under the new covenant.[61] This observation leads us to explore the overall place of promise language in Hebrews' narrative world. Primarily, there is a real continuity among the people of God under both covenants. The cloud of witnesses in Heb. 11 all died without having received the promises (11:39), because God 'foresaw' something better, namely, to perfect all believers through Christ in the new age. This 'waiting' of the Old Testament saints implies a plan on God's part, a continuity in salvation history between the old age and the new. Since Enoch, Abraham and the patriarchs, Sarah, Moses – in short, all those examples of faithfulness in the first twenty-nine verses of Heb. 11 – since all of these lived before Israel failed to enter into rest (3:7–11) and did not remain in God's first covenant (8:9), one can assume that it was not the failure of the wilderness generation or of Israel at any other time that brought about some ad hoc addition of God's second covenant. Rather, the implication is that God had planned all along to perfect his people through Christ. When we come to discuss the correspondence between the old cultus and Christ, this fact will come even more clearly into focus.

The promise remaining for the people of God, therefore, is an eschatological promise, one made as a part of God's overall plan for salvation history but reserved for 'these last days'. As Käsemann pointed out long ago, 4:2 and 6 virtually equate the reception of God's promise with the verb εὐαγγελίζομαι, indicating that promise is in fact an overarching category for the author.[62] The message of God to his 'people' both then and now is really the very same promise, although for the wilderness generation the hearing of it was not mixed with faith. God never intended to give the promise through Joshua, for if he had, he would not have spoken of another day (4:8).[63] Even when it is not explicitly mentioned, it can

---

[61] Käsemann, *Wandering* 30 (esp. n. 23), has noted that in 8:6, the new covenant is said to have been enacted on the basis of 'better promises', confirming the close relationship between promise language and the new covenant.

[62] *Wandering* 19, 26. So also Rose, 'Verheißung' 186.

[63] The people of God are destined to receive these promises as 'heirs'. Repeatedly throughout the epistle, the notion of inheritance is joined to that of promise (6:12, 17; 9:15; 11:9). This fact indicates that the people of God receive the promises as sons and children of God, as seed of Abraham. The connection between sonship and inheritance thus is that of those who have been perfected to that which is promised to them. Technically, of course, such sonship and heirship was not possible until the sacrifice of Christ, meaning that the faithful in the old age had to wait (11:39–40).

be assumed that the author of Hebrews is always thinking in terms of a plan in the mind of God. God has planned and promised from the very beginning a new covenant which will bring finality and perfection to his purposes in the world. The motif of promise, therefore, implicitly stands in the background of all the different contrasts of the book, providing continuity to the plot of salvation history.

Accordingly, the content of God's promise to his people in Hebrews is none other than all that is associated with salvation. It is, first of all, that perfection which God effects through Christ, the setting of the one who believes in a proper relationship with God through cleansing, resulting in access to the heavenly realm. This perfection will of course be 'complete' when the people of God find their rest in that heavenly homeland, the lasting city prepared for them, and thus when they will attain the 'glory and honour' promised in Ps. 8 in victory over death. This promise did not arise haphazardly, but has a constant place in the salvific purpose of God, who foresaw that it would be best to perfect all the people of God with the one sacrifice of Christ.

Conclusion

The purpose of this chapter was to gain a sense of the overall direction of salvation's plot and thereby of the story's overarching goals. I have argued both generally and exegetically that the 'initial sequence' of the plot involved God's intention to present humanity with glory and honour in the creation. We find this overarching goal encapsulated and implied in the author's understanding of Ps. 8. God created humanity for glory, but we do not yet see humanity with that glory. Instead, mortals suffer death and live in fear of death their whole lives. The fact that the Devil holds the power of death implies that he probably is responsible in some way for the failure of the initial sequence. At the very least, he is the current 'opponent' who stands in the way of the plot's fulfilment.

It thus comes as no surprise that Hebrews looks to this current period of time as a time of incompleteness and imperfection. Nor is it surprising that it speaks of the final sequence in terms of perfection and rest. It fits this general pattern that the author applies imperfection language to elements of the old covenant, while perfection language consistently applies to the new. The law made nothing perfect (7:19) nor did Levitical sacrifices perfect those who approached God by that method (10:1). For the fulfilment of these goals, we must look to Christ.

Yet despite such discontinuity, the 'sender' of the plot remains the same. From the very first verse of the epistle, it is the same God who spoke through the prophets, through the angels and the Law which they delivered, through Moses, through the Levitical cultus and, most importantly of all, through Christ. The old covenant was not a mistake, but part of the overall plan of God to lead the people of God, the faithful, the heirs of the promise to their destined honour and glory in victory over the power of death. This continuity is especially seen in language of promise in the epistle. The author clearly believed that the new covenant was a promise for all who become enlightened and are sanctified through the sacrifice of Christ.

The author speaks of such promise in several ways. It is the future rest of the people of God in the heavenly city. It is the perfection of believers as they attain their appointed end within the scheme of God's purposes. The 'goal' which can be applied to every instance of perfection language in the epistle is the appropriate status for any given thing within the purpose of God. Whether the reference is to Christ or believers, to be perfected is to reach one's appointed place within God's intended order. And God guarantees all of his purposes with an unchangeable oath, giving strong encouragement to those who believe.

The author of Hebrews also implies that the old covenant anticipated the new, that it was in fact patterned after the true and ultimate covenant in an imprecise way. It was not the failure of the first ones to receive God's promise which led to the need for a second and different promise. Rather, from the beginning God was ordering the first covenant as an illustration of the second, bringing things to pass in accordance with the necessities and prerogatives of his plan. While the first covenant was an imperfect shadow of God's work in Christ and not a mirror image, it pointed to this work in a God-ordained way. All of this implies a certain '*logos*' to the world. When one notes the wisdom language used of Christ in 1:3 and the author's repeated use of the motif of God's 'speaking' (cf. 4:12), the likelihood of some sort of conception of God's *logos* on the part of the author becomes more and more likely. God's plan and purposes in creation and salvation history give rise to the entire plot and unify the story.

Hebrews is not very explicit about the specifics of the ultimate glory to which Christ is leading the many 'sons'. From the perspective of this current world and the coming judgement, this glory involves salvation. Hebrews 12:28 implies that humanity will experience this glory in an unshakeable kingdom, but the author is ambiguous on the location. The imagery of Hebrews in general points toward heaven as the place where the spirits of the perfected righteous will find themselves (12:23). Presumably the audience knew the answers to these questions well enough that the author did not need to state them explicitly. I will address these sorts of questions more thoroughly in my consideration of the spatial settings of the plot in chapter 5.

4

THE TWO AGES

The 'topical sequences' of the plot

The previous chapter argued that Ps. 8 gives us the 'initial sequence' of the story behind Hebrews' argument, the starting point for understanding the story of salvation. God intended humanity to have glory and honour in the creation. But because of death, humanity does not experience such glory. Hebrews points to the Devil as the one who holds the power of death. Accordingly, we should see humanity's ultimate attainment of glory as the appropriate end of the story, the final sequence of the plot. Hebrews is almost as vague about the particulars of that future glory as it is about the opening sequence when humanity failed to attain it. We can only make educated guesses about its precise nature on the basis of images like the 'heavenly city', an 'unshakeable kingdom', 'rest' and a heavenly 'homeland'.[1]

For Greimas, any number of 'topical sequences' occur between the initial and final sequences of a story. In his analysis, the key topical sequence of a story is when the opponents who prevented the initial success of the plot are overcome. In the case of Hebrews, the key topical sequence is thus when Christ defeats death and the Devil. We would thus expect the key topical sequence of Hebrews to look something like the following:

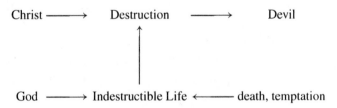

---

[1] And as with the sermon's protology, we must leave open the possibility that the author's eschatology is not fully consistent.

The structuralist system makes the diagram look somewhat more obtuse than its explanation need be. Its thrust basically amounts to the final part of Heb. 2:14: 'in order that through death he might destroy the one who holds the power of death: that is, the Devil'. In some way that Hebrews does not fully explain, Christ's death without sin (cf. 4:15) defeats the power of the Devil over his death. Christ's cry to be saved out of death is heard because of his εὐλαβεία (5:7), and God brings up from the dead the 'great shepherd of the sheep' (13:20). Thus glorified, he is now able to lead many other sons to glory (2:10).

The topical sequence I sketched above is accurate to the theology of Hebrews and the dynamics of its plot. The actual story world of Hebrews, however, as all New Testament theology, is complicated by the separation in time of Christ's death/resurrection from his parousia and the final accomplishment of the plot. The result is that Hebrews presumes two key topical sequences in the resolution of the story. The first takes place with the definitive sacrifice of Christ. This sacrifice inaugurates a period in which the final age has begun but is not yet fully here (cf. 8:13). The second key topical sequence is then when God finally sets the entire universe to rights, completing the plot (cf. 12:25–7).

Surrounding these two key topical sequences are numerous other events in the plot. For example, before Christ's sacrifice we find any number of events from the old covenant. We might speak of a typical sequence from the old covenant in which an earthly priest offers a sacrifice unable to cleanse the human conscience (e.g. 10:1–2). Similarly, we might speak of typical sequences from the new covenant between the ages in which individuals like the audience of Hebrews appropriate Christ's cleansing in anticipation of the promised rest.

It is the purpose of this chapter to explore the way in which these sequences divide up time for Hebrews and thus move the plot toward its final goal. The previous chapter implicitly set the bulk of Hebrews' story in between some pristine 'before' and 'after'. The central dynamics of Hebrews' partition of time, however, derive from its topical sequences. The most important division takes place with Christ's death and sacrificial offering, for this 'event' marks the turning point between the old and new covenants, the beginning of the end. The second most important event is the completion of this process at the shaking of heaven and earth (12:26). Between these two events is a time in which the new is here, but not fully here. Similarly, the old is obsolete, yet not completely gone (8:13; see fig. 4.1).

These are the settings in time presupposed by the story world of Hebrews. I should mention at this point that the sequences I am about

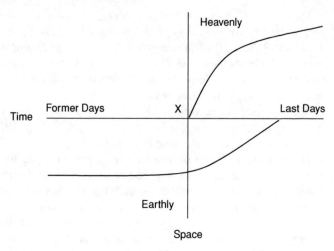

Figure 4.1.

to unfold relate to the way Hebrews understands the dynamics of its underlying story. Because Hebrews presents its audience with a complex argument and because Hebrews does not actually narrate the full story, it actually looks at the same events in multiple ways and does not 'lock' the story world into a single narrative form. The result is that I will at times be able to parse and diagram the structure of events and sequences in more than one way.

The turning of the ages

From the beginning of Hebrews, the fundamental argument is structured on the basis of a contrast between the old and the new, the former age and the new covenant as it has been effected through Christ. In this respect, the first four verses not only provide the main theological theme of the book, they also set its eschatological context by contrasting God's former manner of 'speaking' with his most recent agent of revelation: 'Although at many times and in many ways God formerly spoke to the fathers by the prophets, in these last days he spoke to us by a Son.' The fact that the author begins Hebrews in this way, making this contrast the setting for all that follows, argues that any metaphysical contrast the book might have should be interpreted squarely within this eschatological framework.

The exordium of Hebrews thus divides salvation history into two categories of divine revelation. First of all, there was the former period of God's 'speaking'. Significantly, this epoch was characterized by a multiplicity and diversity of the times and ways in which God's revelation occurred (πολυμερῶς καὶ πολυτρόπως – 1:1). The prophets in particular are mentioned in the proemium as the means by which God spoke to 'the fathers'. All of this diversity is contrasted with a single avenue of divine communication by which God has spoken 'to us'. In contrast to former revelations to the fathers, God has spoken ἐπ' ἐσχάτου τῶν ἡμερῶν τούτων to us by a Son (1:2). This Greek phrase is a Septuagintalism of באחרית הימים, which is found in several places in the Old Testament, notably in the LXX of Jeremiah.[2] It thus ties in closely with the quotation of Jer. 31:31–4 (38:31–4 LXX) in Heb. 8. This phrase in Jeremiah, along with the related clause ἡμέραι ἔρχονται and similar language, is used to refer to the time when God will have accomplished his purposes in the judgement and restoration of Israel and its surrounding nations.[3] It is thus thoroughly eschatological in nature and would probably have had Messianic overtones for our author.[4]

As an expression of eschatology, the 'last days' phrase relates to the covenant language which the author will use later in the epistle. Whereas the discussion in the central portion of Hebrews will deal with *cultic* themes, the exordium implicitly relates the covenant scheme to *revelatory*

---

[2] As, for example, F. F. Bruce notes, *The Epistle to the Hebrews* (Grand Rapids, MI: Eerdmans, 1964) 3. G. W. Buchanan, 'Eschatology and the "End of Days"', *JNES* 20 (1961) 190, notes that the Hebrew phrase is translated four times by ἐπ' ἐσχάτου τῶν ἡμερῶν (Num. 24:14; Jer. 23:20; 49:39 [25:18 LXX]; and Dan. 10:14); seven times by ἐπ' ἐσχάτων τῶν ἡμερῶν (Gen. 49:1; Deut. 4:30 (the phrase here is actually ἐπ' ἐσχάτω τ. η.); Jer. 30 [37]:24; Ezek. 38:16; Dan. 2:28; Hos. 3:5; and Mic. 4:1); and once by ἐν ταῖς ἐσχάταις ἡμέραις (Isa. 2:2). In his study he has denied any *fixed* eschatological content to such phrases either in the Old or New Testaments, *pace* W. L. Lane, *Hebrews 1–8* (Dallas: Word Books, 1991) 10, who read Buchanan as saying that the term 'came to possess technical significance' of an eschatological nature. I hold, contrary to Buchanan, that the term in the New Testament (and in Jeremiah in a different way) *always* has eschatological significance, although I accept that the meaning of the original Hebrew phrase must always be determined in context.

[3] Jer. 7:32; 9:25 (24 LXX); 16:14; 19:6; 23:5, 7; 30 (37 LXX):3; 31 (38 LXX):27, 31, 38; 48 (31 LXX):12; 49 (30 LXX):2; 51 (28 LXX):52.

[4] Whether we choose to define the term 'eschatological' in such a way that it applies to Jeremiah itself, these texts certainly fit any normal definition of the word in terms of the way *our author* would have understood the prophet. For example, Jer. 23:5, one of the 'days are coming' passages, speaks of God raising up to David a ἀνατολὴν δικαίαν who will reign and perform judgement and righteousness upon the land (if the author knew Philo, cf. *Conf.* 62–3). Lane, *Hebrews 1–8* 10, has noted the occurrence of similar expressions in Sir. 48:24–5 and especially 4QFlor 1:15, where the Hebrew phrase occurs in a Messianic context.

motifs by its use of the expression, as we shall also see of the angels.[5] These diverse 'speakings' through the prophets were the way in which God revealed himself formerly to those who were within the old covenant, while his more recent agent of revelation is himself the mediator of a new covenant. We thus find covenant-related imagery throughout the whole book, where two epochs of salvation history with contrasting features are distinguished. In particular, the Jeremiah citation in Heb. 8 serves as a scriptural basis for the claim that God has enacted a change for the better in the way in which he relates to his people, and the author accordingly places the quotation at the very centre of his argument.

The use of Jer. 31 in Heb. 8–10 thus provides an authoritative basis for the distinction which the author has already made in the exordium and upon which, as I shall claim, he has built his argument in Heb. 1. As a result, the use of Jeremiah in these chapters provides the best insight into how the author understands the phrase ἐπ' ἐσχάτου τῶν ἡμερῶν τούτων in 1:2. In Heb. 8, the Jeremiah citation occurs in the middle of the author's central theological discourse on the high priesthood of Christ.[6] The author had already introduced the idea of the new covenant in 7:22 in conjunction with Christ's superiority to Levitical priests. As a Melchizedekian priest whom God has 'sworn into office' and who continues in this role forever, Christ has become the pledge (ἔγγυος) of a better covenant. Hebrews 8 expands upon this covenant motif and sets the stage for the argument in chs. 9 and 10 which follows. The earthly priests serve 'the heavenly things' only 'by shadowy illustration' (8:5). In contrast, Christ 'has obtained a superior ministry, in as much as he is also mediator of a new covenant, which has been put into effect on the basis of better promises' (8:6).[7] Here one sees the close connection in

---

[5] A distinction made by Vos, 'Hebrews, Epistle of the *Diathêkê*', *PTR* 14 (1916) 43, 52. I suspect strongly that a general division of the earlier part of Hebrews structurally into revelation (chs. 1–4) and priesthood (chs. 5–10) stands behind Vos' treatment of the covenant motif and thus that of Lehne, since she is following him (*New Covenant* 94). Vos thus foreshadows in general my relation of the angels to the new covenant motif.

[6] I would place the boundaries of this section as 4:14–10:18, with 5:11–6:20 as a striking paraenetic interruption used in part to retain the attention of the audience (cf. Aristotle, *Rhetoric* 3.14.9: ἔτι τὸ προσεκτικοὺς ποιεῖν πάντων τῶν μερῶν κοινόν . . . πανταχοῦ γὰρ ἀνιᾶσι μᾶλλον ἢ ἀρχόμενοι). This is similar in some ways to the analysis of W. Nauck, 'Zum Aufbau des Hebräerbriefes', *Judentum, Urchristentum, Kirche: Festschrift für Joachim Jeremias*. Ed. by W. Eltester (BZNW 26; Berlin: Alfred Töpelman, 1960) 203–4; and that of G. H. Guthrie, *The Structure of Hebrews: A Text-Linguistic Analysis* (SNT 73; Leiden: Brill, 1994) 79–82, 102–3; although Nauck places the end of the unit at 10:31. Guthrie leaves these boundaries somewhat fluid.

[7] For a justification of this translation of ὑποδείγματι καὶ σκιᾷ, see ch. 5, as well as L. Hurst's article, 'How "Platonic" are Heb. viii.5 and ix.23f?', *JTS* 34 (1983) 156–68.

Hebrews between cult, covenant and Law, as well as promise, a complex of ideas to which we will later return.[8]

In this context, the citation from Jeremiah provides divine authentication of the author's argument, demonstrating that the first covenant was not ἄμεμπτος (8:7) and that God 'found fault' (μέμφομαι) with its recipients.[9] In 'coming days', God will establish a new covenant, different from the previous one, because the *fathers* did not remain faithful to the former one (8:9). 'After those days', God will write his laws upon the very minds and hearts of his people, making it so that they need not teach one another to know him (8:10–11). God will be merciful toward their iniquities and no longer remember their sins (8:12). Finally, after citing this passage, the author concludes by noting that when God has called this covenant a 'new' one, he has implicitly declared the former one 'old'. So the one which is old and aging (τὸ παλαιούμενον καὶ γηράσκον) is about to vanish (ἐγγὺς ἀφανισμοῦ – 8:13).

There are several points of interest in regard to the author's citation of these verses. First of all, we must take extreme caution when interpreting citations, for not every aspect of a quotation is equally significant for an author. The author has a sense, for example, that the new covenant was always a part of God's plan rather than some *ad hoc* solution to a scheme gone wrong. Accordingly, this particular dimension of the citation was not the focus of the author. Rather, the author's interest in the citation comes out clearly in his recapitulation of it in 10:16–17.[10]

Secondly, because the author has modified the 'last days' phrase in 1:2 with the adjective 'these', the author identifies the 'speaking' of God through a Son with the 'coming days' and 'after those days' of the

---

[8] Susanne Lehne, *New Covenant* 26, in particular, has drawn attention to the interrelatedness of these concepts, claiming both that 'the author subsumes the Law under the rubric of cult' and that in Hebrews 'the Law ultimately becomes synonymous with the old covenant' (23f., following M. R. D'Angelo, *Moses in the Epistle to the Hebrews* (SBLDS 42; Missoula, MT: Scholars Press, 1979) 243–6). Indeed, here Christ's high priestly service does seem to be identified with his mediation of a new covenant, which is spoken of in legal terms (νενομοθέτηται) and related to God's promises (Lehne, *New Covenant* 26f.). These are of course the corresponding uses of these concepts in relation to the new covenant rather than the old, but they serve to illustrate the general truth of Lehne's claims.

[9] The actual subject of this sentence is unclear. Christ is the immediate antecedent, but the context would seem to require God or the Holy Spirit, as is confirmed by the author's summary of the quote in 10:15, where it is the Holy Spirit who is said to witness this.

[10] H. Attridge, 'The Uses of Antithesis in Hebrews 8–10', *HTR* 79 (1986) 6, has also implied a summarizing function to the recapitulation when he notes that one of the functions of the Jeremiah citation is 'to indicate what are the "better promises" (8:6) on which the new covenant is based. These promises are implicit in the two verses of the citation from Jeremiah which are repeated at 10:16–17', namely, that the covenant is an 'interior affair' and that sin will be effectively forgiven.

Jeremiah passage. As Heb. 8–10 makes clear, the promises of forgiveness and a 'clean conscience' are already realities for those who hold fast their confession of faith. In fact, these promises (in addition to the author's general polemic in favour of the new covenant) seem to be the main points which the author wished to bring out of the Jeremiah quotation, as can be seen from his recapitulation of it in 10:16–17:

> But as for this covenant which I will make with them,
>   after those days, says the Lord:
> I will put my laws in their hearts
>   and I will write them upon their mind,
> and their sins
>   and their transgressions will I remember no more.[11]

That the author considers these promises a present reality for the people of God is evident from the verses which follow (e.g. 10:19–25), which serve both as the hortatory conclusion of the preceding exposition and the beginning of a new paraenesis.[12] Here, the recipients are encouraged to have boldness to enter the holy of holies (10:19) and to approach God 'with a true heart' which *has been* purified from a wicked 'conscience' (10:22). Clearly the people of God already enjoy these benefits of the new covenant.

While the new covenant may be a present reality, an equally important aspect of the author's treatment of the Jeremiah quotation is the fact that the author cannot say that the new has arrived without reservation. Rather, he says that the old is just that: old, and ἐγγύς to its disappearance. He thus does not say that the old has completely vanished. Herein lies the main complexity of the plot and eschatology of Hebrews. In his exposition, the author clearly wishes his recipients to rely upon the finality and presence of the new covenant, but his paraenesis clearly reflects the element of expectation and of that which has not completely disappeared. Accordingly, the phrase 'in these last days' takes on a dual sense. In the

---

[11] There are a few changes here from his earlier citation, apart from its abridgement: (1) he substitutes 'with them' for the 'house of Israel', possibly because 'the new covenant is of more universal scope' (so Attridge, *Hebrews* 281); (2) he switches the objects of giving and writing; (3) he inserts ἀνομιῶν in parallel to ἁμαρτιῶν; and (4) he changes the aorist subjunctive μνησθῶ to a future indicative μνησθήσομαι, perhaps to make the promise 'more vivid and emphatic' (Attridge, *Hebrews* 281).

[12] Although I would place the structural division break after 10:18 due to the change in genre (see n. 6 above), I affirm the continuity in content between what follows in 10:19 and the preceding argument. The preceding exposition lacks something without the hortatory conclusion, and the exhortation is incomplete without the preceding argumentation. Guthrie, *Structure* 103–4, has made a similar claim, terming this unit an 'overlapping constituent' belonging both to what begins and follows.

context of Jeremiah and the new covenant, the coming days are here, and that which they have accomplished is present. At the same time, the people of God are still in the 'last days' of the old, which has not completely disappeared.

We therefore find two broad epochs of salvation history in the eschatological scheme of the author, with two corresponding covenants. These two ages overlap to some extent, however, in terms of the story's overall plotline (see fig. 4.1 above). The very situation in the background of the sermon is a consequence of the fact that the recipients live in the overlap of the two periods. On the one hand, Christ has come, and the new age and its covenant have begun, granting present access to God and forgiveness for sins. In this sense, the old covenant has effectively ended, implying that the recipients have no need to depend on the Levitical cultus and its priests. In the visible realm, however, the world has not yet seen the full effects of the change. This understanding of salvation history, divided into two epochs with two contrasting covenants, underlies the whole of the author's thought, whether it is expressed explicitly or left implicit.

Mediation in the former age

Hebrews retells and alludes to a number of stories from the first epoch of salvation history. Some of these stories are meant to inspire emulation in the audience, particularly the examples of faith in Heb. 11. Others dissuade the audience from actions of faithlessness. The deaths of the wilderness generation in Heb. 3:7–19 serve such a function.

But when it comes to the temporal settings of salvation's plot, I am chiefly concerned with two types of sequence that took place under the former covenant. The first type consists of sequences in the old age where God revealed truth to some old covenant mediator, often truth that anticipated the new covenant. The second type primarily consists of 'failed' cultic sequences of the old covenant which did not accomplish the cleansing which might have seemed to be their purpose. Of course the author of Hebrews reveals that God in fact never intended such events to take away sin. They were only shadowy illustrations of what was to come in Christ.

This section of the chapter focuses primarily on the revelatory sequences of the old covenant, approaching these by an examination of the old covenant mediators mentioned in Hebrews. I have already hinted that the contrast between the old and new age is not restricted to the central chapters of Hebrews. I believe, for example, that it also relates to the author's argument in the catena of Heb. 1. The division of salvation history into old and new covenant is key to the author's contrast of the Son with the angels.[13] The author finds such a contrast relevant to his discussion in part because he associates the angels with the ministration of the old covenant, while Christ as enthroned Son inaugurates the new. The Law is thus the 'the word spoken through angels' (2:2), and the angels are 'ministering spirits sent for service on account of those about to inherit salvation' (1:14). The angels are hereby connected with the old covenant and with service in this world. They will presumably have different functions in the heavenly assembly (12:22) of the 'world which is coming'. The coming world will not be subjected to them (2:5), but rather to the 'seed of Abraham', whom God is leading to glory through Christ (2:16). These verses indicate that the author views the angel/Son contrast in ch. 1 primarily from an eschatological perspective, even if he does not bring this aspect of the contrast to the fore. The angels revealed the old covenant (they 'spoke' it; 2:2), while the Son is the revelatory agent and effecter of the new.

While Christ and the angels contrast in general as the revealers of two different covenants, the author also found the contrast between them a rhetorically effective way to introduce his homily, particularly in the light of Ps. 8. Although Christ was 'lower than the angels for a little while' in his earthly life (2:9), he is now the enthroned Son at the right hand of God, the mediator of a new covenant better than the one spoken through angels. Although it is not always recognized, language about the Son in Heb. 1 is primarily focused on his 'enthronement' as royal Son at the point of his exaltation.[14] This fact made the contrast between Christ and the angels an appropriate introduction to the homily, announcing the exalted status which Christ has now achieved in fulfilment of his salvific destiny. Since Christ's high priesthood is in part a metaphorical restatement of this exaltation, the appropriateness of the catena as an introduction is even more apparent.

This locus of Sonship in ch. 1 is borne out throughout ch. 1. As Bertold Klappert has written, 'Ps 2,7 eröffnet und Ps 110,1 schließt diese

---

[13] Perhaps even the majority of interpreters currently disagree with this analysis. For example, Guthrie, *Structure* 121f., sees Heb. 1 as the Son's pre-existent superiority over the angels, which is then followed in ch. 2 by the Son becoming lower than the angels. This line of interpretation misses the author's point, which is to show that the Christ who was lower than the angels for a little while (2:9) is now exalted above the angels and is the mediator of a new covenant greater than the one for which they were responsible.

[14] For a full defence of this position, see my 'The Celebration of the Enthroned Son: The Catena of Hebrews 1:5–14', *JBL* 120 (2001) 469–85.

Schilderung des Inthronisationsaktes sinnvoll ab'.[15] Even in Heb. 1:1–4, the main clause is the statement that the Son has spoken in these last days (1:2, placing the Son in the new age in contrast to former days). In addition, the main verb of the relative clause in v. 3 places the locus of its exalted descriptions at the point of Christ's session at the right hand of Majesty. I conclude that Christ is most truly the ἀπαύγασμα of God's glory when he has the All under his feet after he has ascended to God's right hand and is thus mediator of the new covenant. In more than any other way, it is Christ as the embodiment of God's wisdom for humanity in redemption who is the wisdom of God, making it possible for the author to speak of him as God's agent in creation.[16]

Similarly, it is in this exalted state that Christ has *become* better than the angels (1:4), assuming the role of royal Son, a name which the angels do not have (1:5). The very first mention of the angels in 1:4 is thus clearly in the context of Christ's exaltation to the right hand of God as he in his glory is no longer 'lower than' them. There are several associations which the author will bring into play in connection with this exaltation of Christ, one of which is the attainment of glory and honour in fulfilment of Ps. 8.[17] I believe it is this psalm, along with the tradition associating the deliverance of the Law with angels, which gives rise to the contrast in Heb. 1.[18] When this psalm is read Christologically, it seems clear that whenever the Christ is crowned with glory and honour, he must become better than the angels. The fact that Christ was lower than the angels in his earthly life thus argues for a post-exaltation context for Heb. 1.

Accordingly, whenever God leads this firstborn into the world (1:6), it is certainly at a point when the angels must give way in worship to the one who is now to be exalted above them and whose 'covenant' supersedes the one which they revealed. The meaning of this verse is highly debated, hinging on what one considers the οἰκουμένη to be, as well as how one

---

[15] *Die Eschatologie des Hebräerbriefs* (Munich: Chr. Kaiser Verlag, 1969) 22. See also my 'Keeping his Appointment: Creation and Enthronement in the Epistle to the Hebrews', *JSNT* 66 (1996) 91–117.

[16] An interpretation reflected by Heb. 2:10, where it is said that 'it was fitting for him, because of whom the All exists and through whom the All exists, to perfect the leader of their [humanity's] salvation through sufferings while leading many sons to glory.' God is here the one 'through whom' everything exists, in distinction from Jesus, who is the one God perfected through sufferings. A natural inference is that the pre-existent Christ as creator exists in some way within God. The leading of many sons to glory takes place in the 'fitting' wisdom of God, which he accomplishes through the perfection of Jesus. Christ thus embodies God's wisdom in his governance of 'the All' when in the 'consummation of the ages' (9:26) he initiates a new covenant based upon better promises (8:6).

[17] See the previous chapter.

[18] So Caird, 'Method' 49 and Hurst, 'Christology' 154ff.

takes πάλιν. On the one hand, this entrance is not likely to be the birth of Christ, because that occurred during the time when he was 'a little lower than the angels'.[19] If the birth of Christ is excluded, the verse either refers to his second coming or relates directly to the use of οἰκουμένη in 2:5, implying that the entrance is in fact the exaltation of Christ to God's right hand.[20] My interpretation of ch. 1 favours this last reading the most. The angels must worship Christ as he enters into heaven as the exalted Son. We should be careful, however, not to stake our claims too heavily on such a highly debated passage. There are also good arguments for understanding 1:6 as a reference to the parousia.[21] And in all three

---

[19] I therefore disagree with C. Spicq, *L'épître aux Hébreux*, vol. 2 (Paris: Gabalda, 1953) 17; H. Montefiore, *The Epistle to the Hebrews* (London: A. & C. Black, 1964) 45; and Attridge, *Hebrews* 55, all of whom believe this verse to be such an allusion. J. C. Meier ('Symmetry and Theology in the Old Testament Citations of Heb 1,5–14', *Bib* 66 (1985) 507–33) suggests a chiastic structure to the catena that some have used to support an overall exaltation framework while allowing for movement to other points of Christ's existence in the middle of the catena (e.g. Victor Rhee in a paper presented to the SBL Hebrews Consultation in Philadelphia, Fall, 2005: 'Chiasm and Christology in Hebrews 1:1–14'). My argument here and in 'Celebration' point out that such an interpretation ultimately results in conflict between the catena and the author's theology elsewhere in the sermon, whereas a consistent exaltation context does not.

[20] Second coming: B. F. Westcott, *The Epistle to the Hebrews: The Greek Text with Notes and Essays*, 2nd edn (Grand Rapids, MI: Eerdmans, 1892) 37; O. Michel, *Der Brief an die Hebräer*, 13th edn (Göttingen: Vandenhoeck & Ruprecht, 1984 (1936)) 113; E. Käsemann, *The Wandering People of God: An Investigation of the Letter to the Hebrews* (Minneapolis: Augsburg, 1984 (1939)) 98–101; J. Héring, *The Epistle to the Hebrews* (London: Epworth, 1970 (1954)) 9; F. Schröger, *Der Verfasser des Hebräerbriefes als Schriftausleger* (BU 4; Regensburg: Pustet, 1968) 51; and H. Braun, *An die Hebräer* (HNT 14; Tübingen: Mohr/Siebeck, 1984) 37; exaltation: F. J. Schierse, *Verheissung und Heilsvollendung: Zur theologischen Grundfrage des Hebräerbriefes* (Munich: Zink, 1955); A. Vanhoye, 'L'οἰκουμένη dans l'épître aux Hébreux', *Bib* 45 (1964) 248–53; G. Theissen, *Untersuchungen zum Hebräerbrief* (SNT 2; Gütersloh: Mohn, 1969) 122; P. Andriessen, 'La teneur judéo-chrétienne de Hé 16 et II 14B–III2', *NovT* 18 (1976) 293–304; W. R. G. Loader, *Sohn und Hoherpriester: Eine traditionsgeschichtliche Untersuchung zur Christologie des Hebräerbriefes* (WMANT 53; Neukirchen: Neukirchener Verlag, 1981) 23–5; D. Peterson, *Hebrews and Perfection: An Examination of the Concept of Perfection in the Epistle to the Hebrews* (SNTSMS 47; Cambridge: Cambridge University Press, 1982) 214 n.19; Meier, 'Symmetry' 507f.; Lane, *Hebrews 1–8* 27; and P. Ellingworth, *The Epistle to the Hebrews* (Grand Rapids, MI: Eerdmans, 1993) 117. All of these would view the location of πάλιν in terms of the postpositive δέ, as did those who saw the verse as a reference to the entrance of Christ into the world at his birth.

[21] The position of πάλιν within the temporal clause and immediately preceding εἰσαγάγη is sometimes used to argue that this is Christ's second entrance at the time of the parousia. The author may be drawing from the Song of Moses in a form used by the early church. See the discussion in S. Kistemaker, *The Psalm Citations in the Epistle to the Hebrews* (Amsterdam: Soest, 1963) 20–3. Although the LXX of Deut. 32:43 diverges slightly from the quotation here, the Odes following the Greek psalter render the verse almost exactly the same as Hebrews (only without the article on ἄγγελοι) and may represent a form used in Christian worship. Such an allusion fits well into a parousia context, where the ambiguous αὐτῷ might be taken of Christ, who then comes to repay δίκην τοῖς ἐχθροῖς, a motif which would relate to the putting of Christ's enemies under his feet (e.g. 10:13).

interpretations, the entrance relates either to the approach, inauguration or full arrival of the new age in contrast to the former one.

At first glance, the citations of 1:7–12 might seem to relate more generally to Christ's identity than specifically in reference to his exaltation. But a closer look demonstrates that their primary focus is on the permanence of Christ's now realized kingship in contrast to the passing mediation of the angels in the old covenant. The author has the enthroned Christ in view just as he did in 1:1–4. This Son has been anointed and enthroned for eternity by God in the presence of his companions (the other sons? the angels? 1:9) and the years of his reign will never come to an end (1:12). The angels, on the other hand, are servants (1:14) whose ministry to humanity will end with the termination of the first age and is transitional, as indicated by their comparison with winds and flames (1:7). I will further defend this interpretation in ch. 5.

The chain of citations then ends as it began, with a reference to the exaltation of Christ to God's right hand in enthronement, with Christ now higher than the angels in his glory and honour. The angels have never achieved such a status. 'God's word' has never entailed such a role for the angels (1:13a). The appointed place of angels in the order of things with regard to humanity was as ministers while the people of God wait for salvation (1:14). But when salvation comes, the angels will clearly no longer be able to function in such a role and presumably even the other sons will be greater than them in fulfilment of the psalm.

The preceding interpretation does not require that we posit any polemic against an angel Christology or angel veneration in the audience, although it is certainly possible that angels played a significant role in the thought of the community addressed.[22] But we lack the evidence or impetus to consider parallels relevant that we might find in the *Songs of the Sabbath Sacrifice* at Qumran, or in the philosophy at Colossae (cf. Col. 2:18), or even in the apparently propitiatory role of angels in *TLevi* 3. We can sufficiently account for the presence of this contrast (1) because of Ps. 8's implication that Christ's exaltation placed him higher than the angels in the fulfilment of humanity's intended glory and (2) because of the relationship between the angels and the Law. This last fact feeds an association

---

[22] R. G. Hammerton-Kelly, for example, suggested that 'the author found it necessary to combat an "angel Christology"', *Pre-existence Wisdom and the Son of Man: A Study of the Idea of Pre-existence in the New Testament* (Cambridge: Cambridge University Press, 1973) 244. L. Stuckenbruck gives a full delineation and evaluation of the suggested reasons for the contrast between Son and angels in *Angel Veneration and Christology: A Study in Early Judaism and the Christology of the Apocalypse of John* (Tübingen: Mohr/ Siebeck, 1995) 124–39, concluding that there may have been a polemical source behind Heb. 1–2 (137) which the author takes over 'to sharpen his readers' perception of the message given through Christ' (139).

between angels and the old covenant about which the author spends the better part of his exposition arguing.[23] Hebrews 1, while it does not focus directly on this eschatological contrast, presupposes it, for it has only the exalted Christ in view. The author can thus proceed naturally into Heb. 2 with an exhortation based on the covenant distinction (2:1–4).[24]

In the story world of salvation history, the angels were the closest equivalent to Christ in the old covenant, the 'patrons' of the old age. Not only were they the ones through whom the Law was delivered (2:2), thus contrasting with Christ in that way,[25] but they also may have been considered in some way as 'guardians' of the kind of ceremonial purity and ritual cleansing which the author associated with the Law.[26] The angels were only temporary stewards of humanity under the old covenant, which was a mere foreshadowing of the permanent covenant God was going to make with humanity through Christ. In every way, the mediator of the new covenant is superior and more lasting than those who delivered the previous 'word' (2:2).

The distinction between the angels and Christ, therefore, presupposes the fundamental eschatological contrast between the covenants, at least in part a contrast of revelation, mediation and governance.[27] Once one has noted the connections which can be made between ch. 1 and new covenant language and once one accepts that Christ and the angels are the 'revealers' of their respective covenants, one begins to see how Keijo Nissalä

---

[23] See Hurst, *Background*, 45, 78.

[24] Stuckenbruck, *Angel Veneration* 128, argues that there is a 'certain logical distance' between the argument of Christ's superiority over angels' in Heb. 1 and 'accountability to the new covenant' in the exhortation of 2:1–4 (128), thereby precluding that the latter is a basis for the former. I would argue that this 'logical distance' is rather a shift in focus from Christ as the now enthroned one in a contrast which *presupposes* the eschatological contrast between old and new, to the difference between the work of Christ and the work of the angels *explicitly* contrasted in the following verses. There is a shift, but it does not preclude my understanding. Heb. 1 is a rhetorically effective presentation of the exalted Christ in his new role, a role which will form one of the principal bases of argumentation throughout the epistle.

[25] Cf. also Gal. 3:19.

[26] As in 9:10. Such an association with ritual and ceremonial purity may be relevant to such cryptic and allusive comments as 1 Cor. 11:10 and statements in Qumran such as are found in CD 15:17, 1QSa 2:8–9, 1QM 7:6. L. Stuckenbruck presented this possibility in a paper delivered to the New Testament Seminar at the University of Durham, Winter 1995. He raised the possibility that angels might in some way have been considered the guardians of proper order within worshipping communities.

[27] This contrast could be considered a spatial contrast, particularly if the angels were to be associated with an οἰκουμένη in the *earthly* realm in 1:6 and could therefore be associated cosmologically with the earthly realm and its transience. It should be noted, however, that the angels are present in the heavenly assembly (12:22), and I prefer a reading of οἰκουμένη which refers to the heavenly world of 2:5.

and Walter Übelacker could consider 1:5–2:18 as a *narratio* presenting the basic picture for the argument which is to follow. In my opinion, Heb. 1 serves as a rhetorically effective introduction to the cornerstone of the author's Christology and argumentation: Christ is the now exalted Son, the one who has caused a final, eschatological shift in the relationship between God and humanity. The first two chapters of Hebrews thus constitute a rhetorically effective, though not summary, overview and introduction to who Christ is and what he has done, using more traditional language than the following chapters, which will reformulate this language through the metaphor of high priesthood.

Certainly angels are present throughout the whole story. Within the author's story world, however, their principal function is in association with the former age, the first part of the plot. They, like the prophets, served to reveal God's 'word' to his people. Unlike the prophets, they revealed the Law, which was a valid revelation intended to point toward the coming new covenant in which Christ would reveal God's will. Although their function as ministers to those about to inherit salvation seems to continue into the 'today' of the present, it will end when the old age finally vanishes.

Cultic sequences in the former age

The principal function of covenant language in Hebrews is to contrast the Law and its cultus with the one-time offering of Christ. To understand more specifically what the author is getting at in this discussion, we need at least some sense of how he related the 'high priesthood' of Christ, which he places at the centre of the new covenant, to the cultus of the old covenant and its Law. It is, after all, the Christ-sequence of the new covenant that puts the cult-sequences of the old covenant into perspective for him. When the author speaks of the high priesthood of the earthly priests or of the covenant inaugurated by Moses, he uses these terms in their normal sense (cf. 8:4). When he speaks of Christ as a high priest who ministers in a heavenly tabernacle as a mediator of a new covenant, however, he uses these words in a new way, in an unusual sense, a *metaphorical* sense.[28]

---

[28] To say that language of Christ as high priest is metaphorical does not of course imply that the realities to which he refers are untrue or that the author was using such language in anything other than its truest sense. From the standpoint of English usage, I accordingly find E. W. Stegemann and W. Stegemann's use of the term 'metaphorical' slightly odd in 'Does the Cultic Language in Hebrews Represent Sacrificial Metaphors? Reflections on Some Basic Problems', *Hebrews: Contemporary Methods – New Insights* (Leiden: E. J. Brill, 2005) 13–35.

It goes without saying that, in the ancient world, the *customary* referents of terms like 'sacrifice', 'high priest' and 'offering' were various components of earthly sacrificial cults.[29] Accordingly, when we deem capital punishment on a cross a cultic sacrifice or when we refer to Christ's ascension to heaven as an entrance into a heavenly holy of holies, we are giving these words a 'new semantic pertinence by means of an impertinent attribution', which is the definition of a metaphor.[30] To speak of Christ as a high priest is thus *by definition* to speak metaphorically of Christ's work on the basis of a comparison with the earthly cultus.

At the same time, precedents certainly existed for such metaphors. We must subsequently decide whether Hebrews draws on Jewish traditions about a literal temple in heaven (in ch. 6). But I have already mentioned in ch. 2 that Christ's death was viewed as a sacrifice offered by God even at the time of Paul (cf. Rom. 3:25). More ambiguously, Rom. 8:34 speaks of Christ as an intercessor on our behalf at the right hand of God. This comment may allude to Christ in a priestly role in heaven, probably on the basis of Ps. 110.[31] Nevertheless, Hebrews is the only instance in the New Testament where such priestly imagery is explicit, let alone developed in terms of the Day of Atonement sacrifice. Further, Hebrews uniquely considers Christ a *high* priest who offers *himself*. He becomes both the offering and the offerer.[32] We cannot be absolutely certain that the author himself is responsible for these metaphorical extensions, but no evidence exists to the contrary.[33]

---

[29] Although the idea of a heavenly tabernacle certainly predates the epistle, the way in which the author connects traditional language about Christ to this idea is in any case a new way of speaking of these events in the New Testament.

[30] So P. Ricoeur, *Time and Narrative*, vol. 1, K. McLaughlin and D. Pellauer, trans. (Chicago: University of Chicago Press, 1984) ix. See also ch. 3 of *Interpretation Theory: Discourse and the Surplus of Meaning* (Fort Worth, TX: Christian University Press, 1976) 45–70; and ch. 3 of *The Rule of Metaphor* (London: Routledge & Kegan Paul, 1978 (1975)) 65–100.

[31] Whether 8:34 is in fact such an indication, however, is unclear. J. Fitzmyer, *Romans* (London: Geoffrey Chapman, 1993) 533 does not think so, and J. D. G. Dunn, *Romans 1–8* (Dallas: Word, 1988) 504, suggests that other traditions might explain the datum, such as Paul's last Adam Christology, similar to *T.Abr.* 11.

[32] Attridge, *Hebrews* 146–7, makes this distinction between what he considers the traditional priestly tradition as found in Rom. 8:34 and Hebrews' Yom Kippur development of the motif. It is not completely certain, however, that Rom. 8:34 is speaking of Christ as priest at all.

[33] I agree with the arguments of G. Cockerill, 'Heb. 1:1–14, *1 Clem.* 36:1–6 and the High Priest Title', *JBL* 97 (1978) 437–40, that *1 Clement* is dependent upon Hebrews rather than there being a common tradition upon which both draw. Once this proposal is rejected, Rom. 8:34 would seem to be the only evidence for prior tradition concerning Christ as a high priest (cf., however, the arguments of Attridge, *Hebrews* 97–103). The 'confession' mentioned in Hebrews arguably referred to Jesus' sonship rather than to his high priesthood

If the author is largely responsible for the choice and development of this metaphor, then the question of purpose comes to mind. I believe that the author is addressing a real situation which he perceives among his audience. Accordingly, the development of this metaphor – the main point of his exposition (cf. 8:1) – is surely relevant in some way to the perceived needs of the audience.[34] In particular, the author uses the high priestly motif to contrast Christ directly with the entirety of the old covenant, including the Levitical cultus. By choosing this metaphor, the author could argue that Christ had replaced the entire Law with its cultic acts and sanctuary. In ch. 2 we already began to reflect on the kinds of situations that might have driven such a context, not only polemic but also potentially apologetic in nature.

Hebrews 9 and 10 give us both a good sense of how the author of Hebrews understood the cultic sequences of the old covenant to work (or rather, not work), as well as a sense of how the sacrifice of Christ was in fact effective. The numberless sacrifices under the old covenant, for example, were attempts to perfect or cleanse the consciences of the worshippers by way of animal sacrifices like the blood of bulls and goats (e.g. 9:9–10; 10:1, 4). Hebrews considered such sequences unable to take away sin. They might cleanse the flesh (e.g. 9:10), but they were unable to cleanse the consciousness of its sins (e.g. 9:9; 10:2). We might diagram a typical old covenant sacrificial sequence in the following way:

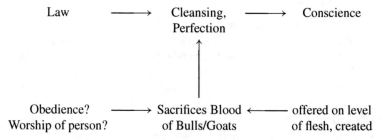

Hebrews seems careful to affirm such sacrifices in so far as their divine intent. They were never meant truly to take away sins. Rather, they were shadowy illustrations of the reality that would be brought about by Christ. The law only had a 'shadow of good things to come', but it did not include 'the image of the things' (10:1). Accordingly, we might also

(4:14; 10:23). Regardless of the position one takes on these issues, however, the author is sufficiently original in his development of the motif and the priestly nuance is sufficiently new to consider the motif a 'live' metaphor in terms of the author's use of it.

[34] Cf. 8:1.

picture the new covenant equivalent of the preceding sequence in the following way:[35]

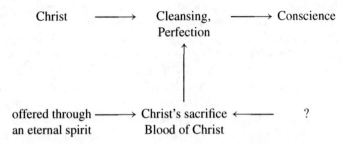

The remainder of this section will explore the dynamics of these sequences in the thought of Hebrews. I want to understand precisely how the author related the work of Christ to the old cultus and covenant so that I can fully understand what the author meant when he spoke of Christ as a high priest of a new covenant. The meaning of the latter was in many respects lockstepped with the former. This study will proceed, therefore, by examining the author's use of νόμος and his utilization of cultic imagery before returning to summarize how high priestly language functions in terms of the new age and its covenant.

νόμος in Hebrews

The first occurrence of the word νόμος in Hebrews comes at 7:5, although it is alluded to as early as 2:2. There, the 'word' spoken through angels is contrasted with the salvation which was first spoken by the Lord. The fact that the author speaks there of παράβασις and παρακοή, as well as μισθαποδοσία, demonstrates that, for the author, the Law functions to identify what sin is and what is to be punished. These functions are in addition to its prescriptions for the Levitical sacrificial system, which foreshadows sin's later 'atonement' through Christ (cf. also 10:28 and 12:18–21). Nevertheless, the principal concern of the author so far as the Law is concerned is its sacrificial system and its priests.

Hebrews 7:11 notes that the people of God were given the law (νενομο-θέτηται) on the basis of the Levitical priesthood (ἐπ' αὐτῆς). There thus exists an intrinsic relationship between the two such that if this priesthood should be changed, the Law must also be changed (7:12). This statement

---

[35] Here is an example of how the same basic event in the story can be diagrammed in more than one way. In many respects, the diagram that follows is another way of understanding the sequence I diagrammed at the beginning of the chapter.

is very significant for apprehending the author's thought, for it indicates that whatever the Law might be for the author, it contains in its essence the Levitical priesthood. Remove the cultus, and the Law ceases to exist. They cannot be materially differentiated.

The author uses this inextricable connection to prepare his audience for his point. The change in priesthood has occurred. The former commandment (of sacrifice), that is, the Law, has been nullified because of its weakness (7:18, 28) and inability to perfect those who depend upon it (7:19). The author can support this claim via Ps. 110:4 and God's appointment of a royal priest after the order of Melchizedek. This order is superior because it is constituted by a priest who does not have an end to his life (7:3), who 'lives' (7:8) by the power of an 'indestructible life' (7:16), always 'living to intercede' for his people (7:25). By contrast, the earthly priests could not offer such an eternal service because they were always hindered by death (7:23). One begins to sense how important Christ's victory over the one having the power of death (2:14) is for the epistle's soteriology. This victory seems the main content to what the author understands by a Melchizedekian priesthood. This priesthood apparently serves as somewhat of a metaphor for more traditional Christian language, allowing the author to contrast Christ directly with the Law and Levitical cultus.

Hebrews 10:9 states in stark terms that Christ in fact 'took away' the sacrifices which were offered according to the Law when he obeyed the will of God by offering his own body (10:8). Therefore, the Law belongs squarely to the old covenant and has been cancelled along with the Levitical cult which stands as its foundation and with which it is virtually interchangeable.[36] Neither of these two need play a role any longer in the life of the people of God. They are truly past, as is seen by the author's concluding exhortation in 13:9–16, where the author denies the efficacy and relevance of the Levitical altar and its sacrifices to the audience, exhorting them to go 'outside the camp' (13:13) to Jesus instead.[37]

[36] I would reverse Lehne's comment and say that Hebrews subsumes the cult under the rubric of Law, but in such a way that the Levitical cult is the very substance and foundation of the Law, and thus that the two become nearly synonymous in the author's argument.

[37] The exact nature of that to which the author is referring here is hotly debated, with answers varying from Jewish dietary laws (most patristic commentators (so Attridge, *Hebrews* 394 n.62)) to participation in pagan cultic meals (Moffatt, *The Epistle to the Hebrews* (Edinburgh: T & T Clark, 1924) 233). Another suggestion is that there is a reference here to Jewish synagogue meals of some sort (cf. J. Thurén, *Das Lobopfer der Hebräer: Studien zum Aufbau und Anliegen von Hebräerbrief 13* (Åbo: Åbo Akademi, 1973) 186ff.), perhaps in relation to a group torn between connections with the synagogue over and against their Christian associations. For a different thesis, see B. Lindars, *The Theology of the Letter to the Hebrews* (Cambridge: Cambridge University Press, 1991) 10f.

The Levitical cultus of the old covenant

The author defends his view of the Law in more detail in the argumentation of Heb. 9 and 10, which follow directly upon the Jeremiah citation and the author's claim in 8:13 that the old is obsolete and about to vanish. Here the author is contrasting the first covenant (i.e. the Law and its cultic prescriptions) with the new one in terms of the wilderness tabernacle and Old Testament sacrificial rituals. In this, 9:1–10 (9:1 – μέν) contrasts the Old Testament tabernacle and its sacrifices in general with that which Christ has effected in 9:11–15 (9:11 – δέ).[38] We need not be too concerned with the problems of the author's placement of objects in the tabernacle at this time.[39] What is significant for the eschatology of Hebrews is the author's unique division of the tabernacle into two different tents.

At first, the author sets out the basic scheme of service in the two parts of the tabernacle, providing the basis for his argumentation (9:6, 7). The priests are said to go into the first tent *throughout the year* (διὰ παντὸς εἰσίασιν), while *only* the high priest entered the holy of holies *once* (ἅπαξ) in the year to offer blood for the unintentional sins of the people.[40] The author then concludes that the Holy Spirit is demonstrating by this scheme that 'the way of the holy of holies has not yet been manifested while the first tent still has standing' (9:8). In its immediate context, it is not exactly clear in what way 9:8 follows upon the preceding contrast. In what way does the contrast between frequency of entrance and one time entrance relate to the idea that the way into the holy of the holies has not yet appeared? In addition, how does the existence of the 'first tent' impede such entrance? For that matter, to what does the author refer by the 'first tent'?

The most natural way of taking the phrase 'first tent' here reads it in continuity with the preceding context, which is clearly the distinction between the first and second parts of the wilderness tabernacle. B. F. Westcott long ago noted that it would be difficult to suppose that the author had suddenly changed the referent of 'first tent' from its meaning

---

[38] So J. Thompson, *The Beginnings of Christian Philosophy: The Epistle to the Hebrews* (CBQMS 13; Washington, DC: Catholic Biblical Association of America, 1981) 105; and N. H. Young, 'The Gospel According to Hebrews 9', *NTS* 27 (1981) 206; *pace* G. W. Buchanan, *To the Hebrews* (Garden City, NY: Doubleday, 1972) 139f., who argues that the intervening distance and the inclusion of another μέν . . . δέ construction (9:6–7) preclude such an interpretation. A semantic consideration of the units, however, demonstrates that they do in fact form contrasting units.

[39] For an interesting speculation as to the rise of traditions of interpretation which might stand behind the arrangement of the objects, see Attridge, *Hebrews* 236–8.

[40] For a discussion of whether Hebrews envisages two types of sins, see H. Löhr, *Umkehr und Sünde im Hebräerbrief* (BZNW 73; Berlin: de Gruyter, 1994) 22ff.

in the immediately preceding verse.[41] In addition, this provides some explanation of how the first tent could be figuratively considered a barrier to the holy of holies: because it is – you have to go through it to get to the holy of holies. There is also a prohibition on who can enter this inner sanctum, since *only* the high priest is allowed to enter it (9:7). We can thus hear in this imagery echoes of other imagery in Hebrews: the idea that the high priest of the new covenant is a 'leader' (12:2) and 'brother' to the other 'priests' (2:11 – cf. 13:15); the idea that Christ provides present access to the holy of holies (10:19); and so forth. Therefore, a contrast of exclusion/inclusion seems implicit in 9:8. The way into the holy of holies has not yet been made apparent while the first tent exists.

Lincoln Hurst, however, has argued that the 'first tent' here is a reference to the whole tabernacle. He does so on the basis of supposed ambiguities in (1) the use of πρῶτος in Heb. 9 and (2) the phrase 'present time' in 9:9.[42] These arguments do not seem substantial. For one thing, the author is not really as ambiguous as Hurst claims in his use of πρῶτος in Heb. 9. Hebrews 9:1 clearly refers primarily to the first *covenant*, given that τὴν πρώτη in 8:13 is obviously modifying an understood διαθήκη.[43] Hebrews 9:2 makes a clear shift to the tents of the tabernacle, which we have already noted occurs in the verse immediately preceding 9:8. Unless there are strong reasons to the contrary, it seems most logical to presume that this continues to be the case until 9:15, where the author specifies that he is once again using the term in relation to the first *covenant*.

If the train of thought is complex when the 'first tent' is taken to refer to the outer part of the tabernacle, it becomes even more difficult in Hurst's reading. In what way does the preceding explanation of ministry in the earthly tabernacle demonstrate that the way into the holy of holies will not appear until the whole tabernacle is gone? In my explanation this analogy makes good sense. The author consistently makes a distinction between the 'once for all' sacrifice of Christ and the multiplicity of sacrifices of the old covenant (e.g. 9:25; 10:1, 10, 11–12, 14), so the two parts of

---

[41] *Hebrews* 252.

[42] *Background* 26–7, following in general J. Moffatt, *Hebrews* 117–18; A. Cody, *Heavenly Sanctuary and Liturgy in the Epistle to the Hebrews: The Achievement of Salvation in the Epistle's Perspectives* (Meinrad, IN: Grail, 1960) 147–8; Bruce, *Hebrews* 194–5; and Héring, *Hebrews* 183. Hurst's argument at this point is similar to Héring, who notes the facility with which the author 'manipulates expressions with various senses' (*Hebrews* 74).

[43] While it is conceivable that ἡ πρώτη in 9:1 could in some allegorical sense have a dual reference to both σκηνή and διαθήκη, such a suggestion seems a bit speculative. It is puzzling how Hurst (and Buchanan, *Hebrews* 139f.) could miss this fact in the light not only of the antecedent, but also of the fact that if ἡ πρώτη referred to the first tent, then the first tent comes to have an 'earthly sanctuary' (9:1), which would be a rather nonsensical statement.

the tabernacle as the author has explained them in 9:6–7 provide a ready-made analogy for the difference between Christ and the old covenant. My reading in fact provides an explanation of the peculiar language of a first and second tent in the first place, language which becomes irrelevant in Hurst's construal. These factors begin to explain how 9:6–7 might relate to 9:8 in the author's mind.

In any case, the author's main point appears in 9:9, where the division of the tabernacle into a first and second tent is made into a temporal contrast which corresponds to the author's eschatology as expressed by the two covenants. The situation of multiplicity and singularity which corresponds to the first and second tent of the tabernacle is in fact an eschatological parable of the two epochs of salvation history, the first of which had continuously offered sacrifices in contrast to Christ's single offering, as we have seen. The grammar confirms this reading as 9:9 begins with the indefinite relative pronoun ἥτις, which most likely refers to the first tent of the tabernacle in 9:8.[44] Hurst's conjecture that the 'present age' might refer to the time of Moses is not only unlikely on lexical grounds, it misses the entire point the author is making.[45] The author is not speaking about the wilderness tabernacle out of some obscure historical interest, nor is it merely a gloss for the Jerusalem temple. It is representative of an age and of a covenant. The author has never lost sight of the first covenant from 9:1, and he bounds this very section with an inclusio formed between δικαιώματα in 9:1 and 9:10. This repetition of δικαιώματα in particular serves in 9:10 to demonstrate that the present age of fleshly ordinances is in fact the time of the old covenant, which now more than ever is 'about to vanish'. The 'present time' is thus the time of the 'last days' in regard to the old covenant, which is on the verge of its 'reformation' (9:10). Hurst's suggestion must yield to the pervasive eschatology of the epistle.

In this parable of 9:9, therefore, in which the first tent represents the epoch of the old covenant, there are gifts and sacrifices being offered which are not actually able to perfect the worshipper, for they are only

---

[44] Although scholars such as H. Windisch, *Der Hebräerbrief*, 2nd edn (HNT 14; Tübingen: Mohr, 1931) 77, Michel, *Hebräer* 307, and Bruce, *Hebrews* 195ff., have claimed that it refers to the whole tabernacle. Young, 'Gospel' 201, has argued instead that such an interpretation would run counter to Hebrews' use of ἥτις elsewhere in the epistle, 'for the writer consistently refers back to a specific antecedent and the gender and number are modified accordingly'. He then mentions 2:3; 8:6; 9:2; 10:9[= 10:8], 11, 35; and 12:5.

[45] Attridge, *Hebrews* 241 n.133, has noted that 'the expression is common for "the present"' in the contemporary literature, noting Polybius *Hist.* 1.60.9; Philo *Sacr.* 47; *Migr.* 43; Josephus *Ant.* 16.6.2, 162; and Sextus Empiricus *Pyrrh. Hyp.* 3.17.144, a fact noted of ἐνεστώς as early as Westcott (*Hebrews* 252).

ordinances orientated toward the flesh (9:9–10).⁴⁶ They have only been
imposed μέχρι καιροῦ διορθώσεως (9:10), which is the point at which the
outer tent and its limitations on further entrance will cease to exist (9:8).
At that point the people of God will be able to enter freely into the holy of
holies.⁴⁷ This parable corresponds exactly to what the author has already
said in general about the Levitical cult in Heb. 7. The Law simply was
not capable of perfecting anything. Instead, God has introduced a 'better
hope' of reaching God (7:19).

Hebrews 9:11–15 states exactly what that better hope is. Christ himself
has now arrived as a high priest of good things γενομένων (9:11). If this
is the original reading of the verse, then the author points out clearly that
the time of reformation about which he has been speaking is now here,
a claim which we have already seen to be consistent with the author's
thought in general.⁴⁸ The good promises which the Jeremiah quotation
has brought to light are now available, and there is no longer any need
to rely upon the fleshly ordinances of the first covenant. Christ has not
entered into the inner sanctum of the earthly sanctuary, nor has he used the
blood of bulls and goats, but he has entered by means of his own blood into
the true holy of holies (9:11–12). Almost every one of these expressions
has an interpretive problem of some sort which we will eventually need
to address, but for the moment it will suffice to note the eschatological
significance of 9:13–14:

> For if the blood of he-goats and bulls and the sprinkled ashes of
> a heifer on those who have become unclean sanctifies to cleanse
> the flesh, how much more will the blood of Christ, who offered
> himself blameless to God through the eternal spirit, cleanse our
> conscience from dead works in order to serve the living God.

The author has once again contrasted the multiplicity of the old
covenant with the singularity of Christ. He has done so by combining
cultic rituals from the Old Testament.⁴⁹ So, in addition to the goats and
young bulls (τράγων καὶ μόσχων) of the Day of Atonement (Lev. 16:3)

---

⁴⁶ Now taking καθ' ἥν to refer to παραβολή which is the immediate antecedent. Young,
'Gospel' 201, sees καθ' ἥν as also referring to the first tent, which is certainly the basis
for the parable, but this parable (9:9–10) applies to the whole sacrificial service of the old
covenant, not just that performed in the outer tent.
⁴⁷ As the author explicitly states, this is a parable, but cosmological overtones may also
be present, a possibility which we will consider in ch. 5. See also the discussion in ch. 6 of
the idiom ἐχούσης στάσιν.
⁴⁸ The other reading, μελλόντων, also has some significant manuscript support (e.g. ℵ), but
the reading γενομένων seems to fit in even better with the author's eschatological scheme.
⁴⁹ So especially Young, 'Gospel' 205.

which the author mentions in 9:12,[50] he adds the ashes of a heifer from regulations for ritual purification (Num. 19), as well as the more generic 'bulls' (ταύρων).[51] This is similar to what the author will do more strikingly with the inauguration ritual in 9:19. The point the author is making yet again is that the whole of the old covenant cultic ritual is now past in the light of Christ. The Levitical cult contributed only to the cleansing of the *flesh*, while Christ's work is *spiritual* and cleanses the *conscience*. Christ is thus the mediator of a better covenant, because his death has brought about an eternal redemption from the transgressions committed under the first covenant, which leads to the reception of the promise of an eternal inheritance (9:15). The author thus returns to his original covenant theme and completes the contrast begun in 9:1.

Hebrews 9:15 provides a good transition to the next phase of the author's argument, which concerns the inauguration of the two different covenants.[52] It concludes with reference to the 'eternal inheritance' which belongs to those who are called. Verses 16 and 17 then play on this idea by shifting the meaning of the language momentarily to the idea of a 'will' or 'testament' (διαθήκη): 'for with a will, it is necessary to bring the death of the testator, for a will is secure on the basis of the dead, since it is never in effect when the testator lives'. John Hughes has argued temptingly that διαθήκη cannot mean 'will' here, claiming that such an interpretation does not fit syntactically, semantically, or in the light of the historical background.[53] Indeed the sentence is odd in many ways, introducing a new sense to διαθήκη without significant warning,

---

[50] The word for goat in Lev. 16:15 of the LXX is χίμαρος, although Attridge, *Hebrews* 248, and Michel, *Hebräer* 312, note that Aquila and Symmachus use τράγος. This would not be the only place where the author agrees with the LXX revisions, for the term θυμιατήριον is also used by Symmachus and Theodotion in their translation of Exod. 30:1 (Attridge, *Hebrews* 234).

[51] This term is never used in the LXX of the Pentateuch in a sacrificial context, although it does appear in such a connection significantly in Ps. 50:13 (49:13 LXX) (The author alludes to Ps. 50:14 in 13:15 and perhaps also to 50:5 in 9:17, as J. J. Hughes has posited in 'Hebrews IX 15ff. and Galatians III 15ff.: A Study in Covenant Practice and Procedure' *NovT* 21 (1979) 44), and Isa. 1:11, both of which stand in the Old Testament 'anti-cultus' tradition!

[52] It has been noted by Young, 'Gospel' 205, and Hurst, 'Eschatology and "Platonism" in the Epistle to the Hebrews', *SBLSP* (1984) 65–6, that these verses treat the inauguration of the earthly and heavenly tents. Although I accept this notion, I also feel the force of the term καθαρίζω in 9:23 (so Attridge, *Hebrews* 261). In ch. 6 I will consider and modify Attridge's suggestion that the heavenly cleansing has more to do with 'human interiority' and the cleansing of the human conscience than with a more literal interpretation (262).

[53] 'Hebrews and Galatians'. He is followed by Lane, *Hebrews 9–13* 230–2, and Lehne, *New Covenant* 124 n.5.

as well as in its use of φέρεσθαι and the plural νεκροῖς.[54] Hughes has also pointed out that wills in the Hellenistic world were not only valid while the testator lived, but also were quite often put into effect before his or her death.[55] Instead, he argues that Heb. 9:16–17 finds its proper sense against the background of ancient Near Eastern practice, where the death of the victim represented the death of the one making the covenant, and one invoked a curse upon oneself if the agreement was not kept.[56] He posits an allusion to Ps. 50:5 (49:5 LXX), which speaks of the righteous making a covenant with God on the basis of sacrifices (ἐπὶ θυσίαις).[57]

Hughes' argument is tempting, but it runs into difficulty with Hebrews' claim that it is necessary for the one making the covenant to die in order for it to be βεβαία.[58] In order for Hughes' sense to prevail, one must suppose that these words are meant in a rather extended sense. Moreover, the kind of covenant about which Hebrews speaks, one which only God can make (8:9), would require God's death.[59] When we consider how a first-century Greek speaker would likely have heard these words, it seems virtually certain that such individuals would have heard διαθήκη as 'will' and not in terms of ancient Near Eastern practice. Even Hughes admits that 'the author is using Hellenistic legal terminology to describe Semitic covenant practice', so Hughes recognizes that the sentence contains legal terms and has an undeniably Hellenistic 'feel' to it.[60] In addition, Hebrews has just spoken of 'inheritance' in the previous verse, which inevitably would lead in the direction of 'will' rather than toward ancient covenant practice. Finally, the concern of the author is clearly forgiveness

---

[54] Bruce's claim that φέρω is a technical term for registration, which he backs up by a reference to *P.Oxy.* ii (London: 1899) 244, is somewhat dubious (*Hebrews* 207 n.101). The usual words for registration are compounds of γράφω (ἀπογράφω or ἀναγράφω), and papyrus 244 is about a *transfer* of cattle (which would need to be 'brought'), not to mention the fact that the text breaks off soon after φέρεσθαι, leaving its sense somewhat ambiguous. The author may thus only be speaking of the bringing of cattle from one place to another. Finally, the reading φέρεσθαι itself is conjectured, since two of its letters are missing and the others are all uncertain.

[55] 'Hebrews and Galatians' 44 and 60f.   [56] Ibid. 45f.   [57] Ibid. 44.

[58] So also Attridge, *Hebrews* 256: 'Covenants or contracts, of whatever sort, simply do not require the death of one of the parties.' It is possible also that by βεβαία the author does not so much envisage the validity of the will, for the usual word in the papyri here is κυρία (so *passim P.Oxy.* iii (London, 1903) 489, 490, 491, 492, 493, etc.). What the author may mean is that the will is not unchangeable and *fixed* until the testator is dead.

[59] This is all the more significant in light of the limited use of covenant terminology in Hebrews, using it only to refer to the old and new covenants. Although I agree with Lehne (*New Covenant* 17) that the patriarchal 'covenants' are present in Hebrews, *pace* E. Grässer, *Der Alte Bund im Neuen* (WUNT 35; Tübingen: Mohr/Siebeck, 1985) 96, it is significant that the author uses the word *promise* when he refers to them. The word *covenant* is thus restricted elsewhere in the epistle to God's salvific provisions for humanity.

[60] 'Hebrews and Galatians' 63.

(ἄφεσις – 9:22) and cleansing rather than covenant agreement, so Hughes' way of taking the verses also involves a shift in sense from the main argument. For these reasons, we should reject his reading.

In the end, however, the notion of a will here is only superficial. The author really has the two covenants in mind, and he has only shifted the sense slightly because it relates to language of inheritance and the argument he is about to make about the inauguration of the new covenant. The language of 9:16–17 is thus shaped by the covenant idea, and it is not unlikely that the author had Ps. 50:5 in mind as he wrote. This fact might explain some of the peculiarities in wording. The death which brought inheritance (9:15) was like a will. With a will, death brings to fruition the promise of inheritance. In a sense, it 'inaugurates' the promises of its testator. So it is with the death of Christ, which not only brought about redemption for sins committed under the old covenant, but also enacted the promises of the new.

The author shifts back to the initial sense of the word in 9:18–28. This unit also consists of two contrasting parts: 9:18–22 presents the inaugural purification of the old covenant, while 9:23–8 discusses the 'cleansing' of τὰ ἐπουράνια. N. H. Young notes how the author again amalgamates and alters the Sinai covenant of Exod. 24 in 9:19–21:

> To the Sinai limitation to blood (Exod. 24.6ff.), he introduces from the red heifer ceremony (Num. 19) the elements water, scarlet, wool and hyssop. In Exod. 24.6ff. the blood is cast against the altar and over the people, in Hebrews the book of the covenant replaces the altar. The writer also includes a sprinkling of blood upon the tent and cultic vessels by adding details from the consecration service of Lev. 8.[61]

As we have already observed, this amalgamation serves to contrast the old covenant as a whole in all its multiplicity with the singular sacrifice of Christ. It is also significant that the author replaces the altar by the book of the covenant, for it confirms once again that the Law and cult in Hebrews are intrinsically bound together and that the people were given the Law on the basis of the Levitical cult (7:11).

This inauguration is contrasted in turn with the cleansing of the 'heavenly things'. We will have to wait until chs. 5 and 6 to discuss many of the interpretive questions involved with 9:23 and the verses that follow it. Such issues include the question of why τὰ ἐπουράνια needed to be

---

[61] 'Gospel' 205.

cleansed at all and whether we should understand ὑποδείγματα Platonically in 9:23. What is significant for the eschatology of the epistle is the same argument which has already been seen in so many different respects. The new covenant offering is intrinsically superior to the old covenant cleansings because it is made in heaven itself (εἰς αὐτὸν τὸν οὐρανὸν – 9:24) and because it only needs to take place once (ἅπαξ – 9:26). The fact that the inaugurations of the two covenants are contrasted in these verses confirms once more that the whole of the old covenant is inferior to the one which Christ has effected because they contrast in this way from their very foundations.

Therefore, the Law and sacrificial system in Hebrews include elements that are a σκιά of coming good things, but those elements are not an exact εἰκών of those things (10:1). The Levitical priests serve the heavenlies ὑποδείγματι καὶ σκια rather than as its actual ministers (8:5). An understanding of the precise nuance of these terms will be illuminating for the author's combination of spatial and temporal motifs in general. But whether these terms have Platonic/Philonic overtones or not, it is at least clear that the Law only 'foreshadows' its corresponding 'antitypes' (9:24) in the new covenant as an inferior counterpart.[62] Once the real substance has come, there remains no more need for the Law and its sacrificial system.

By contrast, Christ is a minister of the 'true' tent in the heavens (8:1–2) and is now the mediator of a new covenant, which has been put into effect (νενομοθέτηται) on the basis of better promises (8:6). The word νομοθετέομαι, which occurs in the New Testament only in Hebrews, corresponds here precisely to its use in 7:11. There the word speaks of the establishment of the Law on the basis of the Levitical priesthood. In 8:6, it speaks of the establishment of a new covenant on the basis of 'better promises' and a new 'sacrificial system', namely, the 'sacrifice' of Christ. In a sense, the new covenant is put into effect as the 'law' of the new order, with Christ as the sole sacrifice.[63]

---

[62] So, for example, R. Williamson, *Philo and the Epistle to the Hebrews* (ALGHJ 4; Leiden: E. J.Brill, 1970) 95.

[63] Lehne, *New Covenant* 27, holds that there is no law in the new covenant, yet there are certainly aspects of the new covenant which correspond to it, for the Law is a shadow of those things. It is also significant that the author mentions and emphasizes that part of the Jeremiah citation where it is said that God will put his *laws* into the minds and hearts of his people (8:10; 10:16). There also remains the possibility of willfully, and thus accidentally, sinning in the new covenant (cf. 10:26). These factors may imply that the author, as Paul, did not mean to nullify certain aspects of the Law considered essential in the true worship of God.

The Christ sequence of the plot

The beginning of the chapter suggested that the key sequence of the story behind Hebrews should look something like the following:

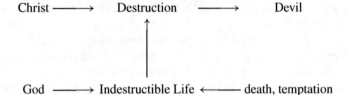

Christ ⟶ Destruction ⟶ Devil

God ⟶ Indestructible Life ⟵ death, temptation

However, as salvation history actually unfolded, the death blow to the Devil became separated in time from humanity's ultimate achievement of glory. What might have been a single event turned out to be at least two: (1) the Christ event in which Christ died and, as high priest, passed through the heavens and entered into a heavenly holy of holies and (2) a final event in which Christ returns a second time, bringing salvation (9:28) from God's judgement when he shakes the created realm (12:26–7).

The term 'Christ event' is thus somewhat ambiguous, and I will use it as a singular reference to what is potentially more than one 'moment' in salvation history. The defining characteristic of this 'event' is the effective defeat of the Devil's power over death. It may of course turn out that these moments are in fact differing metaphorical perspectives on the same basic moment in the story, namely a moment when atonement is accomplished. I diagrammed the basic sequence of Christ's atonement earlier in the chapter as follows:

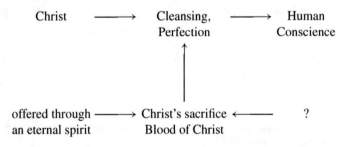

Christ ⟶ Cleansing, ⟶ Human
                    Perfection   Conscience

offered through ⟶ Christ's sacrifice ⟵ ?
an eternal spirit   Blood of Christ

I have already circled this sequence from a number of different directions – and I am not yet finished. I have suggested that the reason we find so many different perspectives results not least from the fact that Hebrews itself views the Christ event from several different metaphorical angles. The death of Christ is an atoning sacrifice (10:14), the enactment of a new covenant and a new law (8:6). It is related to Christ's appointment as a priest after the order of Melchizedek (5:10), not to mention his enthronement as cosmic king (1:5). It relates to his passage through the heavens (4:14) and by way of the greater and more perfect tent (9:11). It is the inauguration of that heavenly tent (9:23), the opening of his flesh as a veil through which we can pass (10:20), and indeed it constitutes the bulk of his ministry in that tent (8:1–2).

We will return to many of these perspectives on the Christ event in ch. 6. For the moment, I limit myself to the image of Christ as a priest after the order of Melchizedek. How does this perspective function in the overall metaphor of Christ's high priesthood? I suggested in ch. 2 that the author pitted Christ against the entirety of the old covenant cultus by suggesting that Jesus had offered (1) a superior sacrifice, (2) as a superior priest, (3) in a superior sanctuary. Chapter 5 will address some of the basis for considering Christ's sacrifice superior to those of the old covenant. Further, ch. 6 will explore the matter of how the heavenly sanctuary functions in the rhetoric of Hebrews. It remains here to mention briefly how the author presents Christ as a superior type of priest.

The author conveniently found in Ps. 110:4 an Old Testament text which provided a biblical basis for a Messianic high priest. Since this psalm was already in use in Christian circles as a Messianic text, the author had a ready-made proof text from which to launch his metaphorical venture. In a situation in which the author felt that his audience needed to be shown the obsolescence of the Levitical cultus, this psalm could have easily inspired the particular form which the author's argument took. Here was a connection between kingship and priesthood. Christ's death was already considered a sacrifice by early Christianity (cf. Rom. 3:25 and Heb. 2:17), so all that remained was for someone to extend the metaphor just that much further. He could easily read the psalm in terms of two appointments: v. 1 in terms of a call to enthroned, royal Sonship (1:5, 13; 5:5) and v. 4 as an appointment to a Melchizedekian high priesthood (5:6).

But what is the 'order of Melchizedek' to which the Messiah will belong? To answer this question, the author understandably turned to the only other text in the Jewish Scriptures that mentions Melchizedek: Gen. 14. On the basis of this text, the author cleverly argued for the superiority of the Melchizedekian order to that of the Levitical priesthood, drawing on the encounter in Genesis between Abraham and Melchizedek. Since Melchizedek blessed Abraham and since Abraham offered tithes to Melchizedek, the author could easily argue that Melchizedek was the superior. And since Levi was, in a sense, in the 'loins' of Abraham, the author could conclude further that a Melchizedekian priesthood is superior to a Levitical one. We can thus far explain the author's rhetoric about Melchizedek without recourse to any extra-biblical material such as we find at Qumran or in Gnostic sources.[64] Thus far we can explain the author's argument simply on the basis of biblical exegesis. Yet we have not yet explained 7:3, wherein we find the basis for what the author understands a Melchizedekian priest to be.

I begin my interpretation of this verse with the observation that the author not only interprets the name of Melchizedek, but even that *of the city* in which Melchizedek is king. He is using allegorical exegesis at these points to address the question raised by Ps. 110:4: What is a priest after the order of Melchizedek? Accordingly, he turns to Gen. 14 with this question in mind. It is crucial to recognize that the author is asking questions of the *text* of Gen. 14 far more than he is thinking of the literal Melchizedek who was king of a particular place.[65] He is using ancient exegetical methods to interpret the deeper meaning of a biblical text.

There are several clues in Heb. 7 which support this general observation. For example, 7:8 notes that while 'here' the Levitical priests die, 'there *it is witnessed* that he lives'. Where is this witness made? Since the author must be referring to an Old Testament text, the only real candidate must be Ps. 110:4, where it is stated that Christ is a high priest *forever*.[66] This everlasting dimension of the psalm text is the point which the author repeatedly brings out in the chapter. Christ, as a Melchizedekian priest, has succeeded in his service because he serves 'according to the power of an indestructible life' (7:16). While the Levitical priests are hindered by death, Christ has a permanent priesthood (7:24), since he always lives to intercede (7:25). Clearly it is the enduring aspect of Melchizedek's priesthood as derived from Ps. 110:4 which is the author's focus in argumentation.

Gareth Cockerill has in fact noted that every part of Ps. 110:4 plays a role in the argumentation of ch. 7.[67] Hebrews 7:11–14, he claims, relates

---

[64] E.g. A. S. van der Woude, 'Melchisedek als himmlische Erlösergestalt in den neugefundenen eschatologischen Midraschim aus Qumran Höhle IX', *OTS* 14 (1965) 354–73. For an overview of suggestions, see F. L. Horton, *The Melchizedek Tradition: A Critical Examination of the Sources to the Fifth Century A.D. and in the Epistle to the Hebrews* (SNTSMS 30; Cambridge: Cambridge University Press, 1976).

[65] Of course the author was easily able to utilize both levels of meaning. He easily shifts from allegorical interpretation in 7:3 to a more literal comment in 7:4, only to return to his more typological use of Abraham and Melchizedek in 7:5–10.

[66] Note the same use of μαρτυρέω in 7:17 of this psalm text! Λέγω is similarly used in 7:21.

[67] *The Melchizedek Christology in Heb. 7:1–28* (Ann Arbor: University Microfilms International, 1979) 18.

to the phrase κατὰ τὴν τάξιν Μελχισέδεκ, 7:15–19 to εἰς τὸν αἰῶνα, 7:20–2 to ὥμοσεν κύριος, καὶ οὐ μεταμεληθέσεται, and 7:23–5 to εἰς τὴν αἰῶνα once again. While some of these connections seem a bit forced, Cockerill has clearly shown that most of the themes treated in these verses arise from an interpretation of Ps. 110:4 and not from extraneous traditions. Indeed, we can adequately explain Heb. 7:3 on the basis of the interpretive rule, *quod non in thora, non in mundo*.[68] This rabbinic and Philonic hermeneutical principal holds that if the biblical text does not explicitly state something, then it can be considered not to exist for the sake of an argument. Since there is no father or mother, birth or death recorded of Melchizedek in the Genesis text, then for the sake of argument we can say he is *without* father or mother and *without* beginning of days or end of life.

Why does the author note these omissions in particular? He argues for these characteristics because he finds them most illustrative of what he wants to argue about Christ, namely, his eternality (cf. 1:3), non-priestly genealogy (7:6), and especially the fact that he has no 'end of life'. The author is thus moving backwards from Christ to Melchizedek rather than vice versa.[69] The author is not really interested in Melchizedek for Melchizedek's sake. Indeed, *the literal Melchizedek would not have qualified as a priest after the order of Melchizedek*. The author's concern is the basis which texts about Melchizedek provide for arguing that Christ is a 'priest' superior to those priests descended from Levi.

From a mainstream Jewish perspective, Heb. 7 is a startling piece of rhetoric.[70] In this chapter, the author argues that Christ is not only a superior priest to any Levitical priest, but he argues that the arrival of a priest after the order of Melchizedek signals a complete change in priesthood and, in turn, of law (cf. 7:12, 18–19). The author thus uses the idea of Christ as a priest after the order of Melchizedek to declare the end of the Levitical cultus *en masse* along with the Levitical priesthood. With the superior priestly identity of Christ established, the author will go on in Heb. 8–10 to show how the sacrifice and sanctuary of Christ were also superior to those of the Levitical cultus.

We have seen how heavily the author draws on non-literal interpretation in his use of Melchizedek traditions in the Jewish Scriptures.

[68] As Thompson notes (*Beginnings* 118f.), referencing Str-B 3.694–5, and Philo's, *Det.* 48 and *Ebr.* 14.

[69] Cf. also Cockerill, *Melchizedek Christology* 187.

[70] I have already suggested in ch. 2 that such rhetoric may make better sense in the period after the temple was destroyed rather than while it was still standing. As such this rhetoric becomes more of a consolation than a polemic.

This observation makes me wonder how literally he meant us to take Christ's Melchizedekian priesthood itself. In a very general way, 5:10 seems to equate Christ's designation as 'priest according to the order of Melchizedek' with the point when he has become a 'cause of eternal salvation' (5:9). In that context, this point is after he has been 'perfected', and is thus post-death. But the imagery can fold in on itself somewhat. In the metaphor of Christ as *high* priest, Christ must be priest to offer himself as sacrifice (e.g. 9:14), which likely included his death.[71] Any such tensions in the timing of Christ's priesthood are likely due to the fact that the author is jumping into metaphors of priesthood from more than one point in the story.[72] The metaphor of Christ's Melchizedekian priesthood is one of priesthood in general and can be correlated directly to the moment Christ is enthroned as royal Son. By contrast, the *high* priestly metaphor is built off imagery from the Day of Atonement and thus interacts both with Christ's death and, arguably, his ascension to heaven.

The penultimate sequence of the plot

The final sequence of the plot is when humanity finally attains the glory initially intended for it. I mentioned at the beginning of the preceding section that Hebrews argues for two events in the lead-up to that final sequence. The most crucial is of course the need for Christ to defeat the Devil's power over death by way of his atonement. But for reasons not fully explained, the end does not immediately ensue upon that event. Hebrews looks for a penultimate sequence of judgement that eliminates the final vestiges of the 'problem' standing between humanity and glory, thus enabling the final attainment of glory sequence. Since the two chapters which follow deal fairly extensively with matters of Hebrews' cosmology, I wish only to present the eschatological dimension of this final event here.

We might diagram the penultimate sequence of Hebrews' plot in the following way:

---

[71] F. Laub accordingly argues against too narrow an equation of Christ's priesthood with his exaltation (*Bekenntnis und Auslegung: Die paränetische Funktion der Christologie im Hebräerbrief* (BU 15; Regensburg: Pustet, 1980) 121 n.222).

[72] Attridge suggests that tensions in the timing of Christ's priesthood in Hebrews are due to the author reinterpreting prior *traditions* relating to Christ's priesthood in the light of the Yom Kippur ritual (*Hebrews* 146). While it is possible that such traditions existed (cf. Rom. 8:34), it is also possible to account for the tensions from the use of varying metaphors.

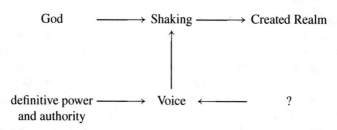

The key passage for this sequence is clearly 12:25–9. This passage is fascinating on a number of accounts. For one, the author seems to connect the need for the heaven and earth to be shaken in some way with the fact that they are πεποιημένοι (12:27). Indeed, unlike Paul, Hebrews gives us no sense of an event after creation that enslaved the creation to futility (cf. Rom. 8:20). The 'feel' of Hebrews is that the creation, by virtue of its very createdness, is in some way a hindrance to the glory intended for humanity. In a comment perhaps more revealing of the author's subconscious than his conscious theology, he suggests that if Christ's sacrifice was needed repeatedly, then he would have had to suffer ἀπὸ καταβολῆς κόσμου (9:26). The image is of one in which the world was in need of atonement from the moment of its inception.

It is best not to draw these conclusions with any certainty at this point. It remains to be seen that the author really would have agreed with these comments. What seems more certain is that these images give us a feel for the author's metaphysics and conception of the world. Paul apparently saw the world, like human flesh, as a slave to the power of sin. In contrast, Hebrews seems to operate – at least on a subconscious level – with a sense that the created realm is also something from which humanity needs to be saved in order to achieve the intended glory.

Conclusion

In this chapter we explored some of the key sequences in the plot of salvation, namely, the sequences in between the beginning and end of the story. We began by considering how the author divides salvation history into two broad epochs: the former days and 'these last days'. The latter phrase was seen to relate to the Jeremiah citation of Heb. 8. This connection demonstrated that the recent speaking through Christ of Heb. 1:2 signified the inauguration of the new covenant and the eschatological age.

We then examined how the new covenant/two age distinction might relate to the contrast of Christ with the angels in Heb. 1. I argued that the author included this contrast because (1) Christ is below the angels 'for a little while' in Ps. 8 and (2) the angels functioned as mediators of the Law, and thus the old covenant. This latter fact in particular shows that the contrast of Heb. 1 is eschatological in nature. The exalted Christ is in view throughout as the one now higher than the angels, since he has now been crowned with glory and honour. We thus see a connection between the catena in Heb. 1 and the new covenant contrast. Hebrews 1:5– 2:18 is a rhetorically effective introduction in more traditional language than the author uses in the following chapters. In those later chapters the author is devolving new metaphors to demonstrate that Christ's atonement eliminates any need for reliance on the cultus of the old covenant.

Following the discussion of the angels, I began to address the author's main use of covenant language, namely, to contrast the high priestly work of Christ with that of Levitical priests. I discussed the author's use of νόμος and the way he understands the Levitical cultus in the light of Christ. The cultic sequences of the old covenant relate to Christ in the relationship of shadow to reality. The author used the Law, Levitical cultus, and old covenant as roughly interchangeable concepts all of which are now obsolete in the light of Christ's singular offering.

The rest of the chapter addressed with broad strokes the two most crucial events of the new age: the 'Christ event' and the ultimate shaking of the created realm. We will explore some of the most important features of these events in the next two chapters. In this chapter, I focused my discussion of the Christ event on the way the author uses Melchizedek in his argument. The author can pit Christ against the entirety of the Levitical cultus by arguing that he was (1) a definitive and superior priest, (2) offering a definitive and superior sacrifice, (3) in a definitive and superior sanctuary. Psalm 110:4 opened the door for the author to consider Christ a 'priest after the order of Melchizedek', an office he explicated with an allegorical interpretation of Gen. 14. Thereby he argues that a definitive change of Law and priesthood has taken place, thus establishing that Christ is a definitive and superior priest vis-à-vis the Levitical cultus. My brief discussion of the shaking of the created realm awaits a more complete analysis in the chapter which follows. This penultimate event of the story apparently reveals the created realm as the last obstacle to humanity's glory in some way.

We can thus divide the plot of salvation into two broad ages corresponding to the two covenants. These two epochs overlap, for the old covenant is only near to its disappearance. In addition, while the new covenant is decisively here, it has not fully arrived. The sacrifice of Christ is the decisive 'curtain opening' of the second act of the drama, for the author emphasizes the completed aspect of Christ's work. Christ's accomplishment is in fact the basis for the author's exhortations. The second act must therefore be seen in two stages, beginning with the 'today' of the story, a time in which the full impact of Christ's work has not reached its completion. The final scene will come when Christ has 'appeared a second time' (9:28).

The Settings of the Story in Space

5

THE SPATIAL DUALISM OF HEBREWS

Introduction

In Hebrews, the central event of salvation's plot pertains to two realms. On the one hand, it involves the death of Jesus Christ, who suffered *physically* 'outside the gate' of the *earthly* Jerusalem (13:12). This event is arguably part of that to which the author refers when he speaks of the offering of Christ. However, in the rhetoric of Hebrews, the offering of the sacrifice also involves Christ's entrance into the holy of holies in *heaven*, an event which I believe corresponds in part to Christ's exaltation to the right hand of God. This death/exaltation sequence constitutes the central event of salvation history.[1]

Further, Christ's high priesthood is a heavenly office, at least in terms of the author's main rhetorical purpose. Hebrews 8:4 leads us to this conclusion when it says that Christ could not have served as a priest upon the earth. We have already seen in ch. 2 that the author uses the metaphor of the high priesthood of Christ in order to contrast Christ directly with the Law and the Levitical order as a whole. This contrast, however, is not simply eschatological; it is cosmological as well. The author is able to undermine the primacy of the old order by positing the invisible, heavenly realm over and against the visible world in which the Levitical priests serve the 'tabernacle'. This distinction between the heavenly and earthly, visible and invisible, pervades especially Heb. 8–10, where the two tabernacles are contrasted. But it is also present throughout the epistle, whether it is explicitly mentioned or implicitly presupposed.

---

[1] I thus disagree with both N. H. Young and W. E. Brooks. The former sees the death of Christ as his offering ('The Gospel According to Hebrews 9', *NTS* 27 (1981) 208–9) and the latter believes the sacrifice to exclude Christ's death ('The Perpetuity of Christ's Sacrifice in the Epistle to the Hebrews', *JBL* 89 (1970) 212 n.101). The author is speaking metaphorically and is thus not overly specific in this language. Viewed traditionally, the sacrifice is on the cross. In the metaphor of high priestly entrance into a heavenly sanctuary, the offering is taken into heaven. The atoning event thus involves both realms in Hebrews' rhetoric.

The previous section of this study has set out the basic 'plotline' of salvation history as the author of Hebrews might have conceived it. It concluded that salvation history could be divided roughly into two broad epochs, each with its respective covenant which God made with his people. Further, these two ages overlap, giving rise to an 'in-between' time. The new age has begun and the old has lost its relevance. Yet the old has not completely disappeared. Accordingly, we might say that the plot consists of the 'yesterday' leading up to the sacrifice of Christ, the 'forever' after Christ has 'appeared a second time', and 'today', the eschatological present in which old and new coincide.

The problem of the delay of the parousia and the death of the first apostles was one shared in common by second-generation Christianity.[2] The plot of salvation history had not seemed to come to its proper conclusion after the resurrection of Christ, and all that the early church had expected to follow upon that event had not yet come to pass. In this period, the author of Hebrews was not the first to use 'cosmological' and 'psychological' imagery to hold this 'now' and 'not yet' of Christian faith in tension. Nevertheless, he clearly used spatial and psychological motifs in a manner unique in the New Testament.[3] He was able to explicate the overlap of the two ages cosmologically, with the old age tied inextricably to the earthly, visible realm and the new tied to the spiritual and heavenly dimensions of existence.

Now that I have laid out the basic contours of the plot of salvation history, I can profitably explore this sermon's cosmology with an appropriate perspective. Without such groundwork, I might have addressed certain passages myopically, particularly those that seem at least superficially Platonic. And it is indeed the cosmological settings of the plot that generate the most pointed background questions. With the narrative of salvation fully in view, we can confront these matters in the context of exegesis. From the very beginning of the study, I have argued that such a text-centred approach is the most legitimate way to conduct such an inquiry, indeed the one which ultimately holds the most promise for overcoming the seeming impasse in the background debate.

---

[2] I would date Hebrews within ten years or so of the destruction of Jerusalem, although the precise date is not essential to my argument. The epistle certainly belongs to second-generation Christianity (cf. 2:3), and the recipients may need encouragement at least in part because of the delay of the parousia (e.g. 10:36–8). In the light of 13:14, I wonder in particular whether the destruction of Jerusalem and its temple may have played a role in the audience's faith crisis. See ch. 7.

[3] Cf., for example, Paul in Galatians when he speaks of the present Jerusalem and the ἄνω Ἰερουσαλήμ (Gal. 4:26), as well as the flesh/spirit distinction of Rom. 7 and Gal. 5.

The purpose of this chapter is to explore one of the two 'settings' of the plot of salvation history in the Epistle to the Hebrews, namely, the created realm. The other setting is of course heaven, where Christ enters into the true holy of holies. Given the eschatological framework of old and new in the epistle, it is not difficult to ascertain to which age the created realm belongs. Hebrews is permeated with both implicit and explicit indications that the created earthly realm has *intrinsic* associations with the old age, a period which is 'antiquated and about to disappear' (8:13). This is not to say that the created realm is 'bad' or 'evil' in some sense. It simply has served its purpose and is destined to be removed/transformed.

In the following pages, I will attempt to flesh out those 'metaphysical' aspects of the author's thought which explain various statements and associations which he makes. These assumptions are not always apparent, since they usually are not stated explicitly. Gaps in the text's meaning may ultimately consign many answers to these questions to the realm of speculation. Nevertheless, I will begin by addressing the age-old matter of Hebrews in relation to Platonism, including a brief discussion of *logos* imagery in Hebrews. Then I will explore language in the epistle which expresses the transience of the created realm, followed by an investigation of the contrast between flesh and spirit. I will then bring these probes together in an attempt to form a coherent picture of how the author might have conceived the creation in relation to soteriology.

Hebrews and Platonism[4]

Vocabulary such as ὑπόδειγμα (8:5 and 9:23 in particular), σκιά (8:5; 10:1), τύπος (8:5), εἰκών (10:1) and ἀντίτυπος (9:24) has often been taken as a straightforward indication of Platonic influence on the author.[5] More than any other person, Lincoln Hurst has addressed certain misconceptions usually involved in such discussions.[6] For example, he argues that '[t]here is no instance in known Greek literature where ὑπόδειγμα

---

[4] For a more detailed discussion of this issue, see my 'Philo and the Epistle to the Hebrews: Ronald Williamson's Study after Thirty Years', *SPhA* 14 (2002) 112–35. See also the discussion in my *A Brief Guide to Philo* (Louisville, KY: Westminster/John Knox, 2005) 81–6.

[5] For example, J. H. Burtness: 'there is no doubt but that he [the author] is using words which are *frequently used by Philo* and which seem to express the antithesis between heavenly realities and earthly copies' ('Plato, Philo and the Author of Hebrews', *LQ* 2 (1958) 58, quoted in Hurst, 'How "Platonic" are Heb. viii.5 and ix.23f?', *JTS* 34 (1983) 156).

[6] Especially in 'How "Platonic"', 'Eschatology and "Platonism" in the Epistle to the Hebrews' *SBLSP* (1984) 41–74, and *The Epistle to the Hebrews: Its Background of Thought* (SNTSMS 65; Cambridge: Cambridge University Press, 1990) 7–42.

can be demonstrated to mean "copy"'.[7] Rather, the word usually signifies the '*basis* for imitation or instruction' in conjunction with the idea of 'showing' present in the δεῖγμα word group.[8] On the other hand, the Platonic and Philonic παράδειγμα is not present in Hebrews, nor is the more typical Platonic word for 'copy', μίμημα.

Harold Attridge has found a few places where ὑπόδειγμα can mean something like 'likeness'.[9] However, none of these refers to a *Platonic* likeness or copy. We might therefore modify Hurst's original suggestion to say that there is no instance in known Greek literature where ὑπόδειγμα is used in reference to a Platonic copy. More often than not it relates, as the δεῖγμα word group in general, to the exemplar rather than the image. Hebrews itself uses the word this way in 4:11, where ὑπόδειγμα refers to an example from the Scriptures. These simple observations call for a more careful reading of these terms in the central section of Hebrews.

The *locus classicus* from which to launch an investigation of possible Platonism in Hebrews is of course 8:5, where it is said that the earthly priests, 'by shadowy illustration[10] serve the heavenly tabernacle, even as Moses has been instructed as he is about to erect the tent'.[11] Hebrews then cites Exod. 25: 'Be careful that you make everything according to the pattern shown you on the mountain.' Hebrews' choice of words in this citation is revealing. The author seems to combine the bulk of 25:40 (25:39 LXX) with the 'all' from 25:9, but he relies more on 25:40 than 25:9. Ironically, it is the latter verse that has the more Platonic term παράδειγμα. So if the author meant his audience to take the verse Platonically, he failed miserably at this point.

In his attempt to move away from a Platonic reading, Hurst has tried to shift the focus of interpretation from the word *pattern* (or rather, τύπος)

---

[7] *Background* 13.

[8] So Hurst, *Background* 13, citing E. Lee, 'Words Denoting "Pattern" in the New Testament', *NTS* 8 (1962) 167–9.

[9] *The Epistle to the Hebrews* (Philadelphia: Fortress Press, 1989) 219 n.41: Ezek. 42:15 (LXX) and Aquila's translation of Ezek. 8:10 and Dan. 4:17.

[10] Hurst, *Background* 15–17, prefers 'outline' as the best translation of ὑπόδειγμα, finding J. Moffatt's interpretation of ὑποδείγματι καὶ σκιᾷ as a hendiadys for 'a shadowy outline' an acceptable translation if the phrase is emptied of Platonic meaning (*A Critical and Exegetical Commentary on the Epistle to the Hebrews* (Edinburgh: T&T Clark, 1924) 105–6). He suggests that the use of ὑπόδειγμα here is related to its occurrence in Ezek. 42:15, where it denotes the outline or outside perimeter of the temple. It seems more straightforward, however, to take the term in a similar sense to its use in 4:11.

[11] The use of the perfect tense here is striking and indicates that the author is interpreting Scripture. So also Attridge, *Hebrews* 220 n.46: 'The perfect tense is used here in the exegetical context.' We must always bear this fact in mind when reading Hebrews. It is not so much the historical earthly priests or earthly tabernacle that Hebrews has in mind but the priests and tabernacle of the biblical text.

to other components of the verse. In particular, he suggests that the author may have focused more on the mountain, the reference to 'all things', or the notion of showing rather than on 'pattern'.[12] In his attempt, he makes a case that the real key to the verse is Ezek. 42:15. His interpretation is not, however, convincing. Since the author will take up the 'type' or 'pattern' motif in 9:23–4 with the same basic language, it seems fairly clear that the pattern-τύπος aspect of the Exodus citation is what is most important for the author.[13] On the other hand, such a focus does not necessarily imply that the author took this language in some straightforward Platonic way.

The general relationship between old and new is well illustrated by the correspondence between 9:11 and 10:1. The latter verse states that 'the Law, having a shadow of good things to come, but not itself being the image of those things . . . is never able to perfect those who approach [God through it]'. For our purposes, the most important aspect of this verse is that *the relation between shadow and image is a temporal one.* The Law, in the past, contains a shadow of the good things in the future. This temporal order in the verse creates a significant problem for a straightforwardly Platonic reading of 10:1. The Law is not said to have had a shadow of something in heaven, as if referring to some Platonic form. Indeed there is no explicit indication that the reality to which it pointed even existed at the time of its institution. Rather, those repeatedly offered sacrifices which the Law did 'have' (10:1b) referred to something which was to come. While 10:1 is vague about what these 'things' might be, they surely must include the atonement provided by Christ.

This reading of 10:1 is substantiated by a comparison with 9:11, where Christ is said to be 'a high priest of good things *having come to be*'.[14] The Law had a shadow of good things *to come*; Christ is the high priest of good things *accomplished*. This correspondence fits well with the theology of Hebrews, as the previous chapters have demonstrated. Hebrews consistently contrasts Christ with the Law as the new covenant equivalent of the Levitical cultus (e.g. 7:11 vs. 8:6). The shadow language thus exists as much or more on the level of event as on the level of entities. It is thus impossible to see this as a straightforwardly Platonic or Philonic contrast, for events do not have Platonic forms.

---

[12] *Background* 15f.

[13] In the next chapter, however, I will argue that the author probably does not have a rigid correspondence between the heavenly 'type' and the earthly 'antitype' in mind. If this is the case, the Platonic reading loses more and more ground.

[14] A textual variant exists of roughly equal manuscript support, with μελλόντων instead of γενομένων. However, since the author emphasizes the completed aspect of Christ's high priesthood (e.g. 9:26; 10:12–14), the latter is more likely.

A further complication for those who would wish to read 10:1 Platonically is the contrast of σκιά with εἰκών. In Plato the εἰκών is associated with the earthly copies rather than the heavenly realities.[15] And while in contrast Philo can refer to the *logos* as an εἰκών because it is an intermediate entity between God and the physical realm, any kind of straightforward Philonic reading of the verse wreaks havoc with its meaning.[16] What are the 'good things' of which the cultic apparati of the Law were shadows and the heavenly things the image, or of which Christ was the image? By the time we have adjusted the Philonic language to fit Hebrews' matrix, it no longer looks very Philonic.[17]

It is much easier to start with the basic notion that the old covenant was only 'shadowy' in its picture of the new covenant. It did not even give a one-to-one image of what the new covenant elements and events were like. The Law with its ministrations was only a shadow cast by the coming good things accomplished in Christ; it did not reflect these things with a mirror image. The following chapter will show further how language of 'type', 'antitype', 'shadow' and 'example' is all imprecise in the relationship portrayed between exemplar and representation.[18] In particular, the author amalgamates all the sacrifices of the old order to pit them against the singular sacrifice of Christ in the new. The old foreshadows the new, but it does so in a shadowy, imperfect way.

Indeed, if we are to find a Philonic precedent for Hebrews' rhetoric, it is in the way Philo treats the literal interpretations of scriptural texts as σκιαί of more substantive *interpretations*. In *De Confusione* 190, Philo encourages those overly wedded to the literal interpretation of Scripture to consider the letters of the oracles as σκιαί of more substantive interpretations (σώματα). Similarly, *De Opificio* 157 tells us that the story of

---

[15] E.g. *Timaeus* 29b.

[16] This is because Philo has a 'three-tiered' system, where the *logos* is both the εἰκών of the divine παράδειγμα and the model for the shadowy, earthly copies (e.g. *Leg.* 3.95–96; *Som.* 1.79).

[17] I find the efforts of Vos to maintain a 'spatial' priority here valiant but inadequate, in *The Teaching of the Epistle to the Hebrews* (Grand Rapids, MI: Eerdmans, 1956) 55–8. He suggests two explanations, the first of which comes from the sphere of art and the second from the sphere of philosophy. In the first, the Old Testament possesses the sketch and the New the true picture of the heavenly realities. In the second, he offers alternatively the idea that Christ is the reality come down from heaven, baldly asserting that εἰκών can mean 'archetype'. In terms of an interpretation built of a Philonic three-tiered model, perhaps one might suggest that with Christ as the χαρακτήρ of God's substance (1:3), God is the heavenly substance, Christ the image, and the Law has the shadow. Such a modified Philonism bears little resemblance to Philo himself.

[18] The author's incorporation of the word 'all' in the citation in 8:5 is the one place where one might argue for a more rigid correspondence between type and antitype. See the chapter that follows.

Adam and Eve in Genesis provides us with δείγματα τύπων, 'examples of types', deep allegorical meanings waiting to be explored. In short, we can make a much better case that Hebrews is employing a Philonic-like *exegetical* approach in these instances than a metaphysical one.

The relationship between shadow/illustration and reality is therefore most significantly one of anticipation. The earthly cultus points toward the heavenly one in a primarily temporal, although also spatial scheme. The earthly cultus and tabernacle are indeed not the 'true' items but are only 'antitypes' of the heavenly realities (9:24). They are neither effective nor lasting. On the other hand, they served a valid function in pointing forward to the realities which were to come. Moses was indeed commanded to build the earthly tent, even if the structure did not truly make atonement possible. The earthly tabernacle has a 'parabolic' purpose (9:9) in teaching us about the true tent and the eternal sacrifice. All of these factors lead us to the conclusion that the old covenant was indeed God ordained and God given as a part of his plan. It was never meant to have any independent value, however. It was meant as an indication, an illustration of that which was to come.

We should not leave this section without at least a brief mention of the *logos* imagery in this sermon. Marie Isaacs has rightly criticized Graham Hughes and Ronald Williamson for seeing in Hebrews an 'all-but explicit Logos Doctrine' in reference to Christ.[19] Her critique, however, does not preclude the existence of 'all-but explicit' – indeed actually explicit – *logos* imagery in the sermon. The clearest instance of such language occurs in 4:12–13 where the 'word' of God is likened to a sword in its ability to discern the thoughts and intents of the heart. The author's language here is reminiscent of Wis. 18:15, where the all-powerful word of God leaps from heaven wielding a sword, bearing God's authentic command. Hebrews thus knows to speak of the *logos* of God as the bearer of his command in accomplishing his will in judgement.

The author repeatedly uses 'word' imagery throughout the epistle, raising further suspicion that he has some notion of a *logos* of God which functions on a broader level. Thus God formerly *spoke* through the prophets, but recently he has *spoken* through a Son. Hebrews 1 is replete with statements which God *says* either to the Son or the angels (1:5, 6, 7, 13). Hebrews 2:2 speaks both of the λόγος which the angels had *spoken* and of that one (i.e. salvation) which began to be *spoken* by Christ. Throughout, verses like 2:6, 3:5, 5:13, 6:1, 7:28, 12:19, and 13:7, to name only a few,

---

[19] *Space* 198f., arguing against Hughes, *Hermeneutics* 5 and Williamson, 'The Incarnation of the Logos in Hebrews', *ExpTim* 95 (1983) 4–8.

demonstrate that the author links the speaking of God with authoritative revelation and the proper ordering of salvation history.

On the one hand, in none of the above instances, not even in 4:12–13, does the author directly equate the word spoken with Christ. Even in 1:2 God has spoken a word *through* him, but Christ is not equated with this word. On the other hand, Hebrews does use *logos* related language in 1:3, where he is deemed an ἀπαύγασμα of God's glory and a χαρακτήρ of his substance. The latter term in particular is reminiscent of Philo's use of *logos* language,[20] and the verse carries overtones of Christ as the wisdom of God. One might reasonably suppose, therefore, that Christ was God's *logos par excellence* for the author. Whether the author had a systematically formulated *logos* concept or not, therefore, he did have a sense of the power and order of God's word as the instrument of his action in the world. This *logos* is not to be exclusively equated with Christ, although verses like 1:3, 2:6–8 and 2:10 indicate that he is the embodiment *par excellence* of God's wisdom for the world. Terminology relating to fittingness, necessity, and impossibility also demonstrate that there is a certain *logical* structure to the world. A certain *logos* proceeds from God in his ordering of the creation, although we must be careful not to over-read such imagery.

The transience of the created realm

There are two key passages in Hebrews which demonstrate that the created heavens and earth are destined to end along with the final remnants of the old covenant and thus that they are associated with the old age in some way. The first of these is 1:10–12, which is one of those fascinating instances in the New Testament when an author transfers to Christ a Scripture from the Jewish Bible which clearly referred to Yahweh in its original context, in this case Ps. 102:26–8 (101:26–8 LXX):

> You at the beginning, Lord, founded the earth,
> and the heavens are the works of your hands.
> They will perish, but you remain,
> and they all as a garment will become worn out,
> and as a covering you will roll them up,
> *as a garment* even they will be changed.
> But you are the same and your years will not run out.

---

[20] For brief arguments that χαρακτήρ in particular is Philonic here, see J. Frankowski's 'Early Christian Hymns Recorded in the New Testament: A Reconsideration of the Question in the Light of Heb 1,3', *BZ* 27 (1982) 186. For the contrary opinion, see Williamson, *Philo and Hebrews* 74–80.

The context of this quotation is of course the contrast in Heb. 1 between the Son and the angels, a contrast which I have already argued is primarily eschatological in nature.[21] The author sets up Ps. 102 in contrast with what he has said in 1:7, where he relates the angels to winds and flames of fire, that is, things which are transitory and 'earthy' in nature.[22] James Thompson believes that the point of this verse is to demonstrate the inferiority of the angels by noting their changeability in conjunction with the created order.[23] Although he seems to exclude angels from the heavenly realm altogether, Thompson is probably correct to associate the angels with the created realm and its transience.[24] He notes, for example, the connection between the angels which are 'flames of fire' in 1:7 and the *tangible* mountain with its 'burning fire' in 12:18, present when the Law was given on Sinai.[25] Although he misses the eschatological overtones of this fire and wind imagery, he catches its cosmological and 'metaphysical' associations.

That the transience of the angels' 'ministry' is the point of the contrast in 1:7–12 is clear when we look more closely at 1:8–12. Here the author uses two other Old Testament passages to contrast the angels with the superiority of the Son.[26] These two citations stand in a μέν – δέ construction with 1:7, a fact which makes 1:7 the governing element in the author's interpretation of Ps. 45 and 102. Thus while the angels have been made 'winds' and 'flames' in association with the material realm, the Son's throne is 'for ever' (1:8 quoting Ps. 45:6–7 (44:7–8 LXX)).[27] Also, the

[21] In the previous chapter.

[22] The word πνεῦμα, of course, could be translated as 'spirit', but in conjunction with the image of a flame, perhaps wind is a better translation in English. Cf. Jub. 2:2.

[23] *The Beginnings of Christian Philosophy: The Epistle to the Hebrews* (CBQMS 13; Washington, DC: Catholic Biblical Association of America, 1982) 133. See also O. Michel, *Der Brief an die Hebräer*, 8th edn (Göttingen: Vandenhoeck & Ruprecht, 1984 (1936)) 117; O. Kuss, *Der Brief an die Hebräer* (Regensburg: Pustet, 1966) 37; and W. L. Lane, *Hebrews 1–8* (Dallas: Word, 1991) 29.

[24] Heb. 12:22 demonstrates invariably that angels will be present in the heavenly Jerusalem. The verb ποιέω in 1:7 should probably be taken in the sense of appointment or assignment, rather than in the sense of creation.

[25] Note also the possible connection between the 'winds' of 1:7 and the 'windstorm' (θύελλα) of 12:18.

[26] Here the author uses some of the 'highest' Christological language in the New Testament, referring to Christ as 'God' (1:8) and applying to him words used of God in the Psalms. C. F. D. Moule, *The Birth of the New Testament* (London: Adam & Charles Black, 1962) 79 and L. D. Hurst, 'The Christology of Hebrews 1 and 2', *The Glory of Christ in the New Testament: Studies in Christology in Memory of George Bradford Caird*, L. D. Hurst and N.T. Wright, eds. (Oxford: Clarendon Press, 1987) 151–64, have suggested, following B. W. Bacon, that the author might have read the LXX of Ps. 101 as God speaking to the Messiah.

[27] It is perhaps worthwhile to note that 'fire' and 'air' were two of the fundamental components of the world in ancient philosophy.

Son will remain and his years will not come to an end, while the heavens and the earth will perish and be rolled up like a garment (1:11–12).

From this common theme of the Son's eternal continuance, it is clear that the author understands 1:7 as an indication of the transience of the angels' role in salvation's history, in contrast to the exalted Christ. In contrast to Christ, the role of the angels in their 'ministry' (1:7, 14) is associated with the transience of the created realm, for otherwise the contrast of the endurance of the Son with the created order would not relate to the angels in 1:7. Although I favour οἰκουμένη in 1:6 as a reference to the heavenly realm, a reading equating it with the earthly realm would fit this general line of interpretation as well, with the world as the locus of angelic operation.[28]

Accordingly, the principal factor behind the author's choice of Ps. 102 has to do with the Son's enduring appointment, in contrast to that of the angels in their appointed role.[29] In terms of the created realm, the focal elements of this psalm for the author are the 'rolling up' of the heavens and earth as one rolls up a covering and the 'changing' of the created realm as a garment. The reading ἑλίσσω here, 'to roll up', is found in some LXX manuscripts, and thus we cannot conclude definitively that the author used it with special significance.[30] On the other hand, the addition of ὡς ἱμάτιον seems the author's own doing. This redaction implies that the author believed that the created realm at some future point would, at the very least, be taken off and changed like a garment.[31] This 'taking off' of the created realm is thoroughly linked to the final disappearance of the old covenant, as is implied by the common use of παλαιόω in 1:11 and 8:13.[32]

---

[28]   Michel, *Hebräer* 121, argues for such a connection when he notes of 1:11, 'Vielleicht darf man gerade hier daran denken, daß die Himmel die Wohnung der Engel sind und ihr Schicksal auch die Engel angeht.' I do not tie the *destiny* of the angels themselves to that of the created heavens, as I have indicated, but I would tie their *role* as the 'ministers' of humanity to the time of the old order. For a more detailed exegesis of this passage, see my 'The Celebration of the Enthroned Son: The Catena of Hebrews 1:5–14', *JBL* 120 (2001) 469–85 and *Understanding the Book of Hebrews: The Story behind the Sermon* (Louisville, KY: Westminster/John Knox, 2003) 40–55.

[29]   The pre-existence of the Son is thus not the main point of this citation, although it is significant that Christ is placed 'outside' of the created order. For a discussion of Hebrews and Christ's pre-existence, see my 'Keeping his Appointment: Creation and Enthronement in the Epistle to the Hebrews', *JSNT* 66 (1997) 91–117.

[30]   Vaticanus (B) and Alexandrinus (A).

[31]   Attridge, *Hebrews* 61, suggests that the word 'change' in this context is too weak and that the word 'remove' fits the context better, especially in the light of 12:26–7.

[32]   Thompson, *Beginnings* 136, once again sees the connection, but fails to emphasize the eschatological point.

The second key passage confirms that the author is implying the *destruction* of the created realm in some way, namely, 12:25–9, where the author quotes Hag. 2:21 (or 6). This is a truly intriguing passage which appears in the context of paraenesis. In the earlier part of Heb. 12, the author has exhorted the readers to endure the discipline of the Lord (12:7) and to beware that they not become like Esau, who sought a place of repentance with tears but failed to find it (12:15f.).[33] The author then reiterates in hortatory form the nature of their belief. They had not arrived at a *tangible* mountain like Sinai with its fire, darkness, gloom and windstorm, whereat even Moses was frightened (12:18–21). Rather, their 'mountain' was 'Zion', the *heavenly* Jerusalem, city of the living God, and they had come to the mediator of a new covenant (12:22–4).

In these verses, the author alludes to his earlier contrast between the old and new covenants and to the Law with its cultic ordinances in contrast to the blood of Christ. The readers are no longer in the assembly of the first covenant, but in the church of the firstborn enrolled *in the heavens*. Implicit in this exhortation is at least a contrast between visible and invisible, between that which is presently upon the earth and that which is associated with heaven and the future.[34] The author then goes on to warn the readers. If those in the old covenant did not escape when they refused *on the earth* the one warning them, how much less will those in the new covenant be excused if they reject the one warning *from the heavens*! Since the author believes that God made both covenants (although the first was spoken 'through angels': 2:2), it is clear that the author considers heaven in some way superior to the present earthly realm.

This supposition is confirmed by the verses that follow. Verses 26 and 27 read:

> whereas the voice shook the earth then, now it has been promised saying, 'yet one more time I will shake *not only* the earth, *but* also the heaven.' Now the 'yet once more' indicates the μετάθεσις of those things which are being shaken, since they are created, in order that those things which are not shaken might remain.

---

[33] Others alternatively take the blessing to be that which Esau could not find. E.g. C. R. Koester, *Hebrews* (Doubleday: New York, 2001) 533. The proximity of μετανοία as potential antecedent and especially the parallel rhetoric of 6:6 tip the scales in our direction.

[34] One is reminded of 11:1, 'Now faith is the substance of those things hoped, the verification of things which are not visible'. As C. K. Barrett points out, this is an eschatological faith, 'which is convinced of future good because it knows that the good for which it hopes already exists invisibly in God' ('The Eschatology of the Epistle to the Hebrews', *The Background of the New Testament and Its Eschatology*, W. D. Davies and D. Daube, eds. (Cambridge: Cambridge University Press, 1954) 381). Perhaps it would have been better to say that it already exists invisibly in heaven *with* God.

One key issue here is the precise meaning of the word μετάθεσις in v. 27. The two primary senses of the word are either 'change' or 'removal'.[35] Further, if a sense of removal is chosen, we are then faced with the question of whether the lower world is then replaced or if some heavenly realm alone continues to exist.[36] All these connotations are lexically possible, and the two primary options seem attested in the two other occurrences of the word group in the epistle (7:12; 11:5). We accordingly cannot determine the meaning on a straightforwardly lexical basis.

If we move from what is more certain to what is less, we should first note differences between the flavour of our author's understanding and that of Paul. Paul seems to have a somewhat neutral view of the created order per se. Indeed, he sympathizes with its plight in Rom. 8 when he says that

> the eager longing of the creation awaits the revelation of the sons of God. For to futility the creation was subjected – not willingly – but because of the one who subjected it in hope that even the creation itself will be freed from the slavery of corruption unto the freedom of the glory of the children of God (Rom. 8:19–21).

For Paul the relationship between the creation itself and the creation in its current state corresponds generally to his distinction between σῶμα

---

[35] Most interpreters have taken the word to mean removal: Moffatt, *Hebrews* 221–2; H. Windisch, *Der Hebräerbrief*, 2nd edn (HNT 14; Tübingen: Mohr/Siebeck, 1931) 115; Anton Vögtle, 'Das Neue Testament und die Zukunft des Kosmos', *BibLeb* 10 (1969) 239–54; A. Vanhoye, *La structure littéraire de l'épître aux Hébreux*, 2nd edn (Paris: Desclée de Brouwer, 1976) 208; W. R. G. Loader, *Sohn und Hohepriester: Eine traditionsgeschichtliche Untersuchung zur Christologie des Hebräerbriefes* (WMANT 53; Neukirchen: Neukirchener Verlag, 1981) 58–59; Thompson, *Beginnings* 48–9; H. Braun, *An die Hebräer* (HNT 14; Tübingen: Mohr/Siebeck, 1984) 442–4; Attridge, *Hebrews* 380–1; W. L. Lane, *Hebrews 9–13* (Dallas: Word, 1991) 482; P. Ellingworth, *The Epistle to the Hebrews* (Grand Rapids, MI: Eerdmans, 1993) 687–9; E. Grässer, *An die Hebräer*, vol. 3 (Zürich: Neukirchener Verlag, 1997); D. A. deSilva, *Perseverance in Gratitude: A Socio-Rhetorical Commentary on the Epistle 'to the Hebrews'* (Grand Rapids, MI: Eerdmans, 2000) 471–2; W. Eisele, *Ein unerschütterliches Reich: Die mittelplatonische Umformung des Parusiegedankens im Hebräerbrief* (BZNW 116; Berlin: Walter de Gruyter, 2003) 119. Some taking a more apocalyptic/renewal approach include E. Riggenbach, *Der Brief an die Hebräer*, 2nd edn (Leipzig: Deichert, 1922) 425; C. Spicq, *L'épître aux Hébreux*, vol. 2 (Paris: Gabalda, 1953) 412; F. Schröger, *Der Verfasser des Hebräerbriefes als Schriftausleger* (Regensburg: Pustet, 1968) 193; G. W. Buchanan, *To the Hebrews* (Garden City, NY: Doubleday, 1972) 136; and Michel, *Hebräer* 474.

[36] Most commentators who argue for removal seem unclear on how the cosmos will look thereafter. M. Isaacs clearly equates removal with replacement (*Sacred Space: An Approach to the Theology of the Epistle to the Hebrews* (Sheffield: JSOT Press, 1992) 207). Meanwhile, Grässer, *Hebräer*; Thompson, *Beginnings* 48–9; Ellingworth, *Hebrews* 687; deSilva, *Persistence* 471; Eisele, *Reich* 119, picture a permanent removal.

and σάρξ.[37] The former has a generally neutral value connotation, while the latter more often a negative evaluative sense.

We should most likely infer that Paul saw the created order, including human flesh, as subject to the power of sin and evil forces in this realm. Our bodies, as part of this creation, are in need of redemption (Rom. 8:23). For those on earth in whom the Spirit dwells, their spirits are alive on the condition that their bodies are dead – because of the sin problem associated with bodies (8:10). Before the Spirit, such individuals formerly had τὰ παθήματα τῶν ἁμαρτιῶν working in their physical members (7:5). But now they serve ἐν καινότητι πνεύματος (7:6). The condition of those without the Spirit is one in which sin reigns over their mortal bodies (6:12). Believers thus were formerly δοῦλοι τῆς ἁμαρτίας (6:17, 20). But now in the Spirit, they are ἐλευθερωθέντες ἀπὸ τῆς ἁμαρτίας (6:22).[38]

As we reconstruct the system of thought that seems to lie behind these comments, we get a picture of a creation that is under the power of sin, including mortal bodies. Σάρξ is thus Paul's term for a physical σῶμα under the power of such sin. But Paul believes that even on earth this susceptibility of the body can be overcome by the power of the Spirit. At least in theory, all believers should have crucified the flesh with its passions and desires (Gal. 5:24). Paul is notably ambiguous with regard to the precise nature of this sin power, which in Galatians may relate to what he calls the στοιχεῖα (e.g. Gal. 4:9; cf. Col. 2:20).[39] But at the very least it is clear that he believed evil forces held significant sway over the material creation. One key aspect of the eschaton will thus be the liberation of the created realm from the enslavement of evil powers.

In contrast, Hebrews looks to the *removal* of the created realm in some way. The author makes a distinction between two different categories, namely, τὰ σαλευόμενα, 'those things which are being shaken', and τὰ μὴ σαλευόμενα, 'those things which are not being shaken'. Only those things

---

[37] Cf., for example, J. D. G. Dunn, *The Theology of St. Paul the Apostle* (Grand Rapids, MI: Eerdmans, 1998) 70–3.

[38] I must thus disagree with Dunn, who at this point suggests that 7:25b gives us a 'statement of calm realism about the continuing state of affairs', a 'sober, but fitting conclusion' (*Romans 1–8* (Dallas: Word, 1988) 411). Dunn does not believe that Paul saw any real resolution while on earth to the human struggle against sin. However, we need not resort to hypotheses of interpolations and transpositions to explain this anticlimactic comment of Paul. After his pertinent exclamation of victory over the power of sin in 7:25a, Paul unfortunately recapitulates his argument in 7:14–24 about the state of the person without the Spirit wishing to keep the Jewish law. It is thus crucial to continue beyond 7:25b into Rom. 8 to remain clear on Paul's train of thought.

[39] Dunn cogently argues that 'Paul himself did not have a very strong, or at least very clear, belief' regarding heavenly powers as a power over the human realm (*Theology* 108–9).

which are *not* being shaken remain. These statements bear further exploration. First, we might translate these two participles in terms of 'those
things which are shakeable' and 'those things which are unshakeable'.
The following verse (12:28) speaks of how the audience has received
a βασιλείαν ἀσάλευτον. The coming kingdom thus fits under the category of τὰ μὴ σαλευόμενα, and the use of ἀσάλευτον implies a distinction between that which is and is not shakeable. In other words, τὰ
μὴ σαλευόμενα are not intermingled with τὰ σαλευόμενα as that which
remains after *everything* is shaken. The distinction is between two distinct
kinds of categories rather than with one category inside another.[40] The
broader context in Hebrews pushes us toward seeing response in faith to
God as the major factor in determining which individuals belong to the
shakeable and which to the unshakeable kingdom (12:25; cf. 2:2–3; 3:19;
4:2).

But strikingly, Heb. 12:27 places the created realm itself in the category
of 'those things which are shakeable': τὰ σαλευόμενα are πεποιημένα.
Since these are things that do not remain, we must infer that the author
envisages the removal of the created order. Some human spirits within the
created order may be part of the unshakeable kingdom, but the created
realm itself is not. Imagery elsewhere in Hebrews coheres well with this
interpretation. We remember the author's specific addition of the phrase
ὡς ἱμάτιον to his citation of Ps. 102 in Heb. 1:12. Harold Attridge draws
the appropriate conclusion, 'As a cloak the heavens will be not simply
changed, but "removed" (ἀλλαγήσονται).'[41]

Indeed, it seems likely that the author, whether consciously or subconsciously, associates the created realm in itself with the human problem.[42]
Again, Attridge correctly notes of this passage that 'the reference here
is best understood to have somewhat pejorative connotations, such as
those found in the description of the true tabernacle as "not of this creation" (9:11)'.[43] One of the most striking instances of such an underlying
bias appears in 9:26, where the author startlingly suggests that if Christ

---

[40] So Thompson, 'The author does not speak of the new heavens and new earth which
follow the eschatological shaking, nor the appearance of the unshakeable world. Instead,
he knows of two worlds already possessing reality . . . When the material world disappears,
only the world that is presently unseen (11:1) and untouchable (12:18) remains' (*Beginnings*
50).

[41] *Hebrews* 61. Cf. also Loader, *Sohn* 59.

[42] Although some have suggested otherwise (e.g. G. B. Caird, *The Basis of a Christian
Hope* (London: Duckworth, 1970) 23; Lane, *Hebrews* 482).

[43] *Hebrews* 381.

needed to suffer more than once for sin, then he would have needed to suffer ἀπὸ καταβολῆς κόσμου! Here we find no sense of a Fall or a creation that, while initially good, has become enslaved to corruption. The author consciously or subconsciously associates the created realm *intrinsically* with the need for atonement.

The author's statement that 'those things which are shakeable' are 'those things that have been created' raises a number of questions. So Hurst notes that the heavenly tent and city are also made by God (e.g. 8:1; 11:10), as are the angels (1:7). For that matter, we might add that even the Son himself seems to be 'made' by God (3:2). Yet Hurst adds that none of these are considered by the author to be 'of this creation' (9:11). The author evidently can distinguish between whether something is of this creation or of the unshakeable heaven.[44] If it is only the unshakeable heaven which will survive in the fullness of the new age, then all the language throughout the epistle which pertains to the coming world and city pertains strictly to the heavenly realm and not to the earthly. The coming world of 2:5, which Christ and the people of God will rule, is the heavenly realm. God is taking hold of the seed of Abraham to lead them to the glory of the true heaven (2:16), and the powers of the coming age of which the enlightened have tasted are 'heavenly' (6:4).[45]

It is in theory possible that the author thought God would replace the first created realm with another. Indeed, we might have expected him to say something of this sort. While most Jews at this time certainly must have believed that God created the world, it is not completely clear that the idea of creation *ex nihilo* even existed at this point in time. Thus the author of Wisdom suggests that God created the world out of ἄμορφος ὕλη (11:17). While 2 Macc. 7:28 and *Aristeas* 136 are sometimes adduced to this end, even Harry Wolfson, champion of the idea that Philo believed in *ex nihilo* creation, did not believe the evidence was conclusive.[46] Phrases like τὰ ὄντα in various places need mean only 'things as they *now* are'. And while Philo's position on this topic is genuinely ambiguous, David Runia and Gregory Sterling likely come closest to Philo's view when they suggest Philo must have held to something like *creation aeterna*, the eternal creation of matter as a by-product of God thinking about (and

---

[44] 'Eschatology and "Platonism"', 72.

[45] The reference to the heavenly gift here is of course probably to the Holy Spirit, but this gift is only a foretaste of the powers which pertain to the coming, heavenly age.

[46] *Philo: Foundations of Religious Philosophy in Judaism, Christianity, and Islam*, vol. 1 (Cambridge, MA: Harvard University Press, 1947) 302–3.

thus organizing) it.[47] In short, it is not really until the late second century that we have undisputable references to *ex nihilo* creation.[48]

In at least one sense, it seems easier to argue for the destruction of the cosmos *ad nihilum* if it had been created *ex nihilo*, since such a view does not view matter as truly eternal.[49] And we must consider Hebrews ambiguous on this score. Hebrews 11:3 says that

πίστει νοοῦμεν κατηρτίσθαι τοὺς αἰῶνας ῥήματι θεοῦ, εἰς τὸ μὴ ἐκ φαινομένων τὸ βλεπόμενον γεγονέναι.

A number of interpreters, including the likes of Ronald Williamson and James Moffatt, have seen *ex nihilo* creation in this verse.[50] But this is not at all the only possible interpretation. Hebrews merely asserts that the visible realm was not created out of 'that which appears', which is likely a reference back to the ῥῆμα θεοῦ. The use of καταρτίζω seems an odd choice for creation out of nothing, since it more generally has the sense of mending something that already exists. It is thus quite uncertain that this verse refers to *ex nihilo* creation.

And it is even more uncertain that Hebrews believes the removed created realm will be replaced. *4 Ezra* 7:31 says that the corruptible will perish, but can still speak of a world not yet awake and even the earth, apparently (7:32). 2 Peter 3:10 and 12 can present a cosmic conflagration in which the elements burn with a fire, but a new heaven and earth is only as far away as the next verse (3:13). In contrast, all the imagery present in Hebrews – and all its subsidiary clues – push us away from any sense of a future for the created realm. The recipients of the epistle are 'partakers of a heavenly calling' (3:1), indicating the direction of their pilgrimage. They are not seeking a place upon the earth, but a heavenly city (11:10) and country (11:14), which is a better home (11:16). In fact, they confess that they are strangers and pilgrims *upon the earth* (11:13). As I have already mentioned, they have not arrived at a *tangible* mountain (12:18), but at the *heavenly* Jerusalem and the assembly of those who are enrolled

[47] Sterling: '*Creatio Temporalis, Aeterna, vel Continua*?: An Analysis of the Thought of Philo of Alexandria', *SPhA* 4 (1992) 15–41; Winston: 'Philo's Theory of Eternal Creation: *Prov.* 1.6–9', *The Ancestral Philosophy: Hellenistic Philosophy in Second Temple Judaism: Essays of David Winston*, G. E. Sterling, ed. (Providence, RI: Brown Judaic Studies, 2001) 117–27. This explanation fits well with a Platonic reading of Philo at this point.

[48] See Winston, 'Creation Ex Nihilo Revisited: A Reply to Jonathan Goldstein', *Ancestral Philosophy* 79–80, responding to J. Goldstein, 'The Origins of the Doctrine of Creation Ex Nihilo', *JJS* 35, 2 (1984) 127–35.

[49] On the other hand, one might argue that God might be inclined to destroy some eternally existent formless matter for the very reason of its innate imperfection.

[50] E.g. Williamson, *Philo and Hebrews* 372–85; Moffatt, *On the Epistle to the Hebrews* (New York: Scribner, 1924) 161 n.2.

in the heavens (12:22–3). Here on earth, on the other hand, is no lasting city (13:14), in contrast to the heavenly kingdom, which is unshakeable (12:28). These statements do not present any role for the created heavens and earth in the coming age, nor any need for their existence at that time.

I have already mentioned that the author frequently writes in a way that assigns intrinsically negative connotations to the created realm in contrast to heaven.[51] This is particularly true of the central, theological section of the epistle, where the undebatable superiority of the heavenly tent over the earthly, κοσμικόν sanctuary (9:1) is repeatedly implied. The tabernacle in which Christ's ministry occurs is the 'true tent', which was not pitched by a human (8:2). The author makes much of this fact, noting not only that the 'greater and more perfect tent' is not made by hands (χειροποίητος) but that in fact it is 'not of this creation' (9:11, 24).[52] Here again is the distinction between the creation, which is inferior, and the unshakeable heaven. The earthly tent and its functions only point to the heavenly, true ministry; they have no independent significance. Christ, thus, is not a high priest *upon the earth* (8:4), where the priests serve τὰ ἐπουράνια by way of a 'shadowy illustration' (8:5); and Moses was only able to construct the earthly tent on the basis of a τύπος which was shown him. This earthly holy place was only a sketch or example of the heavenly one, an 'antitype' of the true sanctuary (9:23). The greatness of what Christ has done, on the other hand, comes from the fact that he is now 'higher than the heavens' (7:26), through which he has passed (4:14) as he entered 'inside the veil' (6:19).

A final passage could allude also to the annihilation of the creation, although a fuller discussion will await ch. 6. I have already discussed 9:8–9 in ch. 4 in the context of the epistle's eschatology. There I argued that the author used the two 'tents' of the earthly tabernacle as a parable for the two ages of salvation history. The way to the holiest place was not yet apparent while the first tent had στάσις. An additional nuance to these verses would follow if the outer tent also represented the earthly cosmos itself in these verses. If the author at least sometimes interpreted the heavenly tabernacle cosmologically, as Philo and Josephus do at times, then it is possible that the outer tent here also represents the created realm,

---

[51] I thus agree with Käsemann, *Wandering* 33f., that the κατάπαυσις of the people of God is ultimately found spatially in the coming world, while contrary to Käsemann I would deny any Gnostic implications to these terms. Cf. O. Hofius, *Katapausis: Die Vorstellung vom endzeitlichen Ruheort im Hebräerbrief* (WUNT 11; Tübingen: Mohr [Siebeck], 1970) *passim.*

[52] This word has regularly polemic connotations and is found several times in the New Testament (Attridge, *Hebrews* 247), such as Mark 14:58; Acts 7:48; 17:24 (of temple); and Eph. 2:11 (of circumcision).

with the true heaven as the holy of holies. This interpretation implies a strong link between the old age and the created realm, as well as between the new age and heaven. The heavenly city is thus invisible and unseen while the creation is still in existence (cf. 11:1, 3, 7, 27), and the people of God must proceed by faith until the creation is removed.

In conclusion, the author of Hebrews considered the earthly, 'created' realm to be inferior in some way to the heavenly, unshakeable realm. Further, he believed the created heavens and earth to be destined for 'shaking' and removal, at the same time giving us no indication of its replacement. As a covering, God would eventually wrap up the created heavens and earth, leaving only the heavenly Jerusalem, the city of the living God, and those who have been perfected. This contrast between true heaven and creation at the very least associates the characteristics of the old age with the creation and those of the new with heaven. Heaven becomes the realm associated with completion and permanence. While the earthly is changing and the visible will pass away, the audience has a better possession which will *remain* (10:34). The contrast between multiplicity and singularity also accrues to the created and heavenly realms respectively. These distinctions seem to have metaphysical overtones, just as the distinction between unity and multiplicity is used outside Hebrews as an expression of the difference between the material and noumenal.[53]

Having identified and highlighted the contrast in Hebrews between the heavenly and the created, we have yet to explain *why* the creation is inferior and why it is destined for destruction. This is a particularly difficult question, since the epistle nowhere discusses this issue. The author seems to presuppose at every point that the creation *qua* creation is automatically and intrinsically destined for destruction and that any human within that domain is automatically in need of atonement. The author seems to state without second thought that if Christ's sacrifice was not a once and for all offering, then he would have had to have suffered 'from the foundation of the world' (9:26). There is no mention of a Fall or of Adam, only an oblique reference to the Devil as the one holding the power of death. This puzzle begs for further exploration.[54]

---

[53] Cf., for example, several examples in Philo given by L. K. K. Dey in *The Intermediary World and Patterns of Perfection in Philo and Hebrews* (SBLDS 25; Missoula, MT: Scholars Press, 1975) 129f., including *Ebr.* 36, 85–7; *Plant.* 44; *Somn.* 2:10; *Mig.* 152–4. Dey notes significantly that 'imperfection does not mean something bad or evil in this tradition' (134).

[54] One possibility is that the destruction of Jerusalem and the failure of the Christ to appear to establish an earthly kingdom led some to reorient their eschatology around heaven rather than earth. The Gospel of John might also fit in this category.

Flesh and spirit in Hebrews

The author of Hebrews considered the created realm inferior in some way to the heavenly and taught that the creation would be removed when the old age reached its final end. He associates the earthly and heavenly with the old and new covenants respectively. Further, he uses the 'foreignness' and transience of this earthly realm as a basis for encouraging his readers to orientate themselves toward the other, heavenly world. These are all cosmological distinctions which the author makes either explicitly or implicitly.

In addition, the author's distinction between flesh and spirit is a 'psychological' contrast which also relates to the cosmological framework of the epistle.[55] Indeed, the author seems to associate flesh with the created order and spirit with the heavenly one, providing further insight into the nature of the creation/heaven contrast. He clearly considers the spiritual dimension of humanity the truly significant aspect, even though he does not completely disparage the 'fleshly' component of human personality. He does not use the term σάρξ as the human body under the power of sin, as Paul does. For him, body itself seems innately inferior to spirit, even if these two are not in opposition in the way they will be for the later Gnostics.

In the central theological section of the epistle, the author repeatedly argues for the superiority of Christ's sacrifice because it is effective in cleansing the *conscience* in contrast to the mere washing of the *flesh* which the Levitical cultus effected. The author does not feel the need to argue that such an 'inner' cleansing would be far more valuable to the readers than a mere outward cleaning. *He assumes that such an order of creation is self-evident and innate.* So in 9:9 and 10 the author notes that the gifts and sacrifices which the Levitical priests bring are not able to 'perfect' the worshipper in terms of their 'conscience' or 'consciousness' of past sins, but that these cultic ordinances are merely 'regulations of *flesh* imposed until the time of reformation'.[56]

Similarly in 9:13–14, the author contrasts the blood of bulls and goats and the ashes of a red heifer, which sanctify in the cleansing of the *flesh*, to the blood of the Christ, who *through eternal spirit* offered himself blameless to God, leading to the cleansing of one's *conscience* in terms

[55] It will be important to distinguish the way Hebrews contrasts flesh and spirit from the way that Paul does.

[56] For the connotations of συνείδησις in Hebrews, see the latter part of this section. The author's use of this term is another indicator of the author's Hellenistic background as the word is relatively scarce in the Septuagint, but common in Hellenistic moralist circles. Cf. Attridge, *Hebrews* 242.

of the 'dead works' or sins which one has committed.[57] In both these instances, the author assumes that a cleansing of the flesh is not an effectual cleansing, as he confirms repeatedly by his intimations that the old covenant was not actually able to take away sins. This makes it clear that to the author the physical dimension of a person is not the truly significant aspect. The human body belongs to the realm of the transitory, material, earthly world. The important part of a human being is the spirit, which is that which is capable of reaching heaven, both in the present and in the coming world.

Throughout Hebrews, the author conceives of at least these two dimensions to human personality, namely, the body and the spirit. The role of the soul is more difficult to place, although it is interestingly used only of a person while 'in the body'. Ψυχή seems to be used only when the author is speaking of the encouragement or preservation of the recipients with respect to their need for endurance (6:19; 10:39; 12:3; 13:17).[58] On the other hand, πνεῦμα has an almost exclusively 'heavenly' connotation. Aside from the author's reference to the ability of God's word to divide soul and spirit (4:12), none of the other uses of 'spirit' in Hebrews seem to apply to human personality in general, but are limited to those righteous who have been 'perfected'. Its heavenly connotations thus allow it to carry the same overtones of alienation from the earthly realm which we have already noted.[59]

In 6:4, therefore, one of the images used of 'conversion' is that of tasting the heavenly gift, which is further described as partaking *of holy spirit*. Although the author likely alludes to *the* Holy Spirit, the absence of the article should not be passed over too hastily. The author uses the article quite consistently elsewhere when he refers to the Holy Spirit (3:7; 9:8; 10:15, 29). Here, the absence of the article highlights the nature of the thing rather than the specific thing itself.[60] The *heavenly* gift which is so exalted is a gift of spirit, and holy spirit no less. This verse thus seems to connect spirit and heaven. Further, the parallelism continues to describe

---

[57] One should be careful not to take dead works here as Paul's 'works of law' (e.g. Rom. 3:22; Gal. 2:16; so B. F. Westcott, *The Epistle to the Hebrews*, 3rd edn (London: Macmillan, 1903) 145; K. Nissilä, *Das Hohepriestermotiv im Hebräerbrief: Eine exegetische Untersuchung* (SFEG 33; Helsinki: Oy Liiton Kirjapaino, 1979) 190). The dead works here are that which is cleansed, namely, sinful acts.

[58] We should note that when Philo is showing his 'Stoic' side, he considers the larger portion of the soul to relate to a person's animal part, while for him the spirit is the 'soul's soul'. Cf. *Leg.* 1:11; *Det.* 167–8; *Agr.* 30; *QG* 1:75; *Her.* 55; *Spec.* 1:333.

[59] So also in Philo it is not all human spirits that reach to the heavens (e.g. *Somn.* 1:151; 2:133; *Praem.* 152).

[60] So also with the anarthrous υἱός in 1:2, 5:8 and 7:28.

this experience as a tasting of the good word of God and of the powers of the coming age. This implies once again an association between the Spirit of which believers partake and the heavenly realm, which is likely the sole realm of the coming age. Their spirits have been empowered by holy Spirit, which is but a taste of heavenly stuff and of that heavenly city toward which they are wandering.

This 'birth' of human spirit, so to speak, can also be seen in the paraenesis of 12:9. In this verse, the author contrasts the discipline which fathers *of flesh* administer with that of the father *of spirits*, that is, God. It is perhaps noteworthy here that God is only the father of his children; that is to say, the spirits of which God is father are only the spirits of his people. Hebrews does not emphasize πνεῦμα in a general psychological sense with reference to all humanity. The use of this phrase in Hebrews differs in this respect from the way it is used in Numbers, from which the author has borrowed it (16:22; 27:16). God disciplines the spirits of his 'sons', or children, so that they might live.[61] This demonstrates that the association of spirit with the heavenly realm is not a general correspondence but is limited to those who have partaken of the Christ. The only spirits which reach 'inside the veil' are those of the perfected.

Another connection in 12:9 is between spirit and life. The life here is presumably eternal, heavenly life, which the father of spirits is ensuring through his discipline. This life can be seen against the background of Heb. 2, where the author explains how Christ, by tasting death for all (2:9), transformed those who were subject to slavery all their lives because of the fear of death (2:15). The disciplining of the spirits of the people of God ensures that they will indeed be saved 'out of death' (5:7).

The author need not have spoken of God's discipline in this way. That he does so underlines the role that the contrast between flesh and spirit has in his thinking. It demonstrates a fundamental distinction in his mind between flesh as a part of the created realm and spirit as more at home in the heavenly realm.[62] So the author can not only encourage the readers on the basis of the foreignness of the earthly realm in a cosmological sense, he can urge them as well by implying that the physical and fleshly is not the most important part of the person. It is rather an aspect of humanity which will eventually be discarded with the created realm.

---

[61] For a comprehensive treatment of discipline in Heb. 12, see N. C. Croy, *Endurance in Suffering: Hebrews 12:1–13 in its Rhetorical, Religious, and Philosophical Context* (SNTSMS 98; Cambridge: Cambridge University Press, 1998).

[62] Remembering that spirit at this time was largely conceived in material terms as well, but as much thinner or even fiery material. See D. B. Martin, *The Corinthian Body* (New Haven, CT: Yale University Press, 1995) 3–37.

Another reference to the spirits of the people of God occurs in 12:23, where the recipients are said already to have come to the *heavenly* Jerusalem, to the assembly of the first born who have been enrolled *in the heavens*, and to the *spirits* of righteous ones who have been perfected. Once again, the connection between spirit and heaven is confirmed. The temporal element of this statement is blurred to include both events which are already past, such as the blood which sprinkles, and events which are future, such as God the judge. But all these events are connected to the consummation of the new covenant, both those aspects which have already been accomplished and those which will soon come to pass.

The author thus emphasizes the surety of them all with the perfect tense – 'you have come to' (12:22). 'The spirits of righteous ones who have been perfected', therefore, represents all of those who will be faithful and attain to the heavenly city. In one sense this perfection is accomplished already on earth in the spirits of those who have been sanctified by the sacrifice of Christ (10:14). But presumably this company also includes the heroes of faith from Heb. 11 who were not able to be perfected before Christ (11:40).[63] What is noteworthy for this study is the fact that physical bodies are in no way associated in the epistle in any way with this heavenly congregation, only the *spirits* of the righteous.[64]

A picture emerges of a basically dichotomous view of the person in Hebrews, namely, a body and a spirit. How exactly the spirit is to be conceived, for example in its relationship to the soul or to rationality, is difficult to delineate, given the sparse and allusive nature of the text in this regard. However, it is clear that it is distinct from the earthly body. The body is throughout associated with the transitory and temporary, while the spirit is the important aspect of humanity and the part which is potentially eternal. The body is thus mentioned either as a passing phase and perhaps even as a hindrance to righteousness.

Accordingly, death is only possible because of the physicality of a human being. And Heb. 2 focuses on death more than anything else as the focal problem that Christ solves.[65] Jesus is crowned with glory and honour through the suffering of death, so that he can taste death for all (2:9). He is perfected through suffering (2:10; 5:8–9) and partakes of flesh and blood with the express purpose of destroying the one who has the power of death, the Devil (2:14). The connection between the Devil and death as a function of corporeality provides a marked illustration

---

[63] Cf. Käsemann, *Wandering* 141f.

[64] The author never uses the language of Paul in 1 Cor. 15 when he speaks of a spiritual *body*, although it is possible that the occasion simply did not present itself.

[65] For a more general discussion, see my *Understanding* 24–39.

of the relationship between embodiment and the need for redemption in the author's mind. It was of no mean value to the author that his text of Psalm 40 read that God had prepared a *body* for Christ (10:5). This was the essence of what the heavenly high priest needed in order to be a proper sacrifice, and Christ speaks of this corporeality as he enters *into the world*, making an implicit connection between embodiment and the created realm. Christ frees from the fear of death by defeating the one who has power over bodies and opens up the possibility of endless life (2:15).

Christ's victory over death is also one of the most highlighted aspects of the superiority of his high priesthood in Heb. 7. Although this chapter states that Christ was 'without beginning of days' in some way (7:3), it focuses particularly on the fact that he has no end of life and that Christ remains a priest forever (7:3). The Levitical priests are hindered in their service, because they die (7:8, 23). This is not a problem for the heavenly high priest, because he always lives to intercede for his people (7:8, 25). Christ is according to the likeness of Melchizedek, an order which is characterized by 'indestructible' life, a life which is explicitly contrasted with the Law consisting of *fleshly* commandments (7:16).

He offers himself through 'eternal spirit', which could very well refer as much to his own everlasting life as to the Holy Spirit (9:14).[66] Regardless of how one takes this odd expression, it is certainly meant to contrast the generally fleshly orientation of the earthly sacrificial system in contrast to the spiritual orientation of Christ's sacrifice. Although there may be some sense in which immortality is implied in all these passages, the most important element of the argument is that Christ does not die like earthly priests do. He, on the contrary, has been saved 'out of death' (5:7). This sometimes unrecognized aspect of the author's soteriology demonstrates the connection between the Devil, death and corporeality. Something about the earthly realm and creation implies sin and death and, therefore, the need for redemption. Accordingly, 13:3 can urge sympathy for those who are in prison and who are treated badly, since the readers are also 'in the body' and can thus understand those challenges which come because of physicality.

Likely related to Hebrews' contrast between flesh and spirit is the *rational* orientation that peeks through from time to time in its rhetoric.

---

[66] Attridge, *Hebrews* 251, writes, 'the spirit here most likely refers to Christ and to the interior or spiritual quality of his sacrificial act'. On the other hand, perhaps Hebrews is saying something akin to the odd anarthrous construction in Rom. 1:4. For the history of this verse's interpretation, see J. J. McGrath, *Through Eternal Spirit: An Historical Study of the Exegesis of Hebrews 9:13–14* (Rome: Pontificia Universitas Gregoriana, 1961).

Although it is not completely clear what the connection between rationality and human spirit was for the author, it seems quite possible that they were overlapping categories.[67] The author repeatedly indicates the importance of 'rationality' in defining both sin and salvation. We have already encountered the term 'conscience' in relation to that which is cleansed in contrast to the flesh. As 10:2 and 3 make clear, συνείδησις is conceived by the author largely in cognitive terms and is (at least in these verses) best translated 'consciousness'. Thus the sacrifices of the old covenant were never able to perfect those who drew near, 'since otherwise, would they not have stopped offering them, because they would no longer have had any *consciousness* of sins, those who worship having been cleansed once and for all? But in these sacrifices is a *remembrance* of sins yearly.' The parallelism between συνείδησις and 'remembrance' demonstrates that the conscience is primarily conceived in these verses as that rational faculty which remembers past sins.[68]

In addition to the rational flavour of conscience, the author's conception of sin itself also has a rational taste. No doubt following well-developed tradition, the author uses the image of 'enlightenment' twice in reference to conversion (6:4; 10:32), and he makes the striking claim that the Day of Atonement only provided for 'sins committed in ignorance' (9:7), something which not even Philo taught.[69] This image of wilful sin in the light of knowledge occurs again at 10:26, where the author notes that wilful sinning after one has received a *knowledge* of the truth exhausts the effectiveness of Christ's sacrifice. The author's use of Jer. 31:31–4 (38:31–4 LXX) in Heb. 8 also highlights the fact that in the new covenant, God will place his laws upon the *minds* of his people, a fact the author emphasizes by his inclusion of the same verses in his recap of the citation in 10:16–17. In the new covenant, God's people will no longer need to teach one another about the Lord, because everyone will *know* him, from the smallest to the greatest (8:11). Further, the perfect in that covenant have disciplined their *senses* so that they might be able to *discern* good and evil (5:14).[70] All of these images have strong rational overtones. Perhaps it is no coincidence that the author uses lengthy theological exposition in

---

[67] Philo can speak of mind as the heavenly part of the soul, the soul of the soul (*Opif.* 66; *Gig.* 60; *Deus* 46; *Plant.* 18; *Congr.* 97; *Somn.* 1:34, 146; *Spec.* 3:207) just as he can speak of spirit as the soul of the soul (see n. 57 above). Mind and spirit proper thus are basically interchangeable for Philo.

[68] For historical background on the term συνείδησις, see C. A. Pierce, *Conscience in the New Testament* (Chicago: Allenson, 1955).

[69] Attridge, *Hebrews* 239, draws attention to *Post.* 48 and *Spec.* 2:196.

[70] Cf. 4 Macc. 2:23.

order to exhort his readers to endure. For him, there is a natural connection between knowledge and action.

I am now in a position to summarize the 'psychological' contrast between flesh and spirit in Hebrews in terms of the cosmological distinction between the created realm and heaven. First of all, it should be noted that, while there is a one-to-one correspondence between the fleshly and the created, earthly realm, there is only a correspondence between the spirits of the *righteous* and heaven. When spirit is contrasted with flesh in Hebrews, it is always done either in terms of Christ or of those who have been perfected through his sacrifice, having offered himself through an eternal spirit. Although Hebrews has a clearly rational flavour, the mind does not automatically belong to the heavenly realm.

On the other hand, those who have partaken of Christ are able, through his intercession, to reach heaven and penetrate 'inside the veil' (9:19; 10:20). The faithful are thus exhorted repeatedly to 'draw near' to the heavenly realm. So while the spirit of an individual does not automatically attain to the heavenly realm, heaven is certainly where the spirit finds its most appropriate place. The material seems to be the tool by which the Devil is able to hold the power of death, first over the body, but by inference over the spirit as well.

The spirit of a 'son of God', therefore, 'has partaken' of a body (2:14), just as Christ figuratively declared as he entered the world, 'you prepared a body for me'. However, to be 'in the body' is a temporary state which does not represent the individual in his or her truest self. The 'fleshliness' of the Levitical priests and their sacrifices contrasts with the indestructible life and eternal spirit of Christ. God is the father of spirit, a far higher paternity than that of the fathers of flesh. The flesh is just another aspect of the corporeal, created realm which is destined to be destroyed. Although the flesh/spirit contrast may not tell us much about heaven, it confirms my previous conclusions about the created realm.

God's purpose in creation

In ch. 3, I discussed the continuity between the old and new covenants in terms of the constant purpose of God. There, I argued that the story of salvation history was always destined to move toward the atonement provided by Christ, who represents the wisdom and purpose of God. We can note in Hebrews the recurrence of phrases of necessity and suitability with regards to the plan and purpose of God, indicating a certain '*logos*' to the world. The old age and covenant was not an aberration, but rather an intended part of salvation history. Earlier in this chapter I mentioned that the wisdom 'hymn' of 1:3 applies most of all to the exalted Christ as the fulfilment of God's purpose for humanity. These aspects of salvation history are God's *logos* for salvation, and remember the recurrent use of speaking imagery in Hebrews. God's speaking includes Christ, but is not limited to him.

But how does this continuity in salvation history relate to the creation? Correspondingly, what is the relationship between Christ and the creation? The author does not speak of a Fall or of any particular cause of the need for redemption from the created realm, although it may simply not have been to the author's purpose to mention such on this occasion. If the author stands in some relation to the Pauline circle, perhaps we can infer Paul's sense of Adam as the origin of sin and death.[71] The gaps the author has left in the text preclude any certain answer to these questions. On the other hand, it is intriguing that the author speaks of the need for redemption 'from the foundation of the world' (9:26). If taken literally, this comment implies a need for atonement from the very creation, as if corporeality and the created realm are intrinsically sinful. Perhaps we should rather take the comment as hyperbole or perhaps a fascinating revelation of the author's underlying biases.

The author did likely see a kind of *logos* to the plot of salvation history. I begin with the observation that the creative role of Christ in creation is not as clear as one might think in Hebrews. Verses such as 1:2 and 1:10–12 do speak of Christ either as the creator of the world or as the agent of creation, but these are highly poetic contexts and the only instances in the epistle where Christ is connected to creation. In contrast, a number of passages speak rather of God as creator, 2:10 in particular.[72] Here, it is stated that *it was fitting* for God, for whom and *through whom* the All was created, to perfect Jesus through sufferings.[73] This verse seems to imply a certain *logos* of God in his governance of the creation. It suggests that God was the one for whom the creation exists and that he was the one through whom the creation exists. What is interesting here is the fact that God is the one 'through whom' the universe exists in distinction from Jesus. This use of the phrase 'through whom' is thus interestingly different from the same statement in 1:2, where the phrase refers to Christ.

---

[71] I work through what this option might look like in *Understanding* 24–39.

[72] For a more detailed exploration of this issue, see my 'Keeping his Appointment'.

[73] G. E. Sterling parses these differences by seeing Hebrews sometimes using more Middle Platonic, at other times more Stoic formulas in its prepositions ('Prepositional Metaphysics in Jewish Wisdom Speculation and Early Christological Hymns', *SPhA* 9 (1997) 233). Here he would say that the Stoic categories are in use.

In 2:10, in distinction from 1:2, *Christ is not connected with the act of creation, but with the purpose of God in creation.* There is something about the way in which God made the world which made it appropriate for Christ to redeem humanity from the death associated with their corporality. While the appropriateness of such salvation could be taken to refer to the desirableness of the *restoration* of God's original intent, it could rather denote the final *fulfilment* of God's purposes. What I mean is that this verse could be taken to imply that God always had Christ in mind as the mediator of salvation for the creation, that the created realm was destined for destruction from its very inception. Christ would thus be the *logos* and wisdom of God in creation more than the actual agent of creation.

The expression δι' οὗ in and of itself seems to reflect a kind of 'metaphysics of prepositions' which was common in our period, being used in places of the 'instrumental' cause of some particular effect.[74] When one applies this usage to Heb. 1:2 and takes my interpretation of 2:10 into account, an interesting picture begins to form. Christ is indeed the one 'through whom' the worlds were created, but this is primarily as God's wisdom, his *logos* for the world. Such a construal is supported by the immediate allusion to Wis. 7:26 which follows, where Christ is related to the wisdom of God. The application of Ps. 102 to Christ, therefore, not only emphasizes his everlasting existence, but also implies the connection between the Christ who lasts forever and the transient creation whose purpose he completes. The above is at least a possible way of reading the language which speaks of Christ as the agent of creation.

Hebrews thus remains highly ambiguous with regard to Christ's preexistence. On the whole, Christ's relation to creation seems more profound than that of a simple artificer. Outside Heb. 1, Christ is never presented in the role of creator. We see this phenomenon not only in 2:10 where God in distinction from Jesus is the one through whom the All was made, but we see it also in 3:4 where it is *God* who has constructed (κατασκευάζω) everything and 4:3 where *God* has rested since the foundation of the world. Finally, 11:3 states that the worlds were framed

---

[74] So W. Theiler, *Die Vorbereitung des Neuplatonismus* (Berlin: Weidmann, 1930) 31–7 and T. H. Tobin, *The Creation of Man: Philo and the History of Interpretation* (CBQMS 14; Washington, DC: Catholic Biblical Association of America, 1983) 63f. Tobin notes that phrases such as τὸ ὑφ' οὗ and τὸ δι' οὗ, found in writers like Seneca, Aetius and Varro, were commonplaces used in distinguishing the causes which originally derive from Aristotle. Tobin argues that *Cher.* 125–7 in fact derives from pre-Philonic material. This text speaks of the *logos* as the instrument δι' οὗ the world was created, while God was the one ὑφ' οὗ it was made. See also Sterling's article now mentioned in n. 72.

(καταρτίζω) by the ῥῆμα *of God*. The consistency of these references pushes us toward seeing the language of Christ's agency in creation as metaphorical in nature, the pre-existent Christ as a metonym for some function of God, perhaps his wisdom.

It is thus possible that the current state of the creation, its inferiority and destined annihilation, is not the result of something gone awry. While the author may simply not tell us of Adam's sin, it is also possible that these characteristics of the created realm served some purpose in God's plan from its foundation, as was the atoning role of Christ as 'high priest' and redeemer. Psalm 8 becomes both Christological and anthropological to an even more significant degree. It is at one and the same time understood in both ways, for the destined glory intended for humanity was always planned under the mediation of Christ, for whom the psalm would apply most fully.

Conclusion

The 'setting' of the created realm in the plot of salvation history seems to have certain clear associations for the author. In the first place, the created realm is clearly inferior. Its associations are with the old age and the old covenant, with the fleshly and imperfect. It is the realm of physicality where the Devil holds the power of death. I have drawn attention to the importance of Christ's 'life' and living for the author, an often missed element in the author's soteriology. Christ's defeat of death is clearly important for the author. Meanwhile, this earth is a place where the people of God are only foreigners and strangers (11:13). All of these associations, while not marking the created realm as evil, are deprecatory and indicate a clear and innate inferiority.

Another significant aspect of the author's argument is his contention that the created realm will eventually be removed. Some scholars at this point picture an apocalyptic renewal of the creation or a replacement of the old created realm with a new heaven and earth. But if this is the case, the author is unclear about it at best. The text gives us no reason to believe anything but that the created realm will be irrevocably removed. The author distinguishes between the shakeable created realm and the unshakeable dwelling place of God. In his rhetoric, the former is removed and only the latter remains.

The author's flesh/spirit distinction also seems instructive. While we must infer much of the author's perspective on this issue, it seems possible to construct a picture in which spirit is primarily associated (1) with the sons of God and (2) with the heavenly realm where God is. Hebrews gives us no sense of a spiritual *body*, but the spirit of a person alone seems to relate to heaven. Part of this consistent contrast is likely Hebrews' penchant to process sin and conscience in epistemological terms. Sin is a matter of ignorance, and the notion of sin after one has received knowledge of the truth is contradictory. On the other hand, some of the most Platonic sounding imagery in Hebrews proves not to be straightforwardly Platonic in the way sometimes supposed.

Finally, I speculated on the function and nature of the creation within the purposes of God. Gaps in meaning preclude a full understanding of the author's thought, and it is possible that the author saw Adam as the culprit behind the current state of the created realm. On the other hand, it is also possible that the author believed God had planned the redemption of the creation through Christ from the 'foundation of the world'. It may also be the case that he only viewed Christ as the agent of the creation in a figurative, soteriological way, namely, in the sense that he functions to bring the created order to the fullness of its purpose. Christ as the wisdom of God for the creation is thus metonymically referred to as the creator. Hebrews gives us conflicting signals in its language of Christ as creator.

Therefore, the created realm is the setting of the old covenant and is likely related in a fundamental way to its inferiority. There is something intrinsically obstructive to the earthly realm, whether it be the result of a 'Fall' or simply an assumption of the author's world-view. In contrast, the heavenly realm is intrinsically associated with the permanent and complete, the goal of all human existence. The former is an 'opponent' in the structuralist sense, while the latter is the setting for the *denouement*, attained through the story's 'helper', Christ.

6

THE HEAVENLY TABERNACLE
IN HEBREWS

Introduction

The previous chapter discussed several aspects of Hebrews' cosmology, particularly in relation to the way the created realm functions as a 'setting' for the story of salvation history. One of the most striking observations in that chapter was that Hebrews gives no sense that the created heavens and earth will be replaced after their 'removal', after their 'shaking'. If we go only on that which Hebrews explicitly tells us, we will conclude that the earth is removed in the judgement, and only the true heaven beyond the created skies will remain. In addition, the spirit of one who has been perfected is associated with the heavenly realm, while the body seems intrinsically associated with the earthly realm. These factors give a somewhat Hellenistic feel to the epistle and reflect a significant divergence both from the rest of the New Testament and much Jewish literature of the period. We have also noted possible overtones of some sort of *logos* theology on the part of the author, although we have also noted differences between the author and Philo.

In this chapter I complete my picture of Hebrews' cosmology with a discussion of heaven and all that is associated with it. Of principal importance is the heavenly tabernacle in Hebrews. The nature of the heavenly tabernacle has long been a matter of debate, and we cannot at present speak of any consensus on its precise character or background. Indeed, the nature of the heavenly tabernacle has been the focal issue in arguments over the most appropriate background against which to read this sermon. As such, we remind ourselves of the method and caveats set forth at the beginning of this study.

In terms of caveats, we must first not assume that Hebrews draws on a single ideological background for its imagery. Second, we must take into account the rhetorical nature of Hebrews' arguments involving a heavenly tabernacle. We should not assume that such imagery is used uniformly.

Accordingly, in terms of method we must (1) rigorously allow the text to generate its own categories with regard to the tabernacle and (2) we must understand these categories in light of the sermon's overall rhetorical agenda, an agenda I have unfolded throughout this investigation. To this end, we begin with a close look at the way Hebrews uses the expression τὰ ἅγια, demonstrating that the key passages use it in reference to the holy of holies. The second and more challenging task is to determine the precise referent of σκηνή in the sermon. I will conclude that the term usually refers to the tent as a whole, with a few notable exceptions where the author specifies differently. In the process of examining σκηνή, I will run through the relevant passages, considering three major suggestions for the nature of the heavenly tent in Heb. 8–10, namely: (1) a literal structure in heaven, (2) a reference to multilayered heavens, and (3) a metaphor for the highest heaven itself. I will also examine the term οὐρανός in Hebrews, concluding that it can refer either to the created heavens or to the true heaven where the 'throne of grace' is. As we move through the text, we will begin to sense that the heavenly tent is more than a simple metaphor for any one thing and that the idea of a literal structure in heaven certainly cannot adequately account for the author's overall references.

In the end, if we had to choose a single metaphorical referent for the heavenly tabernacle, heaven itself seems to come closest. A close examination of the author's argument pushes us away from any sense of a literal structure in heaven. However, Hebrews' use of the tabernacle in its argument resists the identification of any single metaphorical referent. Ultimately, the tabernacle must be understood for the role it plays in the author's overall *high priestly metaphor*, where it serves as that superior sacred space in which Christ offers his sacrifice in contrast to any earthly sanctuary corresponding to the Levitical cultus. As such, to ask what the heavenly tabernacle represents independent of its place in this overall metaphor tends to skew one's answer from the very outset of the investigation.

τὰ ἅγια

The term ἅγιος is used eighteen times in the Epistle to the Hebrews. Of these occurrences, ten refer in some way either to the heavenly or earthly tabernacle or to a part thereof. All references use the word in the plural, with the exception of 9:1, where the term τὸ ἅγιον is used of the earthly sanctuary as a whole. Most of the remaining incidences arguably refer to the inner sanctuary of the two-part tabernacle, whether it be heavenly or earthly, as the majority of interpreters would agree.[1] The clearest association between the neuter plural of ἅγιος and the second room of the tabernacle occurs in 9:25. Here it is said that Christ does not offer himself frequently, 'as the high priest enters into τὰ ἅγια yearly with the blood of another'. The reference is clearly to the Day of Atonement as mentioned in conjunction with the 'second tent' in 9:7. Since the high priest is singled out and the reference is to a yearly activity, as in 9:7, τὰ ἅγια here clearly refers to the inner sanctum of the earthly tabernacle. Accordingly, it is only natural that ἅγια in the previous verse (9:24) also refer to the holy of holies in the heavenly tabernacle.[2]

It seems likely that Hebrews' other references to entrance into τὰ ἅγια refer also to the holy of holies. For example, 9:12 states that Christ entered εἰς τὰ ἅγια after he had found an eternal redemption. The parallel to 9:7 and 24–5 imply once more that the author refers to the holy of holies. Hebrews 13:11 similarly speaks of the entrance of the high priest εἰς τὰ ἅγια with the blood of animals,[3] and 10:19 encourages the recipients of the epistle also to have boldness in the entrance τῶν ἁγίων. These

---

[1] Some who believe the term τὰ ἅγια to refer consistently to the inner shrine include O. Hofius, *Der Vorhang vor dem Thron Gottes: Eine exegetisch-religionsgeschichtliche Untersuchung zu Hebräer 6,19 f. und 10,19 f.* (WUNT 14; Tübingen: Mohr/Siebeck, 1972) 57; N. H. Young, 'The Gospel According to Hebrews 9', *NTS* 27 (1981) 198; H. Löhr, 'Thronversammlung und preisender Tempel: Beobachtungen am himmlischen Heiligtum im Hebräerbrief und in den Sabbatopferliedern aus Qumran', *Königsherrschaft Gottes und himmlischer Welt im Judentum, Urchristentum und in der hellenistischen Welt.* Ed. by M. Hengel and A. M. Schwemer (Tübingen: Mohr/Siebeck, 1991) 190–91; and H. W. Attridge, *The Epistle to the Hebrews* (Philadelphia: Fortress Press, 1989) 233 n.46, 240.

[2] M. Rissi has argued that it designates 'das *ganze* Zeltheiligtum samt allen gottesdienstlichen Geräten darin' (*Die Theologie des Hebräerbriefs: Ihre Verankerung in der Situation des Verfassers und seiner Leser* (WUNT 41; Tübingen: Mohr/Siebeck, 1987) 38). He bases his conclusion both on the absence of the article, present in every other reference to the inner shrine except 9:3, as well as on the fact that the verse mentions the cleansing of all the heavenly items in correspondence to all the earthly things mentioned in 9:21. However, the author was not comparing the precise things that are sprinkled (e.g. 'the book and all the people' (9:10) or 'the tent and all the vessels of worship' (9:21)), only comparing the need for each sanctuary to be cleansed in general. Others who have taken Rissi's position include E. Riggenbach, *Der Brief an die Hebräer* (KNT 14; Leipzig: Deichert, 1922) 284; O. Michel, *Der Brief an die Hebräer*, 14th edn (MeyerK 13; Göttingen: Vandenhoeck & Ruprecht, 1984) 323f.; O. Kuss, *Der Brief an die Hebräer und die katholischen Briefe*, 2nd edn (RNT 8.1; Regensburg: Pustet, 1966) 125f.; A. P. Salom, 'ΤΑ ΑΓΙΑ in the Epistle to the Hebrews', *AUSS* 5 (1967) 64f., 67–9; H-F. Weiss, *Der Brief an die Hebräer* (MeyerK 13; Göttingen: Vandenhoeck & Ruprecht, 1991) 486 n.46.

[3] Hofius notes that Hebrews uses the plural here instead of the singular in the text to which the author alludes, Lev. 16:27 (ὧν τὸ αἷμα εἰσηνέχθη ἐξιλάσασθαι ἐν τῷ ἁγίῳ, ἐξοίσουσιν αὐτὰ ἔξω τῆς παρεμβολῆς καὶ κατακαύσουσιν αὐτὰ ἐν πυρί . . .), indicating a tendency on the author's part to give the plural rather than the singular (*Vorhang* 57 n.60; So also Löhr, 'Thronversammlung' 191).

instances strongly imply that the author used τὰ ἅγια consistently to refer to the inner, most holy part of the tabernacle, whether heavenly or earthly.

The one incidence in which the word clearly refers to the outer tent occurs in 9:2, where the first tent is deemed Ἅγια in distinction from the second, which is the Ἅγια Ἁγίων. This reading in itself is actually disputed in the manuscripts but otherwise conforms to the general practice of the Hebrew Bible, diverging only in its use of the plural instead of the singular.[4] Otfried Hofius suggests the change is 'keineswegs ungewöhnlich, da im judengriechischen Sprachgebrauch für das Heilige τὸ ἅγιον und τὰ ἅγια, für das Allerheiligste τὸ ἅγιον τῶν ἁγίων und τὰ ἅγια τῶν ἁγίων nebeneinander gebräuchlich sind'.[5] This divergence from the author's usual pattern (taking the reading given) is not overly significant, since the author is simply following more traditional nomenclature.

Only one other instance remains where the meaning of τὰ ἅγια might be in question, namely 8:2, where Christ is 'a minister τῶν ἁγίων and of the true tent, which the Lord pitched, not a human'. This verse serves as a good transition to the following section, where I examine the meaning of σκηνή in Hebrews. Following the precedent established above, it is most likely that τὰ ἅγια in 8:2 is another reference to the holy of holies, where Christ enters to offer atonement and is seated at the right hand of God. It consequently seems quite possible that 'true tent' in 8:2 is an equivalent expression for τὰ ἅγια, implying that the author thought of the heavenly tent simply as a holy of holies without an outer chamber.

ἡ σκηνή

The heavenly tabernacle is one of the topics in Hebrews that has generated great interest over time, and we cannot as yet speak of any real consensus on its precise character. To be sure, the referent in many cases seems clear enough.[6] When the author speaks of Moses 'about to erect the tent', for

---

[4] Attridge suggests that the reading of 𝔓46 (ἅγια ἁγίων and ἅγια, i.e. the reverse of the published text) was the original and proposes an interpretation of Num. 4:17–20 which might justify such a construal (*Hebrews* 233–4, 236–8). Even if the usual reading is original, however, my case for the other references to ἅγια stands. In any case, the use of the plural for the singular is similar to what the author has done in 13:11.

[5] *Vorhang* 56–7. Hofius here follows G. Schrenk, 'ἱερός κτλ.', *TDNT* 3, G. Kittel, ed., vol. 3 (Grand Rapids, MI: Eerdmans, 1965) 234, who notes that Philo can use τὰ ἅγια of everything in the temple precincts (*Det.* 62; *Fug.* 93; *Leg.* 3:135; *Somn.* 1:207; *Spec.* 1:115; *Mos.* 2:114, 155) or of the first sanctuary (*Her.* 226; *Spec.* 1:296), while the holy of holies is also plural when depicted as τὰ ἅγια τῶν ἁγίων (*Leg.* 2.56; *Mut.* 192).

[6] While 11:9 may have overtones of the transience of the earthly tent while waiting for a true home, it clearly speaks of the tents in which the patriarchs camped and thus is not included in the study which follows.

example, he most likely refers to the entire earthly tabernacle (8:5), as he does in 9:21 when he speaks of Moses sprinkling the tent by way of its inauguration.[7] Therefore, 13:10 probably refers to the service of the whole earthly tabernacle[8] and 8:2 to the whole heavenly tent, whatever it might be.

The use of σκηνή in 9:2, 3 and 6 requires more discussion. Hebrews 9:2 and 6 seem to use πρώτη unambiguously to refer to the first part of the tabernacle *as a first tent*. Similarly, 9:3's use of 'after the second veil' seems to indicate a similar reference to the holy of holies *as a second tent*. Nevertheless, this conclusion has been called into question by Hofius and others.[9] Hofius has claimed that language such as that of Hebrews is not without precedence, noting Josephus, *Jewish Wars* 5:193–5, where he speaks of the δεύτερον ἱερόν in reference to the court of the Gentiles as opposed to the outermost court.[10] Hofius concludes that the phrase in Hebrews has the idiomatic sense of 'der zweite Teil (Raum) des Zeltes' rather than 'the second tent'. Hebrews does not, in his opinion, refer to the two parts of the tabernacle as two *separate* entities, but simply to the first and second parts of the *one* tabernacle, thereby making cosmological interpretations of the tabernacle less likely.

In 9:3, however, the adjective *second* does not actually modify the word *tent*.[11] Rather, the author simply states that after the second veil, there was 'a tent, namely, the one which was called "holy of holies"'. Even the word order (as in 9:2 of the first tent) is arranged in such a way as to highlight the fact that these are two tents, placing σκηνή first on its own, in order to set the argument up for the conclusion to come in 9:8![12] That this is the case is definitively shown in 9:3, since the author refers to the holy of holies as a tent in its own right (not as the 'second tent'). Even the so-called idiom in Josephus is not unambiguous – it is

---

[7] If 9:21 refers only to the outer tent, then Moses would not be sprinkling the holy of holies in the inaugural ceremony. Further, the ὑποδείγματα of the realities in the heavens in 9:23 (which is reminiscent of 8:5) seem to include more than the inner sanctum (as is implied in 9:24) even if they point to it more than to the outer chamber.

[8] H. Koester would be a rare exception to this interpretation, since he takes this reference in its 'direct meaning' to refer to the 'outer part of the tabernacle of the wilderness (= πρώτη σκηνή 9.2,6), never the tabernacle as a whole!' ('Outside the Camp', *HTR* 55 (1962) 309). As we shall see, exactly the opposite seems to be the case.

[9] Hofius, *Vorhang* 61, and more recently Attridge, *Hebrews* 232, and W. L. Lane, *Hebrews 9–13* (Dallas: Word Books, 1991) 219.

[10] As opposed to the outermost court (τοῦ πρώτου, 5:195). Josephus, therefore, does not refer here to the two 'houses' (5:208) of the temple!

[11] As even Attridge notes, *Hebrews* 232 n.27.

[12] The normal attributive construction would place an article on σκηνή as well: ἡ σκηνή ἡ λεγομένη Ἅγια Ἁγίων.

not used of the inner and outer parts of the sanctuary. In the end, it seems more likely that the author is deliberately referring to the two parts of the tabernacle as a first tent and a second tent, each in their own right, in order to prepare for the argument he will make in 9:8. So the author's use of σκηνή seems fairly straightforward in a number of instances. The above occurrences alone demonstrate that the author can use the term either of the individual sections of the earthly tent or of the tabernacle as a whole, although when unqualified it tends to refer to the structure as a whole. However, significant debate has followed the two remaining references. Two of the major interpretations of the tabernacle have their respective strongholds in these two verses.

Hebrews 9:8

Lincoln Hurst has taken this verse as a reference to the first, earthly tent as a whole, rather than as that which the immediate context seems to suggest, namely, the first tent in the two-part tabernacle.[13] On the other hand, B. F. Westcott put it well when he noted that 'it is difficult to suppose that it [σκηνή] should be suddenly used in another sense' when it has just referred to the Holy Place.[14] I conclude not only that such is in fact the reference, but that Hurst has accordingly missed much of the author's point in this part of his argument.

The contrast in 9:6–7 is between the continual ministry of the regular priests in the outer tent and the once-a-year entry of the high priest into the second tent. The author makes this spatial distinction into an eschatological contrast between the first covenant, with its multiplicity of sacrifice and imperfection, and the second one, with its one-time offering leading to perfection. The first tent becomes a parable of this present

---

[13] *The Epistle to the Hebrews: Its Background of Thought* (SNTSMS 65; Cambridge: Cambridge University Press, 1990) 26–7; as also J. Moffatt (probably), *The Epistle to the Hebrews* (Edinburgh: T&T Clark, 1924) 117–18; J. Héring, *The Epistle to the Hebrews* (London: Epworth, 1970 (1954)) 74; A. Cody, *Heavenly Sanctuary and Liturgy in the Epistle to the Hebrews: The Achievement of Salvation in the Epistle's Perspectives* (St Meinrad, IN: Grail, 1960) 147–8; and F. F. Bruce, *The Epistle to the Hebrews* (Grand Rapids, MI: Eerdmans, 1964) 194–5.

[14] *The Epistle to the Hebrews*, 3rd edn (London: Macmillan, 1903) 252. Others who have seen the immediate reference of 'first tent' as the first part of the tabernacle include S. G. Sowers, *The Hermeneutics of Philo and Hebrews: A Comparison of the Interpretation of the Old Testament in Philo Judaeus and the Epistle to the Hebrews* (Richmond: John Knox, 1965) 94–5; R. J. McKelvey, *The New Temple: The Church in the New Testament* (London: Oxford University Press, 1969) 148; G. Theissen, *Untersuchungen zum Hebräerbrief* (SNT 2; Gütersloh: Mohn, 1969) 69–70; Hofius, *Vorhang* 62; G. MacRae, 'Heavenly Temple and Eschatology in the Letter to the Hebrews', *Semeia* 12 (1978) 189; Attridge, *Hebrews* 240; Lane, *Hebrews 9–13* 223; Weiss, *Hebräer* 457.

age, which involves multiplicity and imperfection (and, in fact, the whole of the earthly tent), while the 'one-time' nature of the new age is also implied by the second, inner sanctuary. Such a reading explains why the author says that the way *into the holy of holies* (τὴν τῶν ἁγίων ὁδόν), the second part of the tabernacle,[15] is not apparent while the 'first tent', the outer tent, has στάσις. This interpretation also explains why the author speaks of the tabernacle as being composed of a 'first' and 'second' tent in the first place.[16] Hurst's explanation cannot account for the train of thought nearly as well.[17]

The meaning of 9:8–9 accordingly plays out on two principal levels. The first is the plain reference to the first and second halves of the two-part earthly tabernacle. The second and parabolic meaning is eschatological. The two tents represent the two ages and the two covenants. Access into God's presence was not possible in the old age or under the old covenant.[18] As long as the old age and covenant are afforded the status the recipients seem to be tempted to give it, the way into the holy of holies is not apparent.[19]

It is important to note the way in which the author formulates this contrast between the two ages. In the former age, the cultic ministry had not been able to perfect the worshipper in terms of their consciousness of sins but had rather consisted of 'ordinances of flesh' (9:10). The author's primary interest is not in the structure of the tabernacle, whether heavenly or earthly. Rather, the author is interested in humanity reaching its appropriate state in relation to God, which is full acceptability and access to his presence. Nevertheless, the author assumes certain things about the two ages and two tabernacles in his contrast. The domain of the

[15] As I have argued in the preceding section, τά ἅγια regularly refers to the inner sanctum.

[16] So also C. Koester, *The Dwelling of God: The Tabernacle in the Old Testament, Intertestamental Jewish Literature, and the New Testament* (CBQMS 22; Washington, DC: Catholic Biblical Association of America, 1989) 158: '[B]y using these words the author was able to associate the first and second parts of the tabernacle with the first and second covenants'. Hurst's construal misses the significance of this nomenclature.

[17] How, for example, does the basic distinction between the respective functioning of the two parts of the tabernacle lead *in the argument of ch. 9* to the conclusion that the way into the heavenly holy of holies is not apparent while the whole earthly tent possesses στάσις? In contrast, my reading leads naturally to such a 'parabolic' conclusion.

[18] Hofius has drawn our attention to a relevant passage in Josephus (*Vorhang* 63): τὴν δὲ τρίτην μοῖραν μόνῳ περιέγραψε τῷ θεῷ διὰ τὸ καὶ τὸν οὐρανὸν ἀνεπίβατον εἶναι ἀνθρώποις (*Ant.* 3:181). So also Philo in *Mos.* 2:95 locates the ark, ἐν ἀδύτῳ καὶ ἀβάτῳ τῶν καταπετασμάτων εἴσω.

[19] I accept Attridge's observation that the phrase ἔχειν στάσις is somewhat of an idiom for having a certain status or honour (*Hebrews* 240, n.127), as seen in references such as Plato's *Phaedr.* 253D and Epictetus' *Diss.* 1.21.1. However, the ultimate way in which the old age will lose its 'standing' is in its termination.

earthly tabernacle is the realm of flesh, in conjunction with my findings in ch. 5 that the old age is associated throughout with the created realm and with flesh. The domain of the true holy of holies, on the other hand, is the realm of spirit, as I have shown in the previous chapter. This is the domain in which God's presence dwells.[20]

This way of thinking on the part of the author suggests another possible dimension to the contrast between the outer and inner courts of the tabernacle, although one about which we cannot conclude with certainty. It is possible that the author at times draws on a cosmological interpretation of the tabernacle in his argument.[21] This interpretation sees the earthly tabernacle as a representation of the cosmos as a whole and is well summed up by Josephus:

> Εἰ γάρ τις τῆς σκηνῆς κατανοήσειε τὴν πῆξιν καὶ τοῦ ἱερέως ἴδοι τὴν στολὴν τά τε σκεύη . . . τόν τε νομοθέτην εὑρήσει θεῖον ἄνδρα . . . ἕκαστα γὰρ τούτων εἰς ἀπομίμησιν καὶ διατύπωσιν τῶν ὅλων . . . τήν τε γὰρ σκηνὴν τριάκοντα πηχῶν οὖσαν νείμας εἰς τρία καὶ δύο μέρη πᾶσιν ἀνεὶς τοῖς ἱερεῦσιν ὥσπερ βέβηλόν τινα καὶ κοινὸν τόπον, τὴν γῆν καὶ τὴν θάλασσαν ἀποσημαίνει· καὶ γὰρ ταῦτα πᾶσίν ἐστιν ἐπίβατα· τὴν δὲ τρίτην μοῖραν μόνῳ περιέγραψε τῷ θεῷ διὰ τὸ καὶ τὸν οὐρανὸν ἀνεπίβατον εἶναι ἀνθρώποις.[22]   (*Ant.* 3:180–1)

This cosmological interpretation sees the outer court as representing the earth (or the earth and the sea in Josephus' rendition), while the inner

---

[20] So also C. Koester, *Dwelling* 158–9.

[21] Those who think that the two-part tabernacle may (at least at certain points in the author's argument) be analogous to the cosmos in some way include D. A. Seeberg, *Der Brief an die Hebräer* (Leipzig: Quelle & Meyer, 1912) 96; R. Gyllenberg, 'Die Christologie des Hebräerbriefes', *ZST* 11 (1934) 675; E. Käsemann, *The Wandering People of God: An Investigation of the Letter to the Hebrews* (Minneapolis: Augsburg, 1984 (1957)) 209, 223f.; F. J. Schierse, *Verheissung und Heilsvollendung: Zur theologischen Grundfrage des Hebräerbriefes* (MThS.H 9; Munich: Zink, 1955) 168ff.; H. Montefiore, *The Epistle to the Hebrews* (London: A. & C. Black, 1964) 136–7; Sowers, *Hermeneutics* 106f.; Kuss, *Hebräer* 115ff.; F. Schröger, *Der Verfasser des Hebräerbriefes als Schriftausleger* (Regensburg: Pustet, 1968) 230; Theissen, *Untersuchungen* 105; MacRae, 'Heavenly Temple' 184–5, 187–8; and C. Koester, *Dwelling* 174–5, 178–82.

[22] 'For if someone would consider the construction of the tent and would see the garment of the priest and the vessels . . . even he will find that the lawgiver is a divine man . . . for each of these is intended as an imitation and representation of the All . . . for even when he had divided the tent, which is thirty cubits, into three parts and had devoted two to all the priests as a permissible and common place, he signifies the earth and the sea. For these things are also accessible to all. But the third portion he ascribes to God alone because heaven is inaccessible to humans.' See also *Ant.* 3:123 and in Philo, *Mos.* 2:88; *Spec.* 1:66.

court refers to that heaven where God dwells. The veil, therefore, comes to represent the boundary between earth and heaven.[23]

Philo also uses this model, although he expands it to include the distinction between the noumenal and the phenomenal. In *Questions on Exodus* 2:94 he writes,

> the simple holy [parts of the tabernacle] are classified with the sense-perceptible heaven, whereas the inner [parts], which are called the holy of holies, [are classified] with the intelligible world. The incorporeal world is set off and separated from the visible one by the mediating Logos as by a veil.[24]

These two variant understandings of the tabernacle as a representation of the universe are roughly contemporaneous to Hebrews, and they provide us with one of several backgrounds which have been proposed in explanation of Hebrews' tabernacle imagery. On the one hand, Philo's 'cosmological' tabernacle is quite different in some ways from what is found in Hebrews. Philo notes, for example, that the part of the cosmos within the veil is 'without transient events'.[25] Such a realm of intransience, while analogous in some ways to the permanence associated with the heavenly realm in Hebrews, is quite inappropriate as a place for Christ to offer his one-time sacrifice for sins.[26] Events simply do not take place in a realm of eternal archetypes.

On the other hand, the cosmological scheme in Josephus, also found in Philo, holds a bit more promise in elucidating what may have been in the author's mind when he divided the tent into two parts. This cosmological model has sometimes been proposed as an explication for certain parts of the author's argument, including 9:1–10.[27] In such cases the connection between the two-part cosmos and the future destruction of the created realm often has not been made explicit.[28] I have argued that Hebrews foresees the shaking and removal of the created realm, both heavens and

---

[23] So MacRae, 'Heavenly Temple' 185, notes that Clement of Alexandria speaks of the veil as the midpoint between heaven and earth (*Strom.* 5:6).

[24] Taken from Ralph Marcus' translation in the Loeb Classical Library series, *Philo*, Supplement 2 (London: William Heinemann, 1953) 142–3. See also *Somn.* 1:215 where the rational soul is said to be another kind of temple belonging to God, in addition to the universe.

[25] *QE* 2:91.   [26] As noted by Hurst, *Background* 33–4.

[27] MacRae, 'Heavenly Temple' 187–8, sees it behind 9:24; C. Koester, *Dwelling* 174, 178, in 9:24 and also with the realms of being in 9:8–10. Sowers, *Hermeneutics* 106–10, and Montefiore, *Hebrews* 149, also connect it with 9:1–10. Käsemann sees the distinction implicit in the mention of the veil in 6:19, 9:3 and 10:20, *Wandering* 209, 223. Schierse, *Verheissung* 62–3 comes closest to my interpretation.

[28] Schierse, *Verheissung* 52 and Montefiore, *Hebrews* 149 are apparent exceptions.

earth, at the 'time of reformation', leaving only the unshakeable heaven. In this light, an allusion to a cosmological tabernacle, in which the forecourt represented the created realm and the holy of holies the unshakeable heaven, would bring significantly appropriate nuances to some of the author's statements. In particular, the claim that the way into the holy of holies is not apparent while the first tent ἐχούσης στάσιν would take on added significance.

Harold Attridge and others have noted that this is an idiom which means to have a certain status or honour.[29] The author's principal meaning, once again, is eschatological and, thereby, paraenetic. The recipients grant an established status to the Levitical cultus in some way that the author sees as a hindrance to their faith. By contrast, the author insists that true entrance into God's presence cannot actually take place while this is the case. His audience must leave aside their former values and affirm a new paradigm of what is honourable.[30]

This primary emphasis, however, does not preclude wider implications to the statement, particularly in the light of the author's overall theology. The author not only believes that the Levitical cultus should no longer hold a high status in the minds of the readers. He also believes that its existence is destined to come to an end, as he believes the created realm will. The removal of the created heavens and earth is the final termination of the old order and is thus concurrent with the full arrival of the new age and the final entrance of the people of God into rest. It would therefore be consistent with the author's theology to allude to the destruction of the created realm, implying that it is an obstacle to the arrival of the perfected into God's presence. The way into the true holy of holies, into heaven itself, into God's promised rest and heavenly homeland, is not apparent while the created realm of flesh continues to exist. By contrast, when the created realm is removed, full access for those spirits who have been perfected will be unhindered. Such overtones do not say anything which I have not already established in the author's thought but rather substantiate my previous interpretations. This line of

---

[29] See n. 19. References such as Polybius' *Hist.* 5.5.3 and Plutarch's *Quaest. conv.* 8.9.1 (731B – σύστασις) show the close relationship between existence and standing. The first speaks of certain winds having reached sailing force and the second speaks of diseases coming into existence and *becoming established.*

[30] For detailed analyses of honour and shame categories in Hebrews, see the work of D. A. deSilva: 'Despising Shame: A Cultural-Anthropological Investigation of the Epistle to the Hebrews', *JBL* 113 (1994) 439–61; *Despising Shame: Honor Discourse and Community Maintenance in the Epistle to the Hebrews* (SBLDS 152; Atlanta: Scholars Press, 1995); *Perseverance in Gratitude: A Socio-Rhetorical Commentary on the Epistle 'to the Hebrews'* (Grand Rapids, MI: Eerdmans, 2000).

thought is so similar to the author's theology in general that it seems a strong possibility that such a meaning was in his mind, even if he did not bring it to full expression.

Such overtones would illuminate other comments the author makes. Why, for example, does the author speak of the tabernacle in terms of 'the present time' in 9:9? He has elsewhere gone to great lengths to point out the 'presentness' of the new covenant and the already effected obsolescence of the old covenant. The ever present reminder of the foreign, earthly world fits in well with the realization that, in the end, the new covenant has not yet arrived in its fullness.[31] Additional comments in Heb. 9:1–10 resonate with a cosmological reading of the outer tent. First of all, the author's use of κοσμικόν in 9:1 establishes with good certainty that the author associated the wilderness tabernacle with the created realm. The author specifically wished to define this shadowy tent in terms of its association with this world.[32] Much more tenuous, but worth noting, is the fact that both Philo and Josephus have a tendency to see the vessels in the forecourt symbolically. Josephus, for example, connects the lampstand and twelve breads in the Jerusalem temple with the seven planets and the zodiac respectively.[33] For Philo, the lampstand also stands for the planets (*Her.* 221) and the sense-perceptible heaven (*QE* 2:73, 95), while the table represents sense-perceptible and body-like substance (*QE* 2:69, 95). In both of these cases, the items in the outer court are intentionally related to the corporeal, physical world.

However, it is difficult to make much of this potential symbolism, not least because the author places the altar of incense within the holy of holies. While the cherubim and Ark of the Covenant can easily be taken as representative of the throne of God and the angels who surround it, the inclusion of the altar of incense has long been debated. Attridge suggests that the author might have read Num. 18 in such a way as to see the altar of incense in the holy of holies,[34] while Craig Koester hypothesizes a 'hidden vessels' tradition which may have considered the altar of incense to be hidden along with the ark and tent, waiting to be revealed at a future

---

[31] The author's use of the present tense in verses like 9:9 is not a strong argument that the Jerusalem temple had not yet been destroyed (cf. Attridge, *Hebrews* 8, who notes the present tense in *Ant.* 4:102–87, 224–57; *1 Clem.* 40; *Diogn.* 3). The author's association of the 'ideal' earthly cultus as typical of an age which has not fully come to a conclusion (because the created realm still exists) might further help explain this pattern.

[32] Sowers, *Hermeneutics* 108–9, however, goes too far when he interprets τό ἅγιον κοσμικόν as 'the tabernacle with its cosmic symbolism'. Hofius, on the other hand, may limit the meaning too much when he makes κοσμικόν equivalent to ἐπίγειος (*Vorhang* 61). It may imply more broadly that it was the tent within the created world in general.

[33] *War* 5:217.   [34] *Hebrews* 236–8.

time.[35] Neither of these explanations relates very well to a cosmological reading of the tabernacle. The fact that the author is not able to speak about such things κατὰ μέρος, while perhaps principally referring to the time since these items were in existence, may also warn against pressing the symbolism too far.[36] Such allegorizing was not on the author's agenda at this point.

Before I conclude my discussion of 9:8, we should note the general tenor of the author's argument with regard to the outer part of the sanctuary. As far as the earthly tabernacle is concerned, the outer sanctum is associated with multiplicity and imperfection. It can be used to refer to the old covenant in a parable in which the presence of God is obscured by its 'standing'. As with the veil, there seems little use for an outer tent in the heavenly sanctuary. It makes little sense to include things which are symbolic hindrances to God's presence in a theology which has as its basic point the access of the perfected to God's presence in the heavenly holy of holies. This point is worth bearing in mind in the discussions which follow.

The principal significance of the outer tent in 9:8 is eschatological and directed against the Levitical priesthood and earthly cultus in general. The author reinforces his point with flesh/conscience imagery in 9:9–10, parabolically associating the outer tent with the fleshly and the inner sanctum with the realm of spirit. The author does not make further cosmological claims explicit, but it is not unreasonable to conjecture that they were in his mind. At the very least they are consistent with the imagery he does make explicit.

Hebrews 9:11

One of the most controverted of all references to the tabernacle occurs in 9:11–12. Hurst has warned that '[t]he interpretation of this verse [9:11] is so contentious it would be hazardous to build *any* theory on it'.[37] These verses state that,

> Christ, having arrived as a high priest of good things which have come to pass,[38] through the greater and more perfect tent, not

---

[35] *Dwelling* 175–7.

[36] Many interpreters see 9:5 as a conscious avoidance of allegorizing on the part of the author, but νῦν might imply any number of things, such as the fact that so much time has passed since these items actually existed or the inappropriateness of embarking on an allegorical interpretation of the vessels in this sermon.

[37] *Background* 27 (italics his).

[38] I have already argued that the reading γενομένων is more likely the original here in the light of 10:1.

one made with hands (that is, not of this creation), nor through the blood of bulls and goats, but through his own blood, he entered once and for all into the sanctuary, having found an eternal redemption.

The principal difficulty in interpreting these two verses is the meaning of διά in the phrase 'through the greater and more perfect tent'. On the one hand, a number of interpreters take this preposition instrumentally, yielding the somewhat awkward sense that Christ, by means of the greater tent, entered into the holy of holies.[39] In contrast, the majority of scholars, take the διά locally in parallel to verses like 4:14 and 7:26,[40] drawing various implications such as the existence of a multilayered heaven[41] or a mere reference to passage through the outer tent of a real heavenly tabernacle.[42] The wide diversity of interpretations based upon this verse

---

[39] Some of those who take διά instrumentally include a number of those who see the greater and more perfect tent as the glorified (A. Vanhoye, '"Par la Tent plus grande et plus parfaite . . ." (He 9,11)', *Bib* 46 (1965) 1ff.) or eucharistic body of Christ (J. Swetnam, '"The Greater and More Perfect Tent": A Contribution to the Discussion of Hebrews 9,11', *Bib* 47 (1966) 91ff.), his whole humanity (Schierse, *Verheissung* 57; Cody, *Heavenly Sanctuary* 161; F. Laub, *Bekenntnis und Auslegung: Die paränetische Funcktion der Christologie im Hebräerbrief* (BU 15; Regensburg: Pustet, 1980) 190), or even the church as the body of Christ (Westcott, *Hebrews* 260). Many of these interpretations introduce anachronistic elements into the meaning of Hebrews. The parallel use of χειροποίητος in 9:11 and 9:24 demonstrates that Christ enters this heavenly tabernacle not made with hands. It cannot, therefore, be any of these preceding suggestions. Others have read διά instrumentally with more likely interpretations of the tabernacle, including Montefiore (*Hebrews* 152–3), Young ('Gospel' 202–5), R. McL. Wilson (*Hebrews* (Grand Rapids, MI: Eerdmans, 1987) 150), and C. Koester (*Dwelling* 161–2).

[40] The majority of scholars this century seem to have found this option the most plausible one, including Riggenbach, *Hebräer* 220f., 258f.; Moffatt, *Hebrews* 120; Michel, *Hebräer* 310–11; C. Spicq, *L'épître aux Hébreux*, vol. 2 (Paris: Gabalda, 1953) 256; Héring, *Hebrews* 76; Käsemann, *Wandering* 228 n.159; H. Koester, 'Outside' 309; Sowers, *Hermeneutics* 110–11; Kuss, *Hebräer* 117f.; Schröger, *Verfasser* 237f.; Theissen, *Untersuchungen* 105; P. Andriessen, 'Das größere und vollkommenere Zelt (Hebr 9,11)', *BZ* 15 (1971) 76–92; Hofius, *Vorhang* 56, 67; D. Peterson, *Hebrews and Perfection: An Examination of the Concept of Perfection in the Epistle to the Hebrews* (SNTSMS 47; Cambridge: Cambridge University Press, 1982) 143–4; J. W. Thompson, *The Beginnings of Christian Philosophy: The Epistle to the Hebrews* (CBQMS 13; Washington, DC: Catholic Biblical Association of America, 1981) 106; H. Braun, *An die Hebräer* (HNT 14; Tübingen: Mohr/Siebeck, 1984) 265; Rissi, *Theologie* 39; Attridge, *Hebrews* 245–7; Lane, *Hebrews 9–13* 237–8; J. M. Scholer, *Proleptic Priests: Priesthood in the Epistle to the Hebrews* (JSNTSS 49; Sheffield: JSOT Press, 1991) 63; Weiss, *Hebräer* 465–7; M. Isaacs, *Sacred Space: An Approach to the Theology of the Epistle to the Hebrews* (JSNTSS 73; Sheffield: JSOT Press, 1992) 210; P. Ellingworth, *The Epistle to the Hebrews: A Commentary on the Greek Text* (Grand Rapids, MI: Eerdmans, 1993) 450; E. Grässer, *An die Hebräer (Hebr 7,1–10,18)* (EKK 17.2; Zürich: Benzinger Verlag, 1993) 145–8.

[41] E.g. Riggenbach, Gyllenberg, Moffatt, Michel, Héring, Käsemann, H. Koester, Kuss, Schröger, Andriessen, Peterson, Lane and Isaacs.

[42] Especially Hofius, Rissi and Scholar.

demonstrates that it is dangerous ground on which to build any particular understanding of the heavenly tabernacle. The major interpretive options, however, must be explored in turn.

The local reading

I have already mentioned the awkward sense which seems to result from taking διά instrumentally. In contrast, a local reading at least at first glance seems to yield a much smoother sense, one which would also preclude any need to take the tent here metaphorically.[43] Take, for example, 4:14, which states that Christ is a great high priest διεληλυθότα τούς οὐρανούς, and 7:26, which states that Christ is a fitting high priest ὑψηλότερος τῶν οὐρανῶν γενόμενος. If we compare these comments to 9:11, one might make a straightforward correlation between certain conjectured 'lower heavens' and the outer part of the heavenly sanctuary. This line of attack yields a seemingly smooth reading to 9:11–12: Christ, (passing) through the heavenly tent (these lower heavens), entered into the heavenly holy of holies (the highest heaven(s) where God's throne is). This parallel with 4:14 – which appears in a high priestly context and includes the preposition διά – coupled with the better sense which the sentence as a whole seems to have, constitutes some of the primary arguments that διά is local in connotation.[44]

Otto Michel's 1936 commentary provides us with one of the earliest arguments for a local reading understood as a passage through lower heavens to an upper heaven. He wrote,

> Strenggenommen müßten wir also zwischen dem Bereich der Schöpfung (κτίσις), des Zeltes (σκηνή) und des Heiligtums (ἅγια) unterscheiden: Christus war auf Erden Glied der Schöpfung, durchschritt bei der Auffahrt das Zelt und brachte im Allerheiligsten das Opfer vor Gott. κτίσις, σκηνή, ἅγια sind also Sphären, die einander ablösen. Eigentlich müßte man im Hebr auch einen dreifachen Sprachgebrauch vom 'Himmel' unterscheiden: 1. die Himmel, die zu dieser Schöpfung gehören und deshalb vergänglich sind (1.10–12); 2. die Himmel, durch

---

[43] So Lane, *Hebrews 9–13* 236. He alludes, of course, to many of the scholars mentioned in n. 39 who do not take the passage in a straightforward manner. Lane also contests, as we shall see below, that the local reading fits better into the sense of the basic sentence, 'when Christ appeared . . . he entered' (229).

[44] So Ellingworth, *Hebrews* 450, 'There seems little doubt, following extensive discussion, that διά τῆς . . . σκηνῆς is local.'

die Christus hindurchschreitet (4.14, 9.10–12); 3. den Himmel
als den eigentlichen Wohnort der Gottheit (9.24).[45]

This statement by Michel is perhaps the clearest expression of a local
interpretation of 9:11–12 which relates διά to the various senses which
οὐρανός seems to have in the epistle. If the cosmological reading of
the tabernacle finds an easy foothold in 9:8–9, the view which believes
the tent to relate to heavenly spheres in some way most easily springs
from these verses. Those who hold to this interpretation point out that the
tent through which Christ passes is οὐ ταύτης τῆς κτίσεως, a statement
sometimes used against the cosmological interpretation, since it views
the creation as the outer part of the paradigmatic tabernacle.[46]

While there are a few minor variations of Michel's construal, most
interpretations in this category have this same basic cosmological structure and the same basic correlation to the earthly tent. Eduard Riggenbach,
for example, has a different focus, but the same basic structure and correlation.[47] Paul Andriessen supposes that the 'greater and more perfect
tent' might be the heaven which the angels inhabit, but this heaven is
still to be equated with the 'heavens' of 4:14.[48] In addition, most of these
interpretations view the 'greater and more perfect tent' as the *outer* part
of the heavenly tabernacle, while the highest heaven is reserved for God
as the heavenly τὰ ἅγια.[49]

There would seem to be at least three significant qualifications which
should be made, however, if one is to opt for the local reading. The first
is the fact that σκηνή in 9:11 quite probably refers to the *entirety* of

[45] 'Strictly speaking, we must therefore distinguish between the sphere of the creation
(κτίσις), of the tent (σκηνή) and the sanctuary (ἅγια): Christ was a member of the creation
while he was on earth, he passed through the tent in his ascent, and he brought the offering
into the holy of holies before God. κτίσις, σκηνή, ἅγια are therefore spheres one after the
other. One must actually distinguish in Hebrews also a threefold use of the word "heaven":
1. the heavens which belong to this creation and are therefore transitory (1:10–12); 2. the
heavens through which Christ passed (4:14; 9:10–12); 3. the heaven as the actual dwelling
of divinity (9:24)' (*Hebräer* 311–12).

[46] As, for example, Michel himself points out, *Hebräer* 312. One could also argue this
point from 8:5, which seems to see a pattern for the *whole* earthly tabernacle in what at
least seems to be its *heavenly* type. There are possible ways of explaining these factors
which I will give later in the chapter, but they are indeed the strongest arguments against a
cosmological reading of the tabernacle.

[47] As discussed by Hofius, *Vorhang* 50–2. Rather than focus on the relationship between
the 'two tents' in heaven like Michel, Riggenbach emphasizes the nether heavens as representing a mere approach to God, as opposed to the 'Wohnsitz Gottes' itself.

[48] 'Zelt' 85–6.

[49] H. Koester has even gone so far as to say that σκηνή is *never* used in Hebrews to depict
the tabernacle as a whole, a claim which I have already disputed. See n. 8 and 'Outside'
309.

the heavenly tabernacle and not merely to its first compartment. I have already concluded that σκηνή in Hebrews usually refers to the whole tabernacle, with the exception of the occurrences in 9:1–10, where the word is clearly qualified in the context. It would therefore seem likely that the whole heavenly tabernacle is also in view here, since there is no indication to the contrary. Certainly, some have built on the reference to the outer tent in 9:8 to argue that 9:11 only refers to the first chamber of the heavenly tabernacle.[50] But such is not the case if 9:1 and 9:11 are in a μέν/δέ correlation.[51] Accordingly, 9:11 contrasts the *whole* heavenly sanctuary with the whole ἅγιον κοσμικόν of 9:1. By introducing the whole 'greater and more perfect tent' at the very start of the new section, the author effectively shows that the whole tent of the new covenant is superior to the whole earthly tabernacle.

Hofius has also argued that σκηνή in Hebrews refers to the whole tabernacle on the basis of expressions in Lev. 16.[52] He points out the phraseological similarity between 8:2's claim that Christ is a τῶν ἁγίων λειτουργὸς καὶ τῆς σκηνῆς τῆς ἀληθινῆς and phrases in Leviticus used of the Day of Atonement, arguing that this phrase is not a hendiadys as is often assumed.[53] For example, Lev. 16:20 states that the high priest συντελέσει ἐξιλασκόμενος τὸ ἅγιον καὶ τὴν σκηνὴν τοῦ μαρτυρίου.[54] Leviticus 16:16 and 16:33 also refer to τὸ ἅγιον in distinction from ἡ σκηνὴ τοῦ μαρτυρίου. We know from Heb. 13:11 (and 6:19)[55] that the author was acquainted with this chapter and that he understood τὸ ἅγιον to refer to the holy of holies (Lev. 16:17 would also make this clear). Hofius is probably correct about the referent of σκηνή in 9:11, but his argument is not as convincing or definitive as one might think. While the precedents in Leviticus might argue against a hendiadys, it is not completely certain that the author of Hebrews understood the phrase ἡ σκηνὴ τοῦ μαρτυρίου in Lev. 16 in the same way as Leviticus' original author. Riggenbach has shown how easily the author might have taken

[50] E.g. Lane, *Hebrews 9–13* 230, translates σκηνή here as 'compartment'.
[51] So, for example, Michel, *Hebräer* 304f., 309; Hofius, *Vorhang* 65; Young, 'Gospel' 202; Thompson, *Beginnings* 104–5; Attridge, *Hebrews* 238 n.103; C. Koester, *Dwelling* 161; Lane, *Hebrews 9–13* 229; Scholar, *Priests* 159; Weiss, *Hebräer* 462; and Ellingworth, *Hebrews* 448.
[52] *Vorhang* 57, 59–60.
[53] Some of those who take the καί epexegetically include Westcott, *Hebrews* 216; Riggenbach, *Hebräer* 220–31; Moffatt, *Hebrews* 105; Spicq, *Hébreux* 2.234; Michel, *Hebräer* 288; Bruce, *Hebrews* 161; Peterson, *Perfection* 130; Lane, *Hebrews 1–8* 200. In a moment I will also take this position.
[54] For Hebrews' tendency to make τό ἅγιον plural in reference to the holy of holies, see n.3.
[55] Young, 'Gospel' 199 n.12.

this phrase in reference solely to the outer part of the tabernacle (e.g. Lev. 16:23).[56] In fact, the LXX in this chapter refers to the 'tent of witness' primarily to include the Holy Place *in addition to* the holy of holies in the cleansing ritual, making Riggenbach's reading quite plausible.[57] What seems decisive toward taking 8:2 in reference to the whole tent is the fact that σκηνή in 8:5 almost certainly refers to the whole earthly tent, as I have already suggested. Moses is about to erect the tent and is instructed to make πάντα according to the type shown him on the mountain, which implies at the very least that the holy of holies was included in the pattern.[58] Once we accept this fact, it is only logical to assume that the author is using σκηνή in the same general sense in 8:2, since they both occur in the same general context. If the author had understood the phrase in Lev. 16 to refer only to the outer court, he would surely have used σκηνή consistently in Hebrews to refer only to the Holy Place. We have seen, however, that exactly the opposite is the case.

I might add that it is still possible to take 8:2 epexegetically and yet also take σκηνή as a reference to the entire heavenly tent. The reason is that the author never clearly implies that the heavenly tent includes an outer sanctum. Accordingly, the σκηνή of 8:2 would be both the entire tent and the heavenly holy of holies as well. I will consider this possibility more fully below in my discussion of 9:24. There I will argue that the author did not draw careful distinctions between the two expressions with regard to the heavenly tent because there he uses such language metaphorically to refer to the unshakeable heavenly realm in general.

The preceding arguments do not preclude a local sense to διά or even the general interpretation of Michel. Just as the phrase 'tent of witness' in Lev. 16 refers to the whole tent primarily to include the outer compartment in the atonement, one could suggest that σκηνή is used to include the lower heavens through which Christ passed. A few adjustments to the interpretation, nevertheless, follow from the preceding conclusion. For example, one must allow that when the author states that Christ entered the holy of holies through the greater and more perfect tent, he does not mean to imply 'daß Christus die σκηνή wieder verlassen habe, um εἰς τὰ

---

[56] *Hebräer* 220 n.13.

[57] On the other hand, Lev. 16.16, which states that the tent of witness was placed 'among them in the midst of their uncleanness', could easily have been understood by the author to refer to the whole, visible tent.

[58] Since the author cites Exodus to substantiate his claim that the earthly priests serve τὰ ἐπουράνια by way of a shadowy illustration and since the author uses this same language in 9:23–4 where the reference clearly includes the heavenly holy of holies, it seems beyond question that the whole tent is envisaged in 8:5. See also n. 7.

ἅγια zu gelangen'.[59] So Hofius does not think that Christ passed out the other side of the heavens of 4:14.[60] This line of reasoning is a natural consequence of reading 9:11 locally.

A second qualification we must make to any local reading of 9:11 relates to its contrast of the whole heavenly tabernacle with the 'earthly sanctuary' of 9:1, as the μέν/δέ construction indicates. The implication is that the purpose of 9:11–14 is not to delineate the author's cosmology but to show the superiority of the whole of the heavenly cultus to the earthly. We see this purpose most clearly in the chiasm of four phrases inserted between the subject of 9:11–12 (Χριστός) and the verb (εἰσῆλθεν):

A   διὰ τῆς μείζονος καὶ τελειοτέρας σκηνῆς
B   οὐ χειροποιήτου, τοῦτ' ἔστιν οὐ ταύτης τῆς κτίσεως
B′   οὐδὲ δι' αἵματος τράγων καὶ μόσχων,
A′   διὰ δὲ τοῦ ἰδίου αἵματος.

These four measured phrases contrast the 'cultic spaces' and the 'mediums of approach' of the two covenants with each other.[61] Attridge has rightly pointed out that the use of the same preposition in the same context in two different senses is not unusual, so one cannot use the instrumental sense of the διά in the last two phrases to discount a local reading in the first.[62] In the light of the contrast with 9:1, however, it must be borne in mind that the real point of passage through the tent here, if the meaning is indeed local, must be to contrast the tent through which Christ passed with the one in which the earthly priests and high priests performed their duties and through which they passed. Both the sacrifice which Christ offered (A′) and the structure in which he offered it (A) are superior to the sacrifices (B′) and structure (B) with which the earthly priests ministered.

---

[59] Hofius, *Vorhang* 65.

[60] *Vorhang* 67–8. Similarly, he does not take 7:26 as a statement of place but as 'eine Aussage über die unbeschreibliche Machtfülle, die Christus von Gott empfangen hat' (69).

[61] Phrases used by Lane, *Hebrews 9–13* 237, although he sees the tent here as the outer compartment and the nether heavens.

[62] *Hebrews* 245, following Moffatt, *Hebrews* 121 and Hofius, *Vorhang* 67 n.110. Attridge points out Rom. 2:28 (ἐν); 4:25 (διά); 11:28 (διά); Heb. 5:1 (ὑπέρ); 7:25 (εἰς); and 1 Pet. 2:20 (ἐν). Note Montefiore's incorrect comment in *Hebrews* 152: '[I]t would be bad style and unparalleled N. T. usage to use the same preposition twice in the same sentence with the same case but with different meanings'. Attridge also rightly notes that διά should not be taken with anything which precedes it, such as ἀγαθῶν (as also J. C. K. von Hoffmann, *Der Brief an die Hebräer*, HSNT 5 (Nördlingen: Beck, 1873) 335, and A. Nairne, *The Epistle of Priesthood* (Edinburgh: T&T Clark, 1913) 89) or Χριστός (Seeberg, *Hebräer* 100). The balance of the four phrases demonstrates conclusively that they all belong together to modify εἰσῆλθεν.

The third qualification relates to the parallelism of 9:11 with 4:14 and is more of an observation. For many interpreters, this similarity is that which makes the local reading decisive. In the light of the preceding two qualifications, is the parallel as close as is generally thought? Hebrews 4:14 exhorts the audience to hold fast to their confession since they have 'a high priest who has passed through the heavens'. This verse marks the very beginning of the main discussion of Christ's high priesthood,[63] and the author's comment is certainly related to the role of Christ as high priest.

Nevertheless, the question remains: what aspect of Christ's high priestly 'passage' is in view? It is certainly possible that 4:14 relates to the outer tent of the heavenly tabernacle in the light of 7:26, where Christ has come to be 'higher' than (presumably) these heavens. On the other hand, the language may have a slightly different nuance. Although 9:11 and 8:1[64] are similar to 4:14 and 7:26, 6:19 and 10:20 may be even closer parallels. The imagery of 4:14 seems closer to Christ passing through the veil than through the outer tent. The heavens in these two verses are mentioned more as that which Christ has successfully penetrated than as a part of the greater and more perfect tent. The author does not denigrate such heavens, but he does not hold them in the same regard as the heavenly tent in 9:11.

The local reading, therefore, supports at least two plausible interpretive options for understanding the heavenly tabernacle, namely, one which envisages a 'vertical' heavenly structure consisting of lower heavens and the highest heaven and one which sees it as a 'horizontal' structure located somewhere in the heavens.[65] Since most scholars opt for one of these interpretations based on this reading of διά, the local sense should be taken seriously. On the other hand, my qualifications diminish the explanatory power of a local reading. Hebrews 4:14 and 7:26 are not as close parallels as they might at first glance appear, for the author is referring to the whole tent and making a point which is not primarily spatial. Further,

---

[63] W. Nauck, 'Zum Aufbau des Hebräerbriefes', *Judentum, Urchristentum, Kirche: Festschrift für Joachim Jeremias*, Walther Eltester, ed. (Berlin: Alfred Töpelmann, 1960) 199–206, following Michel's division at 4:14, *Hebräer* 29–35, noted the similarity between 4:14–16 and 10:19–23 and claimed that this was an inclusio bracketing the middle theological section of the epistle. G. Guthrie, *The Structure of Hebrews: A Text-Linguistic Analysis* (SNT 73; Leiden: E. J. Brill, 1994) 110, 117, 120, has refined Nauck's observations through a text-linguistic analysis of the epistle as a whole, but he has confirmed that despite the rhetorical interruption of 5:11–6:20, 4:14 does (in one of its functions) serve as the introduction to the central theological argument of the epistle.

[64] So Hofius, *Vorhang* 68.

[65] A distinction made by Rissi, *Theologie* 39, in favour of the horizontal option.

I have significant doubts about the very existence of an outer sanctum in the heavenly tent because of the author's theology of access. These factors lead me to reconsider whether the instrumental reading fits in the context.

The instrumental reading

The principal objection to the instrumental reading is that it results in a sentence which, when taken as a whole, is semantically awkward. Christ, by means of the greater and more perfect tent, entered into the holy of holies. If the heavenly tent has no outer chamber, the meaning boils down to 'by means of the tent he enters the tent', a clearly redundant expression. Accordingly, most who have chosen this interpretive option have taken the tent metaphorically, resulting in readings which see the tent as something symbolic, such as Christ's body.

On the other hand, if one suspends judgement on the sentence as a whole for a moment and looks only up to the point of the main verb, an instrumental reading does fit well with the parallelism of the four measured phrases in 9:11–12. While a shift from a local to an instrumental sense is not impossible, these four phrases form a smooth and coherent whole if they all be taken instrumentally. They would then straightforwardly contrast the 'tools' of atonement used in each covenant, first in terms of the two tabernacles and then in terms of the two kinds of sacrifices. When Christ arrived as high priest, he did his work by means of a greater and more perfect tent (not like the 'hand-made' tabernacle of this creation) and by means of his own, perfected blood (not like the ineffectual blood of goats and bulls). One would suppose that a first-time reader or listener could easily have had such an understanding at least until they arrived at the main verb.

Nevertheless, the semantic awkwardness of the instrumental reading, when one arrives at εἰσῆλθεν, makes it unlikely. It is always possible that the author, after his four chiastic qualifications, lost his semantic sense. It is possible that he had moved in thought so far away from the initial διά that he found himself repeating himself in the main verb. And if the author did largely think of the heavenly tabernacle as a metaphor for heaven itself, then we might give some allowances for awkwardness when the sentence is read on a literal level. We have more reason to think that Hebrews was a carefully planned text, not a text in which the author seems to lose his train of thought. The arguments in favour of a straightforward instrumental reading do not seem strong enough to warrant such interpretive coping strategies.

A modal reading

The difficulties of the instrumental reading are largely removed if we take the first διά of 9:11 modally rather than instrumentally: 'by way of the greater and more perfect tent . . . Christ entered into the holies'. The first phrase highlights the different *way* that Christ has fulfilled the Day of Atonement ritual, *how* he has done it: *via* the heavenly tent rather than the earthly one. The author is not primarily thinking of structures or cosmology. He is making an eschatological argument. The greater and more perfect tent is a better *way* than the ἅγιον κοσμικόν. The first διά expression thus completes the contrast of the heavenly tabernacle with the earthly, the eschatological contrast between the two tents begun in 9:1. The second mention of entering in highlights the superior redemption which Christ has effected, a salvific emphasis. The first continues the imagery of the structure of the tabernacle which the author is using; the second the symbolism of the Day of Atonement which takes place within that structure.

N. H. Young has rightly noted that the διά expressions in 9:11–12 are really about the superiority of the new order, the new eschatological age.[66] Marie Isaacs argues additionally that the author is generally concerned with 'sacred space', that 'which the worshipper wishes to approach in order to gain access to the deity'.[67] The phrases 'greater and more perfect tent' and 'entrance into the holy of holies' are not straightforward literal expressions. They ultimately have slightly different connotations. The tent language serves to contrast the structures of the earthly cultus in order to sustain the rhetoric of the discourse and is somewhat peripheral to the author's main concern. Day of Atonement imagery, on the other hand, stands at the heart of the contrast, having the important function of representing the core of traditional Christian atonement language in terms of the high priestly metaphor. A modal reading of διά thus suits the μέν/δέ contrast with the whole ἅγιον κοσμικόν of 9:1 better than a local reading. While the earthly sanctuary had certain ordinances which included ineffectual sacrifices, Christ performed his sacrifices via a greater and more perfect tent. Such a reading also fits well with σκηνή as a reference to the entirety of the heavenly tabernacle.

Hebrews 9:24

While σκηνή does not actually occur in 9:23–4, these verses tie together several themes relating to the tent and shed light on the previous references

---

[66] 'Gospel' 204.   [67] *Space* 61.

to the tabernacle in chs. 8 and 9. The reference to ὑποδείγματα is reminiscent of 8:5 and Moses' instruction to make the tent like the τύπος shown him on the mountain. The reference to ἅγια which are not χειροποίητα reminds one both of 8:2 and 9:11, while the statement that Christ entered 'into heaven itself' sounds much like the cosmological reading such as may have been present in 9:8. These two verses, therefore, have the potential of bringing together our examination of the heavenly tabernacle up to this point.

The *crux interpretum* of 9:24 is largely the meaning of the statement that Christ did not enter into a handmade holy of holies,[68] but *into heaven itself*. This statement has been taken in three basic ways:[69] as an identification of this holy of holies with heaven as a whole,[70] as an identification of it with the highest heaven,[71] or as a synecdoche in which the whole (heaven) is substituted for its part (the tabernacle in heaven).[72] These three readings of the verse roughly correspond to three general interpretations of the heavenly tabernacle: namely, the metaphorical-cosmological reading (heaven metaphor for whole tent), the view which identifies the parts of the tent with a multilayered heaven (a more literal cosmological reading), and the interpretation which believes there to be a literal structure within heaven.[73] All three interpretations are theoretically possible. We will also need to discuss a Platonic reading, which sees the tabernacle as a Platonic archetype.

ὑποδείγματα

I have already discussed this term in the previous chapter. I observed that it never means a Platonic archetype in all extant Greek literature, although

---

[68] I have already argued above that ἅγια is a reference to the holy of holies, *contra* Rissi.

[69] It is difficult to know how to classify those who read these verses Platonically (e.g. Spicq, *Hébreux* 2.267; Attridge, *Hebrews* 263; Grässer, *Hebräer 7,1–10,18* 190–1). While they are in one sense worthy of being in a category of their own, on the level of the text they could perhaps be placed in the third category.

[70] Riggenbach, *Hebräer* 284–5; Gyllenburg, 'Christologie' 675; Käsemann, *Wandering* 223; Montefiore, *Hebrews* 160; Cody, *Heavenly Liturgy* 149; Sowers, *Hermeneutics* 106; Kuss, *Hebräer* 125–6; MacRae, 'Heavenly Temple' 187; Braun, *Hebräer* 282; Rissi, *Theologie* 39; C. Koester, *Dwelling* 174; Isaacs, *Space* 66 n.1; Scholar, *Priests* 169–76.

[71] Michel, *Hebräer* 312, 323; Hofius, *Vorhang* 70–1; Nissalä, *Hohepriestermotiv* 203; Peterson, *Perfection* 143; Lane, *Hebrews 9–13* 248.

[72] C. K. Barrett (implied), 'The Eschatology of the Epistle to the Hebrews', *The Background of the New Testament and its Eschatology: Studies in Honour of C. H. Dodd*, W. D. Davies and D. Daube, eds. (Cambridge: Cambridge University Press, 1954) 386; Wilson, *Hebrews* 166; Hurst, *Background* 28; Weiss, *Hebräer* 486.

[73] This is only a general correlation, since several interpreters do not fit into this pattern.

it rarely has the sense of a representation.[74] 'Illustration' or 'example' would be more suitable to the context of 8:5 and 9:23. Accordingly, we must seriously question the suggestion that the heavenly tabernacle in Hebrews is an eternal form or archetype. While the language of Hebrews has a Platonic/Philonic 'feel' to it, there are several aspects of the epistle which militate against reading the tabernacle in any straightforwardly Platonic way.

The first is that which I have just mentioned: the language of Hebrews is reminiscent in some ways of Plato/Philo, but it is *only* reminiscent. At every point the author comes close and then turns away from the Platonic, almost as if he is consciously avoiding those implications. He uses ὑπόδειγμα instead of μίμημα or εἰκών, and when he does use εἰκών in 10:1, it has almost the opposite meaning of what we might expect.[75] While he does use τύπος and ἀντίτυπος, he does not use the more obviously Platonic παράδειγμα or ἀρχέτυπος. While he does use σκιά, it is not clear that he utilizes it any differently than it is used in Col. 2:17.[76]

The second and even more damaging argument against a straightforward Platonic tabernacle is the fact that the author's concerns are primarily eschatological in nature. Hurst has rightly pointed out the virtual contradiction in C. K. Barrett's statement that, '[t]he heavenly tabernacle and its ministrations are from one point of view eternal archetypes, from another, they are eschatological events'.[77] Barrett at the time was pioneering the attempt to combine 'vertical' and 'horizontal' elements in Hebrews. We should now go even one step further and note that unless 'archetype' is taken in a general sense, this statement is self-contradictory. Events do not take place in the realm of Platonic archetypes, as I have already noted.[78]

The 'illustrations' and 'shadows' in Hebrews point more to future events than to heavenly structures. Or perhaps even more accurately, the text of the Old Testament provided shadowy examples whose full meaning was to be found in Christ. Hebrews 10:1 states that the Law contained a

---

[74] E.g. in Aquila's translation of Ezek. 8:10 and Deut. 4:17, where ὑπόδειγμα is used instead of ὁμοίωμα and ὁμοίωσις.

[75] Philo can use εἰκών of something which is a pattern (*Leg.* 3:96) or ideal form (*Somn.* 1:79), but the reason is Philo's three-level philosophy in which God himself is the archetype of archetypes, while the *logos* and forms relating thereto are the 'image' of him (cf. *Somn.* 1:75).

[76] So Hurst, *Background* 17. I mentioned in ch. 5 the close parallel in Philo, *Conf.* 190.

[77] *Background* 33–4.

[78] Realization of this fact would seem to sound the death knell for studies such as W. E. Brooks, 'The Perpetuity of Christ's Sacrifice in the Epistle to the Hebrews', *JBL* 89 (1970) 205–14, which tried to relate the eternality of Christ's sacrifice to Platonism in the epistle. If Christ's sacrifice was eternal in this way, it could not have been an event.

shadow μελλόντων ἀγαθῶν, meaning the atonement provided by Christ, not a heavenly building. Hebrews 9:11 confirms this impression when it states that Christ arrived as a high priest γενομένων ἀγαθῶν. These good things are the real atonement and perfection which Christ has provided, an 'eternal redemption' (9:12) involving the cleansing of the human conscience (9:14). The Law had a shadow of these good things in its tent and in the ministry which took place there, but these earthly illustrations were not a perfect 'image' of those things. Hebrews 8:5 speaks of the earthly priests serving the heavenly structures by a 'shadowy illustration', a dative of manner referring more to the way in which their *service* related to that of Christ (his one-time offering) rather than to heavenly structures. Once one sees that the main focus of shadow and illustration language in 8:5 is the events which take place in the heavens rather than the heavenly tabernacle itself, the inadequacy of the Platonic model in elucidating the argument of Hebrews becomes more and more apparent.

Indeed, all of the various ministries which are a part of the earthly cultus, all of the 'gifts and sacrifices' offered by the priests and high priest (5:1; 8:3–4), all of these find their heavenly correspondent in the once and for all offering of Christ in the heavenly holy of holies. The author amalgamates numerous Levitical rites together in his contrasts of the Levitical cultus with Christ. All of these liturgical functions in the offering of gifts and sacrifices can be put up against the one offering of Christ. He has no service to perform in the outer part of the heavenly tabernacle; all of the earthly cultus finds its heavenly counterpart in the entrance of Christ into the highest heaven. This point is extremely significant and should be borne in mind in the subsequent discussion.

The use of ὑποδείγματα in 9:23 is slightly different from the dative singular in 8:5. In ch. 8, the term contrasted the *manner* of ministry in the earthly tent with that of the Christ in the heavenly one. By contrast, 9:23 does contrast the *structures and furnishings* of the earthly sanctuary as a whole with the heavenly sanctuary. Even here, however, the author's interest goes deeper than a quasi-literal pitting of structures against structures. The implements both on earth and in heaven are, more than anything else, part of a symbolic world of cultic associations. This fact is clear from the author's enigmatic statement that it is necessary for heavenly 'things' to be cleansed, a datum required by the imagery of a holy of holies.[79] Clearly this statement would not fit well in a Platonic or Philonic scheme.

---

[79] Moffatt writes, 'the idea becomes almost fantastic' (*Hebrews* 132). Hurst's attempt to interpret καθαρίζω as a *mere* synonym for ἐγκαινίζω is not convincing (*Background* 38–9).

Ultimately, the reason the heavenly 'things' need to be cleansed is because the author is developing an extended metaphor. The purpose of this metaphor is to demonstrate that the atonement provided by Christ is the reality to which the Levitical sacrificial system only pointed symbolically. The author constructs a grand metaphor of Christ's high priesthood in which Christ is a superior high priest to any Levitical priest, his sacrifice superior to any earthly sacrifice, and his sanctuary superior to the wilderness tabernacle. I will increasingly argue that the author does not have a literal heavenly structure in mind. At best he is metaphorically thinking of the heaven where God dwells as the heavenly sanctuary. But at times, he is more playing out the overall high priestly metaphor in its sacred space component. When one is playing out an extended metaphor of this sort, the details sometimes come from the world of the metaphor rather than the literal world that one may be using the metaphor to describe. So we should not be surprised to find that the literal correspondent to the heavenly tabernacle in some cases is *the abstract sacred space where Christ's spiritual atonement takes place.*

Hebrews 9:24 seems one place where the author is as much playing out the overall metaphor as thinking of a sanctuary in the heavens. It seems preposterous for the author to suggest that the heaven where God's throne is has some need of cleansing.[80] A better suggestion is that the author is thinking of the cleansing of the conscience. The preceding chapter demonstrated that the author connects the rational and spiritual with the heavenly realm. While the flesh was the only real object of cleansing in the earthly ritual, the heavenly ministry actually perfects the worshipper in terms of their consciences (9:10; 10:22). So it is no surprise that Attridge explains the enigma of 9:23 by suggesting that 'the heavenly or ideal realities cleansed by Christ's sacrifice are none other than the consciences of the members of the new covenant'.[81] But perhaps we should sit even more loosely to the question of what literally the author might have in mind. He has in mind the cleansing of human consciences and spirits. He has in mind that Christ is a high priest in heaven rather than on earth and is speaking of the inauguration of the heavenly sanctuary in contrast to the inauguration Moses performed. These components, which swim in metaphor, are sufficient to generate the imagery of Heb. 9:24.

---

[80] And surely we must locate God's throne in the holy of holies in any scenario of the heavenly tent.

[81] Attridge, *Hebrews* 261–2. So also Schierse, *Verheissung* 48; W. R. G. Loader *Sohn und Hohepriester: Eine traditionsgeschichtliche Untersuchung zur Christologie des Hebräerbriefs* (WMANT 53; Neukirchen: Neukirchener Verlag, 1981) 169–70; and Isaacs, *Space* 212 n.2 (who has a good summary of the other options which have been taken).

τὰ ἐπουράνια

This neuter plural adjective in 9:23 is almost universally taken as a substantive referring to 'heavenly things'.[82] The translation follows from references in the previous verses to several items of the earthly cultus, including the whole earthly tent and its furnishings (9:21). All of these things are certainly the ὑποδείγματα of whatever the heavenly 'items' might be. In the context of a scholarship which often saw this latter term Platonically, it is not difficult to see why most scholars have interpreted τὰ ἐπουράνια as a reference to the originals of the earthly 'copies'.

One should carefully qualify, however, the translation 'heavenly things' by the fact that the function of all the earthly items was to (fore)shadow one event, Christ's entrance into the heavenly holy of holies. There are no other services which Christ seems to perform in the heavenly tabernacle *qua* tabernacle other than this once and for all offering.[83] This fact makes it possible that the author is referring specifically to the heavenly holy of holies, as he is clearly in 9:24, or, if the author is using the heavenly tabernacle metaphorically, to the sacred space which in that metaphor relates to the holy of holies. I have already established that the author uses τὰ ἅγια in general to refer to the holy of holies. Even this expression is a neuter plural substantive of the adjective ἅγιος, possibly indicating that the author uses the neuter plural in general of that which is associated with this sacred space in the heavenly realm, referred to metaphorically as the holy of holies. It is even possible that τὰ ἐπουράνια is a substantive form of τὰ ἐπουράνια ἅγια, although I will not press this possibility. What seems clear enough is that the figurative and metaphorical nature of some of the imagery here implies that we should not necessarily expect

---

[82] E.g. Moffatt, *Hebrews* 131; Michel, *Hebräer* 286, 322; Spicq, *Hébreux* 2.237, 267; Käsemann, *Wandering* 57; Montefiore, *Hebrews* 135, 159; Sowers, *Hermeneutics* 106, 111; Bruce, *Hebrews* 162, 217; Theissen, *Untersuchungen* 92, n.11; Hofius, *Vorhang* 70; MacRae (of 9:23), 'Heavenly Temple' 187; Braun, *Hebräer* 232, 280; Rissi, *Theologie* 36; Wilson (of 9:23), *Hebrews* 164–5; Attridge, *Hebrews* 216, 260f.; Hurst, *Background* 38; C. Koester, *Dwelling* 162; Lane, *Hebrews 9–13* 229; Weiss, *Hebräer* 430, 474; Isaacs, *Space*, 212 n.2; Ellingworth, *Hebrews*, 476; and Grässer, *Hebräer 7,1–10,18*, 77, 186. Cody (*Heavenly Liturgy* 181–4) and McKelvey (*New Temple* 149) may be rare exceptions, although they do not make their translation explicit.

[83] D. M. Hay plausibly suggested that the notion of Christ's intercession in heaven may have been taken over from earlier tradition, since it does not completely fit with the author's strong sense of the completion of Christ's high priestly work after his sacrifice, as symbolized by his session at God's right hand, *Glory at the Right Hand: Psalm 110 in Early Christianity* (SBLMS 18; New York: Abingdon Press, 1973) 149–50. In any case, Christ's intercession also takes place in the holy of holies and arguably has a salvific character. In other words, we should distinguish such *atoning* intercession (cf. Rom. 8:34; 1 John 2:1–2) from that of the Spirit in Rom. 8:26.

the 'heavenly things' to correspond too closely to their earthly, shadowy counterparts.

 Given the faulty translation of ὑπόδειγμα as 'copy' throughout the majority of scholarship, an assumption has resulted that there must be some kind of one-to-one correlation between the 'copies' and the 'originals'. Hofius depicts these assumptions well when he writes,

> Gälte dem Verfasser das irdische Allerheiligste tatsächlich als Abbild des Himmels, so könnte er unter gar keinen Umständen die irdische Stiftshütte mit ihren Einrichtungen (V. 21 f.) als ὑποδείγματα τῶν ἐν τοῖς οὐρανοῖς beschreiben.[84]

Hofius assumes that whatever τὰ ἐν τοῖς οὐρανοῖς might be, they are certainly 'Urbilder' of the earthly 'Abbilder' and therefore that there must be heavenly equivalents for each earthly furnishing.[85] This assumption, however, is not necessarily the case. In its most precise sense, ὑπόδειγμα is a representation or likeness, but it might also be as general in meaning as an example or illustration, as in Heb. 4:11. The author uses this term more to contrast the activities and ministries which take place in the earthly tabernacle than to contrast the precise architecture. The only real correspondent to the activity of the earthly priests is Christ's single offering. This word provides a questionable ground, therefore, on which to base any conception of the precise structure of the heavenly tent. Even the consciences which are the objects of cleansing are purged singularly by Christ's entrance into the heavenly holy of holies. These are several reasons why the heavenly holy of holies, even if not present linguistically, would seem to be the only heavenly 'structure' to which the author could refer in all these statements, and the author may even then be thinking more of the sacred space which τὰ ἅγια signifies than to any specific structure in the heavens.

 At times it is clear that the author is referring explicitly to the holy of holies. Hebrews 9:24, for example, states that 'Christ did not enter into χειροποίητα ἅγια, ἀντίτυπα [ἅγια] τῶν ἀληθινῶν [ἁγίων], but into heaven itself'. It is possible, therefore, that the author also had the holy of holies in mind when he used the neuter plural in the previous verse: 'it was necessary for the illustrations τῶν ἐν τοῖς οὐρανοῖς [ἁγίων] to be cleansed with these, but τὰ ἐπουράνια [ἅγια] themselves with better sacrifices than these'. Again, my argument holds up even if holies merely

---

refer to that sacred space with which the author equates the inner sanctum. Heb. 8:1–5 is an important test case for seeing if τὰ ἐπουράνια reasonably works as a reference either explicitly or implicitly to the heavenly holy of holies. The author begins Heb. 8 with the session of Christ at the right hand of God's throne. This could only be located in the holy of holies, on the right hand of the heavenly counterpart to the ark and mercy seat, God's throne. And Christ's function as a λειτουργός, as in 8:2, can only refer to priestly activities in the heavenly holy of holies, whether his one-time offering or ongoing salvific intercession.

Thus far my interpretation fits the context. I follow the normal usage of τῶν ἁγίων as the holy of holies and τῆς σκηνῆς as the whole tent. This verse thus reads that Christ was 'a minister of the holy of holies and of the true tent, which the Lord pitched, not a human'. We can take the expression as a hendiadys if the author refers to the heavenly tabernacle exclusively in terms of a holy of holies, a possibility I have thought not unlikely in view of the author's theology and seemingly negative attitude toward the outer part of the tabernacle. I can now further suggest that the author may not have an actual structure in view, but heaven itself and, more abstractly, the heavenly sacred space wherein Christ serves as 'high priest'. When we arrive at 8:5, we find that the earthly priests of the old covenant and of the Old Testament text serve this heavenly space in the manner of a shadowy illustration. The comparison between earthly and heavenly cultus makes a reference to the heavenly tabernacle so likely that several interpreters actually translate τῶν ἐπουρανίων in 8:5 as 'the heavenly sanctuary'.[86] Those interpreters who do not translate the phrase in this way would agree that the heavenly tabernacle is the principal thing in view, since the author substantiates his claim by reference to a paradigmatic sanctuary.

Hebrews 8:5, however, stands as the single greatest objection to the idea that the author does not have an actual structure with parts corresponding to the earthly tabernacle in it. The verse has typically been the stronghold of the Platonic interpretation as well, although we saw in the previous chapter that the specifics of the author's citation make this unlikely, particularly his choice of terms from Exodus. The key objection to my line of interpretation is the fact that Moses is told to make πάντα according to the model revealed. Πάντα does not actually occur in our LXX of Exod. 25:40, although it is present in the parallel statement in 25:9. While its presence here could simply represent the LXX version the

---

[86] E.g. McKelvey, *New Temple* 205; MacRae, 'Heavenly Temple' 186; Peterson, *Perfection* 131; Wilson, *Hebrews* 134; C. Koester, *Dwelling* 154; and Lane, *Hebrews 1–8* 199.

author was following,[87] it is quite possible it was included specifically to make the point that *everything* in the earthly tabernacle was constructed to correspond to specific items in the heavenly sanctuary. If so, the tendency to see the heavenly tabernacle as a metaphor for heaven and particularly as a metaphorical space would fail.

Here we face what all interpretations of Hebrews' tabernacle inevitably must at some point face. While all the interpretive paradigms can boast key passages that best favour the paradigm of choice, all must also explain other passages that do not fit as easily. I take this situation as a symptom of the highly metaphorical nature of Hebrews' tabernacle imagery. If a simple referent such as a straightforward heavenly structure were in view, we would not naturally expect so much diversity and complexity. But in the end, the best hypothesis – without having the author present to ask – is the one that can accommodate not only the most favourable passages, but particularly the most unfavourable.

In this instance, we must ask ourselves once again whether Hebrews gives us any reason to believe that the heavenly sanctuary has an outer room. If it does not, then πάντα in 8:5 can only refer to all the things in the *earthly* tabernacle without implying that the heavenly tabernacle had prototypes of *all* the same things. Here we should remind ourselves of my study of Heb. 9:8 earlier in the chapter. There we saw that the author's rhetoric does not see the outer chamber of the earthly tent as representative of anything in heaven but in fact as representative of this present age and earthly ministrations of the earthly sanctuary. The first 'tent' is seen as an obstacle to God's presence. Similarly, the author nowhere mentions an outer room to the heavenly tabernacle, even in 9:11 where σκηνή seems more likely a reference to the whole heavenly tent.

So we must approach 8:5 with the very real possibility that the author does not mean to say that all the parts of the earthly tabernacle correspond to 'parts' of the heavenly tabernacle.[88] The author would be saying somewhat loosely that everything in the earthly tabernacle corresponded *in general* to the τύπος Moses saw on the mountain. Here we remember that the author did not choose to cite the LXX of Exod. 25:9, where the word παράδειγμα might have suggested a more exact correspondence between pattern and shadow. But instead he chose the word τύπος, which is in the singular (i.e. not *types* but singular *type*) and need not correspond quite so exactly to its antitype. After all, the author's purpose in citing

---

[87] It is worth noting, for example, that Philo also quotes this verse with πάντα in *Leg.* 3:102.

[88] Although I do not consider it likely, it is also conceivable that πάντα refers only to the heavenly holy of holies rather than to everything in the entire earthy tabernacle.

this verse is merely to substantiate his claim that the earthly cultus was only a shadowy illustration of Christ's service in the heavenly sanctuary. The πάντα is thus meant to suggest that there is nothing in the earthly sanctuary for which Christ's ministry is not the ultimately reality – not that all the components of the earthly sanctuary have heavenly counterparts.[89] Just as the author amalgamates all the sacrifices of the earthly cultus as the multiple shadows of the singular 'type' of Christ's sacrifice, all the elements of the earthly sanctuary correspond to the singular 'type' of heaven as the place of Christ's offering.

I thus find no reason to reject my sense that τὰ ἐπουράνια in 9:23 and 8:5 refers to anything other than a heavenly holy of holies. Further, we can broadly equate this heavenly holy of holies with heaven itself. If in fact the author understood the skies to be a collection of layers, as seems likely, then we should think of the highest heaven as set off by distinct boundaries in his mind. Further, whatever the throne of God might have signified in his mind, it was surely the reality to which the ark of the covenant in the earthly sanctuary must have pointed.

αὐτόν τόν οὐρανόν

With this phrase, we reach the heart of 9:24 and the crux of the interpretation of this verse. I have already implied that the phrase could be understood in one of three ways: (1) in reference to heaven as a whole, (2) as the highest of a multilayered heaven, with these heavens collectively constituting a two-part sanctuary, or (3) as a synecdoche, with 'the heaven' as a figurative way of referring to the sanctuary *in* the heaven. It is by now clear that I favour the first interpretation.

Of these three readings, the one which views this phrase as a synecdoche seems the least likely, because of indications in the context that the author is saying something more than this figure of speech would indicate. There is, for example, the striking use of the singular here for heaven. Out of the ten occurrences of οὐρανός in the epistle, the author only uses the singular three times (9:24; 11:12; 12:26). Hebrews 12:26 refers to the created heavens and occurs in an Old Testament citation. It thus cannot be taken to indicate the author's usual practice. Hebrews 11:12 also speaks of the created, phenomenological heavens and is not relevant to the context of 9:24. Only in 9:24 does the author use the singular of οὐρανός in reference to the place to which Christ has ascended.

---

[89] I might also mention the possibility that the author did see some allegorical significance in all the elements of the earthly sanctuary.

Even the previous verse uses the plural expression ἐν τοῖς οὐρανοῖς of the location of the heavenly sanctuary. The use of the singular in 9:24 seems to indicate some nuance which the author wants to highlight, a fact emphasized with the use of αὐτόν. The author is making a contrast in which 'heaven itself' is unquestionably better than its alternative. To consider this phrase only a figurative equivalent to 'the sanctuary *in* the heavens' arguably loses some of the meaning: Christ did not enter the sanctuary symbolizing the realities of heaven; he entered heaven itself. The suggestion that *the* heaven here is the highest heaven is somewhat more plausible. In Michel's scheme, Christ passed through the nether heavens (the outer tent) and has entered into the ἅγια, which is the highest heaven.[90] Hofius, taking a slightly different line, has noted a similar alternation from plural to singular in the *Testament of Levi*, where the plural of 2:6 becomes a singular in 5:1 when the angel opens the gates of the highest heaven.[91] He writes,

> [i]n diesem Satz [*TLevi* 5:1] ist mit dem durch kein Attribut näher gekennzeichneten οὐρανός der oberste Himmel gemeint, der "Himmel der Himmel" (οὐρανός τῶν οὐρανῶν), wie er äthHen 1,3f.; 71,5 genannt wird.

Hofius concludes that Hebrews could also signify the highest heaven by its switch to the singular in the context of the inner heavenly sanctum. Such a reading is quite plausible and has precedent. It also can account for the intensive pronoun αὐτόν, since in this scheme the highest heaven is the 'true' type which the handmade holy of holies represents. Hebrews, on the other hand, lacks those distinct indicators of a progression through multiple heavens which *1 Enoch* and *TLevi* clearly have.

Finally, it is hard to deny that a more basic cosmological interpretation of the paradigmatic tabernacle fits extremely well with 9:24. In this interpretation, the holy of holies in the earthly tent is, *in its fundamental significance*, an illustration or representation of heaven, the place where God's throne and presence is, without any distinction between heavenly spheres. The inner sanctum of the earthly sanctuary, therefore, is quite consciously conceived of as a symbol of God's heaven.[92] Christ did not enter into the handmade inner sanctuary, which is after all only a symbolic

---

[90] *Hebräer* 312: 'Auf alle drei Arten von "Himmel" läßt sich sowohl der Singular (οὐρανός) als auch der Plural (οὐρανοί) anwenden (1:10; 8:1; 9:23f.; 11:12).'

[91] *Vorhang* 70–1.

[92] The previous interpretation, where the holy of holies is the highest heaven, can actually be considered a variation of this cosmological reading, the difference being the existence of an outer room.

representation of the true place of God's presence, heaven. Christ did not enter into this imitative structure. Rather, he entered into heaven itself, the true and genuine place of God's presence which these earthly buildings were meant to represent. The cosmological reading might work even if Hofius' idiom should prove to be correct, for the author might only conceive of there being one true heaven, with the lower heavens all being a part of the created realm.

Many statements generally believed to refer to the whole tent throughout Heb. 8 and 9 are said of the heavenly holy of holies in 9:24. Hebrews 8:2 and 9:11, for example, seem to consider the whole heavenly tent as οὐ χειροποίητος, a statement clearly made of the holy of holies in 9:24. While the paradigmatic tent of 8:5 is a τύπος of the earthly tent as a whole, the author specifically focuses on the earthly holy of holies as ἀντίτυπα in relation to the heavenly one in 9:24. Finally, I have argued that the ministry of the whole earthly tabernacle is a ὑπόδειγμα of the heavenly inner sanctum. The fact that the author focuses all of his principal imagery on the heavenly holy of holies supports my claim that it is the true locus of his interest.

καταπέτασμα

Hebrews utilizes imagery of the sanctuary veil at three points (6:19; 9:3; 10:20). Of these three occurrences, 9:3 contributes the least to this discussion, since it simply states the arrangement of the earthly tabernacle. Yet even this verse reminds us that the veil functioned as a barrier to the holy of holies and a statement of the inaccessibility of God's presence. The veil marks the boundary between the outer and inner tent and thus in the author's imagery is potentially parabolic of the transition between the old and new age.

Hebrews 6:19 is of greater import, for the connotations of the veil are more explicit. Here it is stated that we have Christ as an anchor of our soul, steadfast and secure and εἰσερχομένην εἰς τὸ ἐσώτερον τοῦ καταπετάσματος. The phrase 'inside the veil' comes from Lev. 16, and is a roundabout way of referring to the holy of holies.[93] While the statement is roughly equivalent to saying that Christ 'entered once and for all into the holy of holies', as in 9:11, it has further implications.[94] Primarily, it implies that this entrance is the surpassing of a barrier, the possibility of

---

[93] So Hofius, *Vorhang* 88 n.230. I have already noted that the author seems to draw several times upon this chapter, particularly in 8:2, 13:11 and here.
[94] Hofius, *Vorhang* 73.

going where one has not previously been allowed to go. The clear inference is that by means of Christ, the people of God now have unhindered access to sacred space and to God's throne. There is no veil for those who are faithful to the end.

Hebrews 6:19 also seems analogous to 4:14 and 7:26, where it is stated that Christ passed through the heavens or is now higher than the heavens. The passage inside the veil is thus a positive achievement, the surpassing of a barrier or transition. Such a barrier does not seem appropriate to the superior tent of 9:11, which is 'not of this creation'. In the new age, it is difficult to imagine any function for such a veil in a heavenly sanctuary. The other possibility is that the lower heavens are, like a veil, the boundary between earth and the heaven where God dwells; perhaps they are even the created heavens.

The final reference to the veil occurs in 10:20 and is another highly controversial verse in the epistle. Hebrews 10:19–22 reads,

> brothers, since we have boldness to enter into the holy of holies by the blood of Jesus, a new and living way which he inaugurated for us *through the veil, that is his flesh* . . . let us approach [him] with a true heart . . .

The problem centres on how to understand the phrase τοῦτ᾽ ἐστιν τῆς σαρκὸς αὐτοῦ. While the most obvious grammatical reading takes this phrase in apposition to καταπετάσματος,[95] many argue it makes better sense if it is taken with an implied διά or with the verb of the relative clause.[96] Scholarship is roughly equally divided on which interpretation is more likely.

---

[95] E.g. Moffatt, *Hebrews* 143; Michel, *Hebräer* 345; N. Dahl, 'A New and Living Way: The Approach to God According to Hebrews 10:19–25', *Int.* 5 (1951) 405; W. Manson, *The Epistle to the Hebrews: A Historical and Theological Reconsideration* (London: Hodder & Stoughton, 1951) 66–8; Käsemann, *Wandering* 225f.; Koester, 'Outside' 310; U. Luck, 'Himmlisches und irdisches Geschehen im Hebräerbrief: Ein Beitrag zum Problem des "historischen Jesus" im Urchristentum', *NT* 6 (1963) 208–9; Bruce, *Hebrews* 247–9; W. G. Johnsson, 'Defilement and Purgation in the Book of Hebrews' (PhD dissertation, Vanderbilt, 1973) 353–5; N. H. Young, 'τοῦτ᾽ ἐστιν τῆς σαρκὸς αὐτοῦ (Heb. X.20)', *NTS* 20 (1973) 103–4; Peterson, *Perfection* 120; Thompson, *Beginnings* 107; Braun, *Hebräer* 307; Wilson, *Hebrews* 188–90; Attridge, *Hebrews* 285–6; Koester, *Dwelling* 164–5; Isaacs, *Space* 57.

[96] E.g. Westcott, *Hebrews* 320–2; Spicq, *Hébreux* 2.316; Héring, *Hebrews* 91; Cody, *Heavenly Liturgy* 161 n.29; Montefiore, *Hebrews* 173–4; J. Jeremias, 'Hebräer 10,20: τουτ᾽ ἐστιν τῆς σαρκὸς αὐτοῦ', *ZNW* 62 (1971) 131; Hofius, *Vorhang* 81–2; Nissalä, *Hohepriestermotiv* 250; MacRae, 'Heavenly Temple' 188; Rissi, *Theologie* 42–3; Hurst, *Background* 28–9; Lane, *Hebrews 9–13* 273; Weiss, *Hebräer* 520, 525–7; J. Dunnill, *Covenant and Sacrifice in the Letter to the Hebrews* (SNTSMS 75; Cambridge: Cambridge University Press, 1992) 234; Ellingworth, *Hebrews* 519–21.

We need not repeat the customary arguments.[97] In my opinion, the grammatical and contextual evidence is so strong[98] that we must take Christ's flesh as the veil if we can make any sense at all of such imagery.[99] Joachim Jeremias also made a good case for seeing a parallelism between vv. 19 and 20, with the τοῦτ' ἐστιν phrase in parallel to ἐν τῷ αἵματι Ἰησοῦ in 10:19.[100] In whatever sense the author wishes us to equate Jesus' flesh with the veil, the meaning relates to this flesh as a sacrificial means of access to God. So Nils Dahl suggested that Jesus' flesh is that which, when taken away, provides access to the heavenly world.[101] On the other hand, James Moffatt is often quoted for his sense that it is really a 'daring, poetic touch' without too significant an investment in the image.[102] In any case, the meaning of the phrase surely involves Christ's flesh at least as a metaphorical doorway to the heavenly Presence. What is more significant for my purposes is that the author, as Moffatt put it, 'allegorizes the veil'. W. G. Johnsson rightly points out that the comment supplies 'unambiguous evidence of a "spiritualizing" intent on the part of the author', as we have already seen in his creation of a parable out of the two parts of the tent.[103] More than anything else, this pattern of thought indicates that tabernacle imagery does not stand on its own, but is symbolic of a larger paraenetic purpose on the author's part. The author is not so much interested in the tabernacle as a structure, but as what it can represent in his argument.

οἱ οὐρανοί

I have already had occasion to mention the use of οὐρανός in Hebrews in my discussion of 9:24. Hebrews uses the term seven times in the plural (1:10; 4:14; 7:26; 8:1; 9:23; 12:23, 25), while only three times in the singular (9:24; 11:12; 12:26). Among these references we find some diversity of meaning. Three of them, for example, refer in some way to the heaven (11:12; 12:26) or heavens (1:10) of the created realm.

---

[97] A concise treatment can be found in Young's article, 'τοῦτ' ἐστιν' n.102.

[98] While τοῦτ' ἐστιν could introduce a genitive dependent on an implied διά, the unanimous witness of Hebrews is that the author *always* uses this expression appositionally (2:14; 7:5; 9:11; 11:16; 13:15) with the appositional noun in the same case as that to which it refers! One must therefore either accept the reading as appositional or suppose the author to have made a mistake.

[99] C. Holsten (*Exegetische Untersuchung über Hebräer 10:20* (Bern, 1875) 6) suggested that the author might have had a mental lapse or that this reading to be an interpolation.

[100] 'Hebr 10,20'.   [101] 'New and Living Way' 404–5.   [102] *Hebrews* 143.

[103] 'The Cultus of Hebrews in Twentieth-Century Scholarship', *ExpTim* 89 (1977–78) 107. Hurst also recognizes this implication but is so put off by the image of Christ's flesh as a barrier that he takes an agnostic position on the verse's interpretation (*Background* 28–9).

I argued in the previous chapter that these heavens will be removed at the judgement. They are thus to be distinguished from the heaven of God's presence, which is not of this creation (9:24).

While Christ enters into the (singular) heaven itself (9:24), he is seated at the right hand of God's throne ἐν τοῖς οὐρανοῖς (8:1), and those things (or the holy of holies) which the earthly cultus represents are also 'in the heavens' (9:23), from which God speaks (12:25). The author can therefore refer to the heavenly holy of holies as 'the heaven itself' or as being located 'in the heavens'. He can also speak of it as being located 'above the heavens' (7:26), a statement which seems parallel to Christ's passage 'through the heavens' as he enters the inner sanctum.

The exact nature of these various 'heavens' through which Christ passes, in which he sits, or above which he has risen is not exactly clear. Despite the variety of images used, the picture is not necessarily inconsistent. At several points the author distinguishes between the heaven(s) which is a part of the creation and the one(s) which is unshakeable. In the remainder of references, it is not clear whether there is a third category or whether the author simply does not consistently distinguish between the created and indestructible heavens. I have also mentioned Michel's three-sphere interpretation in which there are three kinds of heaven: those which are created, those which constitute the outer heavenly tent, and that which is the heavenly holy of holies. He writes of Christ's passage 'through the heavens' in 4:14:

> οἱ οὐρανοί ist hier nicht einfach der Himmel als Sitz Gottes, auch nicht nur eine Wiedergabe des hebräischen Ausdrucks, שמם, sondern die verschiedene Schichtung überirdischer Sphären, die zwischen Gott und Mensch, Heiligtum und Erde gelagert sind.[104]

Such a distinction would potentially add significance to verses like 4:14 and 7:26. Christ passes '*through* the heavens', and thus comes to be '*higher* than the heavens'. We might easily understand both comments to imply a cosmology with several layers of heaven and the unshakeable heaven(s) at the top. Since for Michel these lower heavens must be 'not of this creation', he classifies them as a third kind of heaven, neither being a part of the created heavens nor being the heaven itself where God dwells.

The notion of a multilayered heaven would not of course be unique to Hebrews in the literature of the period. The *Testament of Levi* spoke of

---

[104] *Hebräer* 204–5. For a similar interpretation, see Cody, *Heavenly Liturgy* 77ff.; Andriessen, 'Zeit' 83f.; Peterson, *Perfection* 76; and for a distinction between types of heaven, Löhr, *Thronversammlung* 188.

three heavens, with the uppermost as the place where the 'Great Glory' dwelt in a heavenly holy of holies.[105] Paul similarly speaks of a third heaven in 2 Cor. 12:2, demonstrating that the tradition was known within early Christianity. Other documents of the period speak of seven or more heavens.[106] Clearly Hebrews would not be unique if it viewed the cosmos as consisting of 'verschiedene Schichtung der überirdischer Sphären' between God and the earth. I have argued, however, against a relationship between 4:14, 7:26 and 9:11. Michel's interpretation can only be inferred from a supposed outer tent and the use of the plural for heaven in verses like 8:1, 9:23; and 12:25. Since I do not find convincing evidence of an outer tent to the heavenly sanctuary, I find Michel's hypothesis unnecessary, even if the author's use of the plural does make it likely that he envisaged a multilayered heaven of some sort.

We should finally consider the use of the term *heaven* in Heb. 12:23, which states that the audience of the epistle have come to the assembly of the first born who are enrolled 'in [the] heavens' (12:23). I have already argued in the previous chapter that this statement is proleptic since it implies the certainty of the believers' entrance into their future, final rest in the heavenly city as spirits finally perfected. This assembly takes place in the heavenly Jerusalem, the city of the living God. This picture implicitly connects the heavenly Jerusalem with τὰ ἅγια to which those who believe have access. Since these ἅγια are arguably 'heaven itself', the heavenly Jerusalem turns out to be yet another metaphor for heaven itself, the heavenly holy of holies. The image is similar to that of *4 Ezra* 10 or *2 Bar.* 4, where the temple is arguably within the heavenly city or paradise.[107] But unlike these Jewish apocalypses, the imagery of Hebrews

---

[105] *TLevi* 2:7–9; 3:1–4. Although the text was later edited to include seven heavens, the original number seems to have been three. (So H. C. Kee in his introduction in *The Old Testament Apocrypha and Pseudepigrapha*, vol. 1 (New York: Doubleday, 1983) 788–9. For a discussion of the date, see 777–8).

[106] E.g. *2 Enoch* 3–20 (7 heavens, although there are 10 in 22J); *Apoc. Mos.* 35:2 (7); *Apoc. Abr.* 19; *Asc. Isa.* 7–11 (7); *b. Hag* 12b (7); *Pesiq. R.* 5 (7); *Midr. Ps.* 92.2 (7); *Abot R. Nat.* 37 (7); *Pirqe R. El.* 154b (7); *Num. Rab.* 14 (10); *Apoc. Paul* 11, 29 (7); *1 Apoc. Jas.* 26:2–19 (72); *3 Enoch* 48:1 (955!). For a discussion of the various concepts of heaven in this regard, see A. T. Lincoln, '"Paul the Visionary": The Setting and Significance of the Rapture to Paradise in II Corinthians XII.1–10', *NTS* 25 (1979) 211–14.

[107] McKelvey comments of the heavenly Jerusalem in Hebrews (*New Temple* 29): 'how could a Jew think of a descent of the heavenly Mount Zion without having in mind a descent of the heavenly temple?' This comment certainly applies to *4 Ezra* and *2 Baruch*, but the question could equally be asked, 'How could a *Christian* imagine a heavenly Jerusalem which did not have unimpeded access to the divine presence and to the Lamb?' In the end, Hebrews gives no evidence that the author expected the heavenly Jerusalem to descend at some point. The heavens and earth will be removed, not renewed.

is closer to Rev. 21:22, where there is no need for a temple in the heavenly city, 'for the Lord God Almighty and the Lamb are its temple'.

Conclusion

In this chapter I have discussed three plausible interpretations of the heavenly tabernacle in Hebrews. I quickly excluded a Platonic meaning because the terms the author uses are not the terms we would expect on such a reading. A second reason was the fact that events cannot take place in an archetypal pattern. While one might theoretically distinguish between a heavenly tent in which salvific events take place and archetypal forms in the mind of God, this is not a distinction Hebrews ever makes. If the author intended his imagery to be Platonic or Philonic, he arguably failed to convey his intentions.[108]

We can probably eliminate additionally the suggestion that the tabernacle is a free-standing, two-part tent in the heavens. For one thing, Hebrews knows nothing of an outer chamber to the heavenly tabernacle. Hebrews 9:11 associates the outer part of the earthly tent with the present age and sees its elimination as a symbol of the new age's full arrival. Hebrews 9:24 provides a further argument against this position because of the contrast between the earthly, handmade holy of holies and 'the heaven itself'. The intensive αὐτός in this verse emphasizes a contrast between heaven itself and that which only symbolizes heaven. Yet another blow to this interpretation comes in 12:22, where the 'rest' of God for which believers are destined is the heavenly Jerusalem, the city of the living God, Zion. This verse arguably implies the equation of τὰ ἅγια with the heavenly Jerusalem. The picture seems quite similar to Rev. 21:22, where the heavenly city does not have a temple, because God and the Lamb serve in this capacity. Hebrews 12 says nothing of a tabernacle and reinforces my sense that Hebrews' earlier rhetoric was more metaphorical and paraenetic than literal and indicative.

In the end, the best explanation for Hebrews' varied tabernacle imagery and rhetoric is that the primary significance of the tabernacle is located in the rhetorical purposes of the author's broader high priestly metaphor. In other words, the notion of a heavenly sanctuary is not a stand-alone concept for the author – it is a catalyst for a larger rhetorical purpose. The author desires to pit the entirety of the Levitical cultus against the atonement provided by Christ. To do so, he argues that Christ is a superior

---

[108] Nor have we any firm basis on which to conclude that the author was consciously avoiding Platonic language because his audience might find it objectionable.

priest and sacrifice who ministers in a superior sanctuary. The widespread sense that the wilderness tabernacle mirrored the structure of the cosmos, an idea well attested in both Philo and Josephus, easily served the author's purposes. So heaven itself, the highest heaven in particular, is the most literal referent for the heavenly tabernacle. This location of the throne of grace, however the author might have understood it, is at the same time the heavenly tent, the heavenly holy of holies, and the heavenly Jerusalem. It is the τύπος according to which Moses made the whole earthly sanctuary (8:5), so that no function of the earthly sanctuary is left unaccounted for in the heavenly one. The outer chamber of the earthly tabernacle was merely a parable of an age that would pass with Christ (9:8–9) and had no literal correspondent in heaven.

But the author largely used the image of a heavenly tabernacle itself as a metaphorical means to a rhetorical end. He could additionally consider Christ's flesh to be like the veil of a temple which, once removed, provides entrance into the presence of God (10:20). Such an extreme metaphor reflects the highly symbolic and metaphorical penchant of the author. He can easily speak of the inaugural cleansing of the heavenly tabernacle (9:23) – an absurd image for a literal structure in the purest heaven. But the author is not thinking of a literal structure. In the overall high priestly metaphor, the heavenly tabernacle ultimately corresponds to that sacred space in which Christ offers atonement for sin. But the author does not literally picture a structure in heaven or, for that matter, Christ carrying blood or some other item into heaven. These are all various permutations of the basic priestly metaphor by which the author asserts that all the functions of the Levitical cultus have been accomplished and thus replaced.

7

CONCLUSION

Introduction

Hebrews argues from a story. This story is the story of salvation history as the author understood it. His arguments are interpretations of this story in the light of the situation of those to whom he sent this homily. Indeed, both he and his audience were themselves characters within the grand plot. The author would have his audience know that the plot had already reached its climax and would soon see its final consummation.

My study has not focused on all the dimensions of this story. I have focused primarily on the two overall settings of the plot, namely, its temporal and spatial settings. I discussed the former under the heading of eschatology, for the plot of salvation history moves in a specific direction. In former days it moved toward the decisive sacrifice of Christ. Since that time it has moved toward its ultimate consummation in judgement and Christ's appearance a second time.

Chapter 4 analysed how the author divides the story of salvation into two broad 'acts' corresponding to two covenants, the turning point lying with the inauguration of the new covenant. Throughout the plot, however, the story was always moving toward God's intended destiny for humanity, namely, a glory and honour appropriate to those who are the sons of God. Chapter 3 explored this continuity in terms of God's promise to his people and language of perfection in the sermon.

Chapters 5 and 6 then discussed the spatial settings of the plot under the heading of cosmology, the ways in which the created realm and true heaven function within the author's discourse. The earthly realm is thoroughly temporary and destined for ultimate destruction along with the end of the first age. Meanwhile, the heavenly tabernacle must be understood in the light of the author's broader high priestly metaphor. Most precisely, it is that abstract sacred space within which Christ as 'priest' offers his atonement. But it also corresponds generally to the highest heaven itself, as Christ's ascension and exaltation to God's right hand is metaphorically reconceived as an entrance into a heavenly holy of holies. The author uses this language for its rhetorical power, as I set out in my exploration of the author's rhetorical strategy in ch. 2.

These two settings, therefore, entail correlations with the two over-lapping ages. As long as the created realm stands, the old age has not fully reached its conclusion. Access to the heavenly realm, on the other hand, corresponds to the beginning of the new age and will be available to the perfected forever. Just as the new age began with Christ's sacrifice, the old age will decisively end with the removal of the created realm and the 'shaking' of all that is shakeable. Hebrews' motif of high priest-hood, the picture of Christ as a high priest who offers himself as a sacrifice in a heavenly sanctuary, is a metaphor which grew out of a re-presentation of the traditional Christian 'story' in cultic terms because of a perceived need.

In this conclusion I bring together the insights gained through my holistic examination of the epistle into a systematic picture of Hebrews' narrative and rhetorical worlds. In accordance with the guidelines I laid down for this quest, I have conducted a text-oriented study which takes into account the whole of the epistle and is sensitive to possible differences between the author and his audience. The first part of the conclusion re-presents Hebrews' narrative world as best I have ascertained it. The final part then ventures some suggestions about the context against which we might read and further speculate about the significance of this sermon.

The narrative world of Hebrews

Prologue

The story begins with God. It is his *logos* which is the unifying feature of the entire plot. The movement of the story of salvation takes place in accordance with that which he has 'spoken', that which he finds 'fitting' and that which is 'necessary'. He speaks both through the prophets (1:1) and angels (2:2) of the old covenant and the mediator of the new (2:3). From beginning to end of story, God is the director of the drama, the one 'for whom and through whom' everything exists (2:10). He is the 'consuming fire' of judgement (12:29) into whose hands it is a fearful thing to fall (10:31). His *logos* is active and sharper than any sword in its analysis of the thoughts and intents of the heart (4:12).

At the heart of the story is a plan, a purpose which was present before the 'creation' of the worlds. The author's conception of this creation itself lies in obscurity. The textual gaps surrounding the nature of creation and of Christ's role within that process are too great to reconstruct without speculation. Nevertheless, I wonder if the author, whether consciously or unconsciously, considered the created realm to be innately inferior to the heavenly, although not evil. Might this outlook be part of a world-view which the author brought with him to Christianity and which remained as a residue in the midst of his new Christian perspective? Did the author, like the author of Wisdom, picture creation out of formless matter? Did he, as perhaps Philo, hold to God's simultaneous creation and organization of matter from all eternity? In any case it was not a long journey from the author's thought to the Gnosticism of the following century.

The author has an almost deprecatory tone towards 'that which has been created' (e.g. 12:27) and perhaps unconsciously associates the need for atonement with the foundation of the world (9:26). In addition, we hear of no point in God's plan which did not entail the eventual coming of Christ. Death, as a function of the earthly realm, has impeded humanity from reaching its destined glory from its very creation. Hebrews does not speak of a time when Adam fell or when the Devil did not hold the power of death (2:14). The fundamental soteriology of the epistle is tied up with Christ's 'indestructible life' (7:16), his sinless life (4:15) in the midst of his learning of obedience (5:8). This salvation was not previously possible, for the one holding the power of this realm prevented any other possibility.

When the epistle speaks of Christ as the creator of the worlds, therefore, it speaks of him as the wisdom 'through which' God made them (1:2). Christ is also at the beginning and end of the plot, yet Christ as pre-existent creator seems primarily a function of God's wisdom and word, as the language of 1:3 seems to indicate. Jesus is distinguished from God as creator in 2:10, demonstrating that the author could at least subconsciously distinguish the two. Again, the textual gaps probably do not allow a firm conclusion, but one wonders whether Christ is this wisdom and *logos* in the sense that God has created the world with the primary intention of providing salvation through Christ. Christ stands as the true *end* of the creation and thus as its beginning purpose and direction, the very ground upon which the heavens and earth were founded. These are some of the most obscure and unelucidated aspects of the epistle.

Act I: 'Yesterday'

The first act within the drama of salvation history is the 'former' age, the time of the old covenant. At that time, God's word to his people, the fathers of Israel, was 'spoken' through the prophets (1:1), and his Law was a 'word spoken through angels' (2:2). These angels within that age were the 'ministers of those about to inherit salvation' (1:14), servants of the old covenant. As winds and flames of fire (1:7), their function in this role was only destined to last as long as the first act of the plot, when their stewards would inherit salvation. The coming world, as opposed to this one, would not be subject to them (2:5) but to Christ and his brothers.

The Law spoken through the mediation of angels was only a 'shadowy illustration' of the perfect work which God was going to perform in the second act of the story (8:5; 9:23). In every way it was sent as an indication of that which was to come. It was not able to 'perfect' those who wanted access to God (10:1), but awaited the entrance of a more perfect hope (7:19). It only contained a shadow of the good things to come (10:1). It was not a perfect image of those things.

This 'shadow' which the Law contained was the Levitical priesthood, upon which the Law was put into effect (7:11). The relationship between the two is inextricable to the extent that a change of the one necessitates a change in the other (7:12). These priests were hindered in their service by death (7:23), as well as by the fact that they had sins which needed atonement (5:3; 7:26). They nevertheless continued to offer their gifts and sacrifices in a tabernacle which had been built upon God's command through the revelation of the true reality to Moses (8:5), who was yet another servant in the house of God (3:5).

The people to whom Moses ministered did not remain in God's covenant (8:9), but had evil hearts of disbelief (3:12) which prevented them from entering into God's 'rest' (3:18). Yet this rest was not the true rest, for if Joshua had led God's people into their true homeland, God would not have spoken of another day (4:8). The wilderness generation, like Esau (12:16), did not believe (3:19), did not hold the substance of their faith in God unto the end (3:14), and their corpses fell in the desert (3:17).

Nevertheless, there were those who were faithful in the old age, in fact a great cloud of witnesses (12:1) who recognized that they were pilgrims and strangers upon the earth (11:13). They were looking forward to their true, heavenly homeland (11:14, 16), a city which would remain (13:14), the heavenly Jerusalem, city of the living God (12:22). They all died in faith without having received God's promise (11:39–40), which God had tendered to Abraham and to his people throughout the first act of the plot (6:17–18). This was because God had planned all along to bring the perfection of humanity together in the eschaton through Christ (11:40).

The first tabernacle and its services, therefore, served symbolically as an indicator of the two covenants which God had planned (9:9). The outer tent, into which the priests went continually throughout the year (9:6), was a parable of the first age (9:9) in which ineffectual gifts and sacrifices were offered only able to cleanse the flesh (9:10). Indeed, the first age was inextricably associated with the created realm and with the fleshly. As long as this foreign realm continues to stand (9:8), the old age is only 'near' its disappearance (8:13). None of these sacrifices and rituals really take away sins, for bulls and goats are not capable of accomplishing such a task (10:4).

All these aspects of the old age looked forward to something better, something truly efficacious. In and of themselves, they were all 'secure' and every transgression received its due punishment (2:2). But they were innately inferior to the heavenly solution which God was waiting to put into effect through Christ. The second act begins, therefore, as the consummation of the ages (9:26). The beginning of the second act is the climax of the plot, the entrance of the long-expected Christ onto the stage, the attainment of God's purpose through a truly effective work and a true atonement for sins.

Act 2

Scene 1: 'Today'

In the days of his flesh, God's heir apparent had demonstrated by his reverent fear (5:7) and sinless life (4:15) that he was qualified to be a Melchizedekian high priest. The one who was able to save him from death heard his petitions (5:7) and brought to realization his destined 'indestructible life' (7:16). Humanity had been intended for glory and honour, but had 'not yet' achieved this status (2:8) because of the power of death, under the fear of which the seed of Abraham were living their whole lives (2:15). Christ, having been made lower than the angels for a little while, destroyed the one having this power of death (2:14) and was crowned with glory and honour, tasting of death for all of humanity (2:9). 'Today', he enters his destined role and thus leads many sons to their appointed glory (2:10). This 'today' is the 'last days' of Jeremiah, the time of the new covenant (8:8f.), the beginning of the eschatological age.

The rubric under which the achievement of glory and honour can be placed, the ultimate statement of the salvific accomplishment of Christ in Hebrews, is the metaphor of Christ's high priesthood. The implications of this fulfilled priesthood are the ultimate rhetorical purpose of the author's argumentation (8:1). In more traditional Christian language, the author can speak of Christ having made an atonement (2:17) and can utilize texts commonly used within primitive Christianity. These are texts like Ps. 8 (Heb. 2:6–8) and Ps. 2:7 (Heb. 1:5). God has 'begotten' his Son 'today' as he pronounces the royal enthronement of Christ. He who had been heir apparent, awaiting his destined place in exaltation, has now been seated at the right hand of God (1:3, 13; 8:1; 10:12; 12:2), only awaiting for his enemies to be placed under his feet (10:13). All of these themes can be found elsewhere in the New Testament and demonstrate that the author is in touch with the traditions of the early church.

Psalm 110:1 more than any other traditional motif represents for the author the statement *par excellence* of Christ's conclusive achievement of atonement. The author takes this more typical expression of Christ's exalted messianic identity and transforms it into a cultic metaphor. By speaking of Christ's exaltation and session as a metaphor for the entrance of a Melchizedekian high priest into a heavenly holy of holies, the author is able to contrast Christ directly with the Levitical priests and thus ultimately with the Law and 'old covenant' in general. The death and ascension of Christ become a sacrifice which was offered in a heavenly tabernacle, transforming all of these salvific actions into a single eschatological movement, in fact the climactic event of the entire story of salvation history, the very 'consummation of the ages' (9:26) and the defeat of the Devil (2:14). By using this language, the author is able to amalgamate all of previous salvation history into one great shadow of this one consummative moment. The entirety of the earthly tabernacle is simply a shadowy illustration, the antitypes of the singular 'type' shown to Moses on the mountain (8:5).

The formulation of this metaphor is ingenious. The author must first find some basis for considering Christ a high priest, which he conveniently discovers in Ps. 110. This psalm not only speaks of the exalted Messiah at God's right hand, but also refers to this king as a priest, after the order of Melchizedek. By coupling this text with Gen. 14, the author is able to argue that a priest like Melchizedek would be greater than a Levitical priest. From Ps. 110:4 he can also argue the 'indestructible life' of such a priest, finding another point of contrast with Levitical priests. He thus had a proof text which could be used as a basis for contrasting Christ with the Levitical priesthood and the cultic Law of Judaism.

Once the author had established Christ as a superior priest, it was easy to relate the traditional motifs of atoning death and ascension/exaltation to the high priestly metaphor. The common conception of the wilderness tabernacle as a representation of the universe enabled the author to see Christ's exaltation to God's right hand as an entrance into a heavenly holy of holies (9:12, 24) and as the offering *par exellence* of Christ as high priest (9:25; 10:12?). His death outside the camp (13:12) could thus be seen as a sacrifice for sins (10:5, 12?). The ambiguity in the author's thought as to whether the offering is the same as his death (9:27–8) or occurs in heaven (9:25) is a by-product of what is ultimately metaphorical language.

But the author does not have a literal, free-standing structure in view as he speaks of the heavenly tabernacle. He does not, for example, have any place in his thinking or argument for an outer room to such a tent (9:8). While he generally has heaven itself, the highest heaven, in view when he speaks of Christ entering the holies, occasionally he builds on the metaphor in ways that stretch the limits of his theology. Thus he speaks of the inaugural cleansing of the heavenly tabernacle (9:23), an image that seems wholly inappropriate in reference to a structure in the purest heaven. And the author reflects his figurative penchant when he refers to Christ's flesh as a veil through which the audience might find access to God (10:20). In short, the imagery of the heavenly cultus of the new covenant is a metaphorical expansion of more traditional language in order to persuade the audience of the sermon that Christ has made obsolete any need for the Jewish Law, particularly in terms of its cultic dimension.

The high priestly metaphor is thus one of two narrative 'objectifications' of the basic story that Hebrews utilizes. Any story can be expressed in several narrative forms, often turning on factors such as point of view and sequence. The author of Hebrews knows the traditional 'narrative', involving the atoning death, resurrection and ascension of Christ. For the sake of his audience, however, he 'narrates' a form of the story which brings out the ways in which Christ's atonement achieves true forgiveness and cleansing over and against the shadowy, cultic orientation of the old covenant. He narrates the second act in the language of the first.

The sacrifice of Christ is thus the key event of the plot. This offering provided a way 'through the veil' (10:20) and thus made access to God a present possibility for the people of God (10:19). The forgiveness of sins is a present reality through Christ (10:22). In a sense, those who believe have already come to the heavenly Jerusalem (12:22–4) because of the certainty of their salvation. They need only hold the substance of the beginning firm until the end (3:14).

Unfortunately, while the recipients should no longer grant any status to the old covenant (9:8) and should no longer rely upon the Levitical cultus or the Law for their relationship with God (13:9, 13), and even though the old covenant is obsolete and about to vanish (8:13), despite all these truths, the 'present' age has not yet completely vanished (9:9). While the people of God now have a better hope (7:19) and might proleptically be deemed 'perfected' (10:14), they are still living in an in-between time in which they are still strangers and foreigners to the world in which they live (11:13). In the in-between time of 'today', the people of God exist in relation to two different worlds. On the one hand, their physical bodies are in this world, and they still have need of endurance (10:36). On the other, their confidence is focused on hoped-for things which are as yet still unseen (11:1). Their loyalty and allegiance is clearly directed toward their heavenly home (11:14–16) and toward their promised rest. 'Today', God has encouraged them not to harden their hearts as the people of Israel long ago (3:7–8), but to hold fast (2:1) and beware of shrinking back unto destruction (10:39).

As characters in the plot of salvation history, the author and his recipients also live in the 'today' of the story. They too are confronted with the choice either to endure and be faithful or to abandon their confidence. They have positive examples of faith like the great cloud of witnesses (11:1), as well as negative examples (e.g. 3:16). These examples spell out for them the choice they must make as the people of God. The present situation in which the visible, foreign world might lure them away from the invisible, heavenly realities gives rise to the author's homily as he directs their attention toward what is truly lasting. The in-between time is a time in which the visible realm speaks deceptively of the old age and the old covenant and tempts them to a false sense of reality. But in truth the new age has begun and all true hope lies in the invisible, heavenly realm. All those who are truly faithful will abandon their confidence in the earthly and vanishing means of fleshly cleansing and will rely upon the true and permanent 'offering' of Christ.

Scene 2: 'Forever'

In just a little while, the one who is coming will come and not delay (10:37). Christ is only waiting for his enemies to be put under his feet (10:13), when at the appropriate point he will be seen a second time in judgement (9:28). At that time, the consuming fire which is God (12:29) will shake the created heavens and earth, removing all that is shakeable so that God's heavenly, unshakeable kingdom will remain (12:26–7). He will remove the 'outer tent' of the created heavens and earth once and for all, this world in which access to God is obscured by that which has been made (9:8). At that time, the people of God will truly and conclusively enter their appointed rest (4:11). Their perfected spirits will join ten thousand angels in festal gathering in the assembly of first-born sons at the heavenly Jerusalem, the true Zion, the city of the living God (12:22–3). This is the place of glory to which Christ is leading them as brothers (2:10), their destined place in God's order (2:6–8). This coming world of salvation will be subjected to them (2:5) and they, like Christ, will be exalted above the angels (2:16).

The whole of the story moves toward this conclusion. As the beginnings of the story lie largely in the unspoken thoughts of the author, so he does not go into great detail about the end of the story. We have only the broadest hints about the ultimate rest of God's people. What is certain, however, is that the Christ who is present at the beginning of the plot as the wisdom 'through which' God made the world is also present at the end as the Son whom God has appointed as 'heir of all things' (1:2).

The rhetorical situation of Hebrews

In ch. 2, I sketched the basic contours of Hebrews' rhetorical situation. There I mentioned three basic factors in such a situation: (1) the particulars of the audience, (2) the particulars of the rhetor, and (3) what Lloyd Bitzer called the 'exigence', the efficient cause behind the creation of the rhetorical piece.[1] If this study has been successful to any degree, then we should now be able to revisit these issues with a better overall sense of Hebrews' rhetorical world. Without question, our lack of evidence stands as an irremovable veil between us and any certain knowledge on so many matters. But at least in theory, we should now be able to speculate about the possibilities in a more refined and informed way than when we first began.[2]

The particulars of the author

It seems doubtful that we will ever have a probable hypothesis on the identity of Hebrews' author. We can say with a good deal of certainty that he was a he. The masculine singular participle at 11:32 almost conclusively points to this conclusion. To argue otherwise would require a

---

[1] 'The Rhetorical Situation', *Philosophy and Rhetoric* 1 (1968) 6.

[2] Since a full assessment of Hebrews' rhetorical situation requires some discussion of the author and audience, I brainstorm in the following pages well beyond matters discussed in this study. The main positions are of course well argued (see any major critical commentary). My real goal in what follows is to suggest some frameworks in which the rhetoric of Hebrews, as I have assessed it, would be appropriate.

conspiracy theory, that the author veiled her identity from the audience because of her gender. But we have no indication of anything of this sort. If anything, the author demonstrates a familiarity with the audience and seems to assume they will know who he and Timothy are without explanation.

Indeed, it seems almost certain that the author and probably Timothy have already visited the location of the audience and are familiar to them personally. The author speaks of being *restored* to them (ἀποκαθίστημι; 13:19). Yet he does not include himself among the leaders of the church, past or present (13:7, 17). The name *Timothy*, along with the fact that Hebrews holds several traditions in common with Paul, easily suggests that the author was connected to the Pauline circle in some way. If so, the authority with which he speaks would indicate a leader in this circle, an equal to Timothy, more than a minor player.

The quality of Greek and the overall sophistication of Hebrews' argument point toward someone for whom Greek was a first language and, indeed, someone with a significant education.[3] We might easily suppose that the author enjoyed a Greek education and was quite possibly more educated than Paul himself. The argument functions exclusively from the Septuagint – at times where it differs significantly from the Hebrew text – and the author shows no real knowledge of Hebrew.[4] These characteristics point generally, although not definitively, to a Diaspora individual, most likely a Hellenistic Jew. The wealth of biblical knowledge exhibited in Hebrews points with probability to a Jew, but not definitively. David Runia has pointed out that four citations in Hebrews are worded so similarly to Philo that 'coincidence must be ruled out'.[5] The most striking of these is the form of citation in Heb. 13:5, which occurs elsewhere only in Philo's writings. Here the author splices together Josh. 1:5, Deut. 31:8 and possibly Gen. 28:15.[6] A not improbable conclusion is that the author of Hebrews stands in some relation to Alexandria. He could have spent

---

[3] For more detailed support of these claims, see my 'Philo and the Epistle to the Hebrews: Ronald Williamson's Study after Thirty Years', *SPhA* 14 (2002) 112–35. Although my views have developed somewhat, also see my discussion of Hebrews' background in my *Understanding the Book of Hebrews: The Story behind the Sermon* (Louisville, KY: Westminster/John Knox, 2003) 88–105.

[4] Most notoriously in his use of Ps. 40:7 (39:7 LXX) in Hebrews 10:5. The author's allegorical interpretation in 7:1–2 of the Hebrew names in Gen. 14 is no proof of knowledge of Hebrew. Philo clearly had no knowledge of Hebrew yet multiplies these kinds of interpretations constantly.

[5] *Philo in Early Christian Literature: A Survey* (CRINT 3; Minneapolis: Fortress Press, 1993) 76.

[6] Philo's conflation of these verses appears in *Conf.* 166.

time in the synagogues there or have been influenced by someone who had spent time there.[7]

One might also mention the suggestion of William Manson that the author of Hebrews might have been a Hellenist of the sort we see in Stephen's speech in Acts 7.[8] Noting that Acts 6:1 divides Jerusalem Christians into 'Hebrews' and 'Hellenists', Manson explored Stephen as narrated in Acts.[9] He concluded that Stephen was not opposed to the temple per se, but that he believed that the Jewish people (and by implication the Hebrews) had mistaken it for a *permanent* rather than a temporary, symbolic structure.[10] Manson then offered eight similarities between Hebrews and Acts 7,[11] which have been modified and supplemented by Lincoln Hurst.[12]

But we might plausibly reverse Manson's suggestion, in the sense that Manson thought of the historical Stephen as the prototype of the Hellenistic Jewish Christian. Rather, it is more likely that the author of Acts had Christians like the author of Hebrews in mind *as he portrayed* Stephen. Given my analysis of Hebrews, the most interesting parallel is Stephen's attitude toward the Jerusalem temple in contrast to the wilderness tabernacle. In Acts 7:44, Stephen speaks of Moses making the tent of witness according to the τύπος he had seen. His tone toward it is favourable. Yet this tone changes notably when Stephen comes to the temple that Solomon built (7:47–8). The author of Acts seems to indict the Jerusalem leadership of that day for mistaking χειροποίητοι houses for the true dwelling of God. Rather, Stephen proclaims, they should have known that 'the heaven is my throne . . . where is the place of my καταπαύσεως' (7:49).

It would not be appropriate to develop this line of thought in greater detail. But it is more than reasonable to suggest that as the author of Acts pondered how to portray the character of Stephen as a Hellenistic Christian Jew, individuals such as the author of Hebrews came to mind. Indeed, it is not impossible that the author of Acts might have known the book of Hebrews and intentionally echoed its rhetoric in Acts 7. Yet if we take the evaluative voice of Acts as an indication of its author's own theology, he or she does not seem to have shared quite so stark a point of

---

[7] For a more detailed discussion of the relationship between Hebrews and Philo, see my 'Philo and Hebrews', 112–35. See also the discussion in my *A Brief Guide to Philo* (Louisville, KY: Westminster/John Knox, 2005) 81–6.

[8] In the 1949 Baird Lectureship, published as *The Epistle to the Hebrews: An Historical and Theological Reconsideration* (London: Hodder & Stoughton, 1951).

[9] *Hebrews* 27–8.   [10] *Hebrews* 34f.   [11] *Hebrews* 36.

[12] *The Epistle to the Hebrews: Its Background of Thought* (SNTSMS 65; Cambridge: Cambridge University Press, 1990) 94f.

view toward the temple. The author of Acts has Paul offering a sacrifice in the Jerusalem temple in Acts 21:23–6, an act that the author of Hebrews indicates is definitively unnecessary in the light of Christ's sacrifice.

The particulars of the audience

As with the author, we are forced to read between the lines of scattered comments in Hebrews in our effort to peer into the thoughts and concerns of its audience. In Heb. 13:24, the author tantalizingly tells the audience that οἱ ἀπὸ τῆς Ἰταλίας greet them. While it is impossible to be certain, the view commanding the greatest support is that these are individuals 'away from' Italy who are sending greetings back. Accordingly, Rome would be the destination with the largest following. Rome is attractive because we can identify one or two situations in the mid-first century that might correlate with Hebrews' description of the audience's prior sufferings in 10:32–4. Given the traditional association of Timothy with Ephesus (e.g. 1 Tim. 1:3), it is then tempting to see Ephesus as Hebrews' point of origin. Unfortunately, these must remain only possibilities, and we must resist letting such hypotheses unduly bias our exegesis.

Of more significance is the question of the audience's ethnicity. The initial impression when one considers the intense biblical argumentation of Hebrews is that the audience must surely be Jewish. While the author does not directly tell his audience not to rely on Levitical means of atonement, his exhortations to continue in faith must relate to the Levitical system in some way or else Hebrews' argument becomes incoherent. Such rhetoric clearly would make sense to a Jewish audience, particularly one tempted to revert to some prior 'Jewish' perspective.[13]

At the same time, several details in Hebrews make us pause before drawing too simple a conclusion. For one thing, Hebrews never uses the terms Ἰουδαῖος or ἔθνος, and the question of the inclusion of the Gentiles never arises. Yet the argument of Hebrews seems universal in scope. I have argued that the author understands Ps. 8 in reference to *all* humanity, and the implication of Hebrews is surely that Christ's death is efficacious for both Jew and Gentile. We must then conclude that the 'seed of Abraham' in 2:16 includes both Jew and Gentile. As modern readers, we are prone to miss the controversial element to such universal assumption. Certainly none of Paul's writings felt free to pass over this issue, even though they were largely addressed to Gentiles. Still less could he have glossed over

---

[13] E.g. F. C. Synge, *Hebrews and the Scriptures* (London: SPCK, 1959) 44, and many others.

such a controversial point if he had ever written to a predominantly Jewish audience. Again, while these arguments are not determinative, they push the feel of Hebrews (1) later rather than earlier and (2) more likely Gentile than Jewish. It would have been easier to pass over universal inclusion when writing to the 'out' group rather than to the 'in' group.

Still more perplexing for a Jewish audience is the list of items the author includes in ὁ τῆς ἀρχῆς τοῦ Χριστοῦ λόγος (6:1–2). He lists as foundational (1) μετανοία ἀπὸ νεκρῶν ἔργων, (2) πίστις ἐπὶ θεόν, (3) βαπτισμῶν διδαχή (4) διδαχὴ ἐπιθέσεώς χειρῶν, (5) διδαχὴ ἀναστάσεως νεκρῶν and (6) διδαχὴ κρίματος αἰωνίου. As the message of the *beginning* about the Messiah, we immediately note that we cannot easily distinguish most of these items from what a non-Christian Jew might believe.[14] On the whole, the list is far more appropriate to a group of Gentile converts to Christian Judaism than to a group of Jews who had accepted Jesus as the Christ. David deSilva plausibly suggests that the νεκρὰ ἔργα might very well refer to the worship of idols.[15]

Here the possibility that the church at Rome may have had a significant 'conservative' Gentile element is intriguing. While Paul's letter to the Romans seems to address an audience of mixed ethnicity, the Roman church on balance at that time was likely more Gentile than Jewish (e.g. Rom. 1:13; 6:19; 10:1–2). The church father Ambrosiaster, writing in Rome about the year 375 CE, claimed that the Gentile Roman Christians of the first century had a 'Jewish bent' to their Christianity. If indeed Chrsitian Jews were expelled from Rome early on by Claudius, we can hypothesize that the Gentile church that remained may have retained the conservative character of its foundations even in their absence.[16] The Gentile Christians at Rome may thus have borne a strong affinity with the relatively 'conservative' Jewish Christianity of Peter and James.

But these are all speculations that we cannot confirm. What we know with some certainty is that the audience is composed of second generation Christians (e.g. 2:3 – which would include the author in this category as well). They have been Christians for some time (e.g. 5:12; 10:32). The leaders under whom they were initially converted have apparently passed from the scene, most likely through martyrdom (13:7). Perhaps, during

---

[14] So also H. W. Attridge, *The Epistle to the Hebrews* (Philadelphia: Fortress Press, 1989) 163–4.

[15] *Perseverance in Gratitude: A Socio-Rhetorical Commentary on the Epistle 'to the Hebrews'* (Grand Rapids, MI: Eerdmans, 2000) 216–17.

[16] E.g. Raymond E. Brown and John P. Meier, *Antioch and Rome: New Testament Cradles of Catholic Christianity* (New York: Paulist, 1983) 110; Joseph A. Fitzmeyer, *Romans* (London: Geoffrey Chapman, 1993) 33.

those days of crisis, they suffered admirably and materially supported those who were imprisoned (10:32–4). If Rome is the destination, then our main candidates for such crises are, first, the expulsion under Claudius – during which, however, we have no reason to believe that any Christians died. The second candidate is the persecution under Nero, documented by Tacitus and Suetonius.[17] Yet we must also include the deaths of Paul and Peter in this list, since tradition holds that they also died in Rome during the reign of Nero in the 60s. Is it possible that 13:7 is an allusion to one or another of these?

The exigence

I spent some time in ch. 2 unfolding the exigent situation of Hebrews as best I could on the basis of inferences from the text. I concluded, first, that the author believed the audience to be waning in its confidence and commitment to the Christian confession as he understood it. Secondly, he believed he could bolster the audience's confidence by developing their understanding of the atoning efficacy of Christ vis-à-vis Levitical means of atonement. Here I observed that the author never exhorts them *not* to rely on Levitical means of atonement (13:9–10 being a slightly different issue), but he clearly believed that an emphasis on the full sufficiency of Christ's atonement would effectively address the underlying causes of their wavering. Accordingly, the author's rhetorical strategy was to pit Christ against the entirety of the 'old covenant', not only as the reality to which it imperfectly pointed but indeed as its replacement. As the earthly cultus had priests who offered sacrifices in an earthly sanctuary, Christ was a heavenly high priest who offered himself in a heavenly sanctuary. The change of priesthood implied a change of law, making the old covenant with its Levitical cultus obsolete.

As I close this study, we might briefly speculate on what sort of circumstances might give rise to such rhetoric. What exigent circumstances might, first, discourage the audience's commitment to the Christian confession, perhaps even challenging entry-level Jewish beliefs that were generically Jewish in character (6:1–2)? Further, what doubts might be addressed by pointing out the superiority of Christ's atonement to that of the Levitical system? We might also mention a number of other oblique references for which we might account. Hebrews 11 redounds with examples of those who faced death or persecution and yet who carried on in faith. There are vague references to edicts of kings (e.g. 11:23) and

---

[17] Tacitus, *Annals* 14:44; Suetonius, *Nero* 16.

alienation from city and country (e.g. 11:10, 14). One of the most intriguing allusions is that of 13:14: 'we do not have here a city that remains but we are seeking the one that comes'.

The thought of a city that did not remain in the first century of course makes us think immediately of Jerusalem, destroyed in 70 CE. Alternatively, we might think of Roman Christians with some pride in their Roman heritage, perhaps even citizenship.[18] We will not follow this line of thinking too long before we begin to ask how Hebrews' language of the tabernacle might have related to the Jerusalem temple and whether Hebrews was written before or after its destruction. It is indeed striking that the temple is never mentioned throughout this sermon. If the temple were standing, it would be difficult not to see this sermon as an implicit and subversive critique meant to dissuade the audience from its use.

On the other hand, the connotations of Hebrews' rhetoric take on a decidedly different character if the sermon was composed in the aftermath of the temple's destruction. There would be no need in such a context to mention the temple, for a destroyed temple offers no competition to Christ. Indeed, Hebrews more takes on the character of a consolation or an apology in the absence of such a temple. With the temple in Jerusalem destroyed, Hebrews would step back and reflect on the nature of earthly sanctuaries in general, utilizing the wilderness tabernacle as the prototype. It has long been recognized that the present tense of Hebrews' sacrificial imagery is no argument against a post-70 date. Several post-70 authors speak of temple sacrifice in the present tense.[19]

Nor does the comment that the audience has not yet shed blood imply that no Christians had yet suffered martyrdom at their location (12:4). The comment is clearly directed at the audience in whatever current situation of 'discipline' they might find themselves. On the whole, a post-70 date seems to fit these details best. It is not really until the 60s that we know of any significant Christian leaders dying who had been involved significantly in Diaspora mission. The author does not tell the audience not to rely on Levitical means of atonement but instead bolsters their confidence in Christ as the definitive alternative. The reference to strange practices in 13:9–10 seems far more appropriate in a context where Jews are looking to find substitutes for the temple than in one where a Jew could fall back on the daily, constant and dependable sacrifices of an existing one.

---

[18] I tried to develop this latter hypothesis in *Understanding* 88–105. As will quickly become apparent, my views have developed considerably since writing those very tentative suggestions.

[19] E.g. Josephus: *Ant.* 4:224–57 *Ap.* 2:77, 193–8 and Clement: *1 Clem.* 41:2.

I close, then, with more speculation, fully acknowledging the impossibility of reaching any definitive explanation. In my opinion, however, something like the following scenario accounts for all the relevant data in Hebrews. A Gentile Christian community in Rome in the early 70s is waning not only in its commitment to Christ, but indeed is beginning to wonder about its earlier attraction to Judaism itself. One can suppose that many of the earliest Gentile Christians were individuals who had been initially attracted to Judaism, only subsequently to adopt a Christian Jewish perspective. Further, it is quite possible that Roman Gentile Christianity had a character more 'conservative' than even the apostle Paul.

When Rome destroyed Jerusalem, such individuals found themselves caught not only between Rome and Christ, but between the empire and Christianity's Jewish substratum. On the one hand, they faced the shame of association, not only with Christianity, but with the destroyed Israel. They would have witnessed the parading of conquered Jews about the streets of Rome. Was the Jewish Messiah not to reign on earth and Israel to become the renewed nation to which all the peoples of the world would flock? It is not at all clear to what extent Christians before the destruction of the temple expected its destruction.[20] Further, if the earlier writings of the New Testament are any indication, the earliest Christian message did not significantly engage the question of whether Christ's sacrificial death was *fully* sufficient for sins. Indeed, if Acts 21:26 is any indication, Christian Jews must have continued to see a role for the temple within Christianity.

It is into this gap that the author of Hebrews would then interject his radical message. The destruction of the Jewish temple and its sacrificial system did not detract in any way from the validity of true Jewish faith, let alone from the truth of the Christ. The audience obviously found the Jewish faith attractive and no doubt was inclined to accept the validity of its Scriptures if it could only overcome the cognitive dissonance of recent events. In this light, the author infolds an ingenious argument. He does not, as other New Testament authors, focus on the destruction of the Jerusalem temple as the result of Israel's sin or rejection of the Christ.[21] Rather, he argues that the Levitical system was never meant to take away sin.

---

[20] E.g. 2 Thess. 2 gives no indication that the temple will be destroyed even though the 'man of lawlessness' apparently is to set himself up there as god (2 Thess. 2:4).

[21] E.g. Matt. 22:7; 27:25; Luke 21:22; Acts 28:28. It is of course not unlikely that the author had such a perspective. His position might be similar to that of Stephen in Acts 7:48 – Israel is being disciplined in part for its failure to recognize the proper relationship between God and his 'house'.

In the consummation of the ages, Christ has forever atoned for sins. Christ has more than adequately atoned for the prior sins that the audience had committed in ignorance (cf. 9:7) back when they attempted to appease the gods by way of 'dead works' (6:1).[22] Further, they need not worry about any future need for sacrifice to assuage God's wrath as long as they continue in faith.[23] No, the path to wrath would be a failure to endure and to maintain the confession of faith. We have here on earth no remaining city, whether Jerusalem or Rome. And we need not fear the wrath of the king. Sometimes God delivers and sometimes he does not. But a better country awaits and a city is prepared. In just a little while, the one who is coming will arrive and will not delay. In the meantime, the audience must live on in faithfulness.

---

[22] Yet another Gentile theme (cf. Acts 17:30).

[23] Let us not forget that belief in gods was near universal, as was the need to assuage their wrath. Hebrews provides a compelling and holistic termination of sacrifice that surely would have been attractive to any ancient.

BIBLIOGRAPHY

Anderson, C. P. 'Who Are the Heirs of the New Age in the Epistle to the Hebrews?'. *Apocalyptic and the New Testament: Essays in Honor of J. Louis Martyr.* Ed. by J. Marcus and M. L. Soards. JSNTSS 24 (Sheffield: JSOT Press, 1989) 255–77.

Andriessen, P. 'Das größere und vollkommenere Zelt (Hebr 9,11)'. *BZ* 15 (1971) 76–82.

— 'La teneur judéo-chrétienne de Hé 16 et II 14B–III2'. *NovT* 18 (1976) 293–304.

Andriessen, P. and A. Lenglet. *De brief aan de Hebreeën* (Roermond: Roman and Zonen, 1971).

Attridge, H. W. *The Epistle to the Hebrews* (Philadelphia: Fortress Press, 1989).

— '"Heard Because of his Reverence" (Heb 5:7)'. *JBL* 98 (1979) 90–3.

— 'The Uses of Antithesis in Hebrews 8–10'. *HTR* 79 (1986) 1–9.

Bacon, B. W. *The Gospel of the Hellenists* (New York: Holt, 1933).

Barrett, C. K. *Acts.* Vol. 1 (Edinburgh: T&T Clark, 1994).

— 'The Eschatology of the Epistle to the Hebrews'. *The Background of the New Testament and its Eschatology: Studies in Honour of C. H. Dodd.* Ed. by W. D. Davies and D. Daube (Cambridge: Cambridge University Press, 1964 (1954)) 363–93.

— *The Gospel According to St. John: An Introduction with Commentary and Notes on the Greek Text* (Philadelphia: Westminster Press, 1961).

Bauer, D. R. *The Structure of Matthew's Gospel: A Study in Literary Design.* JSNTSS 31 (Sheffield: JSOT Press, 1988).

Bengel, A. *Gnomon of the New Testament.* Trans. by J. Bryce. 6th edn (Edinburgh: T&T Clark, 1866).

Biesenthal, J. *Der Trostschreiben des Apostels Paulus an die Hebräer* (Leipzig: Fernau, 1878).

Bitzer, L. 'The Rhetorical Situation'. *Philosophy and Rhetoric* 1 (1968) 1–14.

Bornkamm, G. 'Das Bekenntnis im Hebräerbrief'. *Theologische Blätter* 21 (1942) 56–66.

Braun, H. *An die Hebräer.* HNT 14 (Tübingen: Mohr/Siebeck, 1984).

— *Gesammelte Studien zum Neuen Testament* (Tübingen: Mohr/Siebeck, 1967)

— 'Die Gewinnung der Gewißheit in dem Hebräerbrief'. *TLZ* 96 (1971) 321–30.

— 'Qumran und das Neue Testament: Ein Bericht über 10 Jahre Forschung (1950–59): Hebräer'. *TRu* 30 (1964) 1–38.

Brooks, W. E. 'The Perpetuity of Christ's Sacrifice in the Epistle to the Hebrews'. *JBL* 89 (1970) 205–14.

Brown, R. E. *The Death of the Messiah: From Gethsemene to the Grave*. Vol. 1 (London: Geoffrey Chapman, 1994).

— *The Gospel According to John*. Vol. 2. Anchor Bible (London: Geoffrey Chapman, 1966).

Brown, R. E. and J. P. Meier. *Antioch and Rome: New Testament Cradles of Catholic Christianity* (London: Geoffrey Chapman, 1983).

Bruce, F. F. *The Epistle to the Hebrews* (Grand Rapids, MI: Eerdmans, 1964).

— '"To the Hebrews" or "To the Essenes"'. *NTS* 9 (1963) 17–32.

Buchanan, G. W. 'Eschatology and the "End of Days"'. *JNES* 20 (1961) 188–93.

— 'The Present State of Scholarship in Hebrews'. *Christianity, Judaism and other Greco-Roman Cults*. Vol. 1. Festschrift for M. Smith. Ed. by J. Neusner (Leiden: E. J. Brill, 1975) 299–330.

— *To the Hebrews: Translation, Comment and Conclusions* (Garden City, NY: Doubleday, 1972).

Burtness, J. H. 'Plato, Philo and the Author of Hebrews', *LQ* 2 (1958) 54–64.

Caird, G. B. 'The Exegetical Method of the Epistle to the Hebrews'. *CJT* 5 (1959) 44–51.

— *The Basis of a Christian Hope* (London: Duckworth, 1970).

— 'Son by Appointment'. *New Testament Age: Essays in Honor of B. Reicke, I*. Ed. by W. C. Weinrich (Macon, GA: Mercer University Press, 1984) 73–81.

Chapman, J. 'Aristion, Author of the Epistle to the Hebrews'. *RBén* 22 (1905) 50–62.

Chatman, S. *Story and Discourse: Narrative Structure in Fiction and Film* (Ithaca, NY: Cornell University Press, 1978).

Cockerill, G. 'Heb. 1:1–14, *1 Clem*. 36:1–6 and the High Priest Title'. *JBL* 97 (1978) 437–40.

— *The Melchizedek Christology in Heb. 7:1–28* (Ann Arbor, MI: University Microfilms International, 1979).

Cody, A. *Heavenly Sanctuary and Liturgy in the Epistle to the Hebrews: The Achievement of Salvation in the Epistle's Perspectives* (Meinrad, IN: Grail, 1960).

Collins, J. J. *The Apocalyptic Imagination: An Introduction to the Jewish Matrix of Christianity* (New York: Crossroad, 1989).

— 'Genre, Ideology and Social Movements in Jewish Apocalypticism'. *Mysteries and Revelations: Apocalyptic Studies since the Uppsala Colloquium*. Ed. by J. J. Collins and J. H. Charlesworth (Sheffield: JSOT Press, 1991) 11–32.

Collins, J. J. and G. E. Sterling. *Hellenism in the Land of Israel* (Notre Dame Press, IN: University of Notre Dame Press, 2001).

Cosby, M. *The Rhetorical Composition and Function of Hebrews 11: In Light of Example Lists of Antiquity* (Macon, GA: Mercer University Press, 1988).

Cotterell, P. and M. Turner. *Linguistics and Biblical Interpretation* (Downer's Grove, IL: InterVarsity Press, 1989).

Croy, N. C. *Endurance in Suffering: Hebrews 12:1–13 in its Rhetorical, Religious, and Philosophical Context*. SNTSMS 98 (Cambridge: Cambridge University Press, 1998).

Cullmann, O. *Christology of the New Testament* (London: SCM Press, 1959).

— *The Johannine Circle* (London: SCM Press, 1976).

Culpepper, R. A. *The Anatomy of the Fourth Gospel: A Study in Literary Design* (Philadelphia: Fortress Press, 1983).

D'Angelo, M. R. *Moses in the Epistle to the Hebrews*. SBLDS 42 (Missoula, MT: Scholars Press, 1979).

Dahl, N. 'A New and Living Way: The Approach to God According to Hebrews 10:19–25'. *Int* 5 (1951) 401–12.

Davies, J. H. 'The Heavenly Work of Christ'. *TU* 102 (1968) 384–89.

Dawsey, J. *The Lukan Voice: Confusion and Irony in the Gospel of Luke* (Macon, GA: Mercer University Press, 1986).

Demarest, B. *A History of Interpretation of Hebrews 7,1–10 from the Reformation to the Present*. BGBE 19 (Tübingen: Mohr/Siebeck, 1976).

Derrida, J. *Of Grammatology* (Baltimore, MD: Johns Hopkins University Press, 1974 [1967]).

— *Positions*. Trans. by A. Bass (Chicago: University of Chicago Press, 1981).

deSilva, D. A. 'Despising Shame: A Cultural-Anthropological Investigation of the Epistle to the Hebrews'. *JBL* 113 (1994) 439–61.

— *Despising Shame: Honor Discourse and Community Maintenance in the Epistle to the Hebrews*. SBLDS 152 (Atlanta: Scholars Press, 1995).

— *Perseverance in Gratitude: A Socio-Rhetorical Commentary on the Epistle 'to the Hebrews'* (Grand Rapids, MI: Eerdmans, 2000).

Dey, L. K. K. *The Intermediary World and Patterns of Perfection in Philo and Hebrews*. SBLDS 25 (Missoula, MT: Scholars Press, 1975).

Dibelius, M. 'Der himmlische Kultus nach dem Hebräerbrief'. *Botschaft und Geschichte: Gesammelte Studien. Vol. 2: Zum Urchristentum und zur hellenistischen Religionsgeschichte*. Ed. by G. Bornkamm and H. Kraft (Tübingen: Mohr/Siebeck, 1956) 160–76.

— *James: A Commentary on the Epistle of James*. Trans. by M. A. Williams. Hermeneia (Philadelphia: Fortress Press, 1976).

Donfried, K. P., ed. *The Romans Debate*. Rev. edn. (Peabody, MA: Hendrickson, 1991).

Dunn, J. D. G. *Christology in the Making: An Inquiry into the Origins of the Doctrine of the Incarnation*. 2nd edn (London: SCM Press, 1989).

— *The Epistle to the Colossians and Philemon: A Commentary on the Greek Text* (Grand Rapids, MI: Eerdmans, 1996).

— 'Once More, ΠΙΣΤΙΣ ΧΡΙΣΤΟΥ'. *SBLSP* (1991) 730–44.

— *The Partings of the Ways: Between Christianity and Judaism and their Significance for the Character of Christianity* (London: SCM Press, 1991).

— *Romans 1–8* (Dallas: Word, 1988).

— *The Theology of St. Paul the Apostle* (Grand Rapids, MI: Eerdmans, 1998).

— *Unity and Diversity in the New Testament: An Inquiry into the Character of Earliest Christianity*. 2nd edn (London: SCM Press, 1990).

Dunnill, J. *Covenant and Sacrifice in the Letter to the Hebrews*. SNTSMS 75 (Cambridge: Cambridge University Press, 1992).

DuPlessis, P. ΤΕΛΕΙΟΣ: *The Idea of Perfection in the New Testament* (Kampen: Kok, 1959).

Eisele, W. *Ein unerschütterliches Reich: Die mittelplatonische Umformung des Parusiegedankens im Hebräerbrief*. BZNW 116 (Berlin: de Gruyter, 2003).

Eisenbaum, P. M. *The Jewish Heroes of Christian History: Hebrews 11 in Literary Context*. SBLDS 156 (Atlanta: Scholars Press, 1997).

Ellingworth, P. *The Epistle to the Hebrews: A Commentary on the Greek Text* (Grand Rapids, MI: Eerdmans, 1993).

Firth, R. 'The Anatomy of Certainty'. *PhRev* (1967) 3–27.

Fish, S. *Is there a Text in this Class?: The Authority of Interpretive Communities* (Cambridge, MA: Harvard University Press, 1980).

Fitzmyer, J. A. *Romans: A New Translation with Introduction and Commentary* (London: Geoffrey Chapman, 1993).

Fletcher-Louis, C. *Luke–Acts: Angels, Christology and Soteriology*. WUNT 94 (Tübingen: Mohr/Siebeck, 1997).

Ford, J. M. 'The Mother of Jesus and the Authorship of the Epistle to the Hebrews'. *The University of Dayton Review* 11 (1975) 49–56.

Fowl, S. E. and L. G. Jones, *Reading in Communion: Scripture and Ethics in Christian Life* (Grand Rapids, MI: Eerdmans, 1991).

Frankowski, J. 'Early Christian Hymns Recorded in the New Testament: A Reconsideration of the Question in the Light of Heb 1,3', *BZ* 27 (1982) 186.

Frye, N. *The Anatomy of Criticism* (Princeton, NJ: Princeton University Press, 1957).

— *Fables of Identity: Studies in Poetic Mythology* (New York: Harcourt, Brace & World, 1963).

— *The Stubborn Structure: Essays on Criticism and Society* (Ithaca, NY: Cornell University Press, 1970).

Funk, R. W. *Language, Hermeneutic, and Word of God: The Problem of Language in the New Testament and Contemporary Theology* (New York: Harper & Row, 1966).

Gelardini, G., ed. *Hebrews: Contemporary Methods – New Insights* (Leiden: E. J. Brill, 2005).

Giles, P. 'The Son of Man in Hebrews'. *ExpTim* 86 (1975) 328–32.

Glaze, R. E., Jr. *No Easy Salvation* (Zachary, LA: Insight, 1966).

Goldstein, J. 'The Origins of the Doctrine of Creation Ex Nihilo'. *JJS* 35 (1984) 127–35.

Grässer, E. *Der Alte Bund im Neuen*. WUNT 35 (Tübingen: Mohr/Siebeck, 1985).

— *An die Hebräer (1–6)*. Vol. 1 (Zürich: Benziger Verlag, 1990).

— *An die Hebräer (7,1–10,18)*. Vol. 2 (Zürich: Benziger Verlag, 1993).

— *An die Hebräer*. Vol. 3 (Zürich: Benziger Verlag, 1997).

— *Der Glaube im Hebräerbrief*. Münchener theologische Studien 2 (Marburg: Elwert, 1965).

— 'Der Hebräerbrief 1938–1963'. *TRu* 30 (1964–65) 138–236.

Greimas, A. *Sémantique structurale* (Paris: Librairie Larousse, 1966).

— *Du Sens* (Paris: Seuil, 1970).

Grotius, H. *Annotationes in Acta Apostolorum et in epistolas catholicas* (Paris, 1646).

Guthrie, G. H. *The Structure of Hebrews: A Text-Linguistic Analysis*. NovTSup 73 (Leiden: E. J. Brill, 1994).

Gyllenberg, R. 'Die Christologie des Hebräerbriefes'. *ZST* 11 (1934) 662–90.

Hammerton-Kelly, R. G. *Pre-existence Wisdom and the Son of Man: A Study of the Idea of Pre-existence in the New Testament*. SNTSMS 21 (Cambridge: Cambridge University Press, 1973).

Hanson, A. T. *Jesus Christ in the Old Testament* (London: SPCK, 1965).

Häring, T. 'Über einige Grundgedanken des Hebräerbriefs'. *Monatsschrift für Pastoraltheologie* 17 (1920–1) 260–76.

Hay, D. M. *Glory and the Right Hand: Psalm 110 in Early Christianity*, SBLMS 18 (Nashville: Abingdon Press, 1973).

Hays, R. B. *The Faith of Jesus Christ: An Investigation of the Narrative Substructure of Galatians 3:1–4:11*, 2nd edn (Grand Rapids, MI: Eerdmans, 2002).

— 'Πίστις and Pauline Christology: What is at Stake?'. *Pauline Theology, Volume IV: Looking Back, Pressing on*. Ed. by E. E. Johnson and D. M. Hays 35–60.

Hengel, M. *Judaism and Hellenism* (Minneapolis: Fortress Press, 1974).

— *The 'Hellenization' of Judaea in the First Century after Christ* (Philadelphia: Trinity Press, 1989).

Héring, J. *The Epistle to the Hebrews*. Trans. by A. W. Heathcote and P. J. Allcock (London: Epworth, 1970 (1954)).

Hofius, O. *Katapausis: Die Vorstellung vom endzeitlichen Ruheort im Hebräerbrief*. WUNT 11 (Tübingen: Mohr/Siebeck, 1970).

— 'Die Unabänderlichkeit des göttlichen Heilsratschlusse: Erwägungen zur Herkunft eines neutestamentlichen Theologumenon', *ZNW* 64 (1973) 135–6.

— *Der Vorhang vor dem Thron Gottes: Eine exegetisch-religionsgeschichtliche Untersuchung zu Hebräer 6,19f. und 10,19f*. WUNT 14 (Tübingen: Mohr/Siebeck, 1972).

Holsten, C. *Exegetische Untersuchung über Hebräer 10:20* (Bern, 1875).

Horton, F. L. *The Melchizedek Tradition: A Critical Examination of the Sources to the Fifth Century A.D. and in the Epistle to the Hebrews*. SNTSMS 30 (Cambridge: Cambridge University Press, 1976).

Hughes, G. *Hebrews and Hermeneutics: The Epistle to the Hebrews as a New Testament Example of Biblical Interpretation*, SNTSMS 36 (Cambridge: Cambridge University Press, 1979).

Hughes, J. J. 'Hebrews IX 15ff. and Galatians III 15ff.: A Study in Covenant Practice and Procedure'. *NovT* 21 (1979) 27–96.

Hughes, P. E. 'The Epistle to the Hebrews'. *The New Testament and its Modern Interpreters*. Ed. by E. J. Epp and G. W. MacRae (Atlanta: Scholars Press, 1989) 351–70.

Hurst, L. D. 'The Christology of Hebrews 1 and 2'. *The Glory of Christ in the New Testament: Studies in Christology in Memory of George Bradford Caird*. Ed. by L. D. Hurst and N. T. Wright (Oxford: Clarendon Press, 1987) 151–64.

— *The Epistle to the Hebrews: Its Background of Thought*. SNTSMS 65 (Cambridge: Cambridge University Press, 1990).

— 'Eschatology and "Platonism" in the Epistle to the Hebrews'. *SBLSP* (1984) 41–74.

'How "Platonic" are Heb. viii.5 and ix.23f?'. *JTS* 34 (1983) 156–68.

Isaacs, M. *Sacred Space: An Approach to the Theology of the Epistle to the Hebrews*. JSNTSS 73 (Sheffield: JSOT Press, 1992).

Iser, W. *The Implied Reader: Patterns of Communication in Prose Fiction From Bunyan to Beckett* (Baltimore, MD: Johns Hopkins University Press, 1974).

— 'The Reading Process: A Phenomenological Approach', in *Reader-Response Criticism: From Formalism to Post-Structuralism*. Ed. by J. P. Tompkins (Baltimore, MD: Johns Hopkins University Press, 1980) 50–69.

Jakobson, R. 'Closing Statement: Linguistics and Poetics'. *Style in Language*. Ed. by T. A. Sebeok (Cambridge, MA: MIT Press, 1960) 350–77.

Jeremias, J. 'Hebräer 10,20: τουτ' ἐστιν τῆς σαρκὸς αὐτοῦ'. *ZNW* 62 (1971) 131.

Johnsson, W. G. 'The Cultus of Hebrews in Twentieth-Century Scholarship'. *ExpTim* 89 (1977–78) 104–8.

— 'Defilement and Purgation in the Book of Hebrews'. PhD dissertation (Vanderbilt, 1973).

Käsemann, E. *The Wandering People of God: An Investigation of the Letter to the Hebrews.* Trans. by R. A. Harrisville and I. L. Sandberg (Minneapolis: Augsburg, 1984 [1939]).

Kennedy, George A. *New Testament Interpretation through Rhetorical Criticism* (Chapel Hill: University of North Carolina Press, 1984).

Kingsbury, J. D. 'Reflections on the Reader'. *NTS* 34 (1988) 442–60.

Kistemaker, S. *The Psalm Citations in the Epistle to the Hebrews* (Amsterdam: Soest, 1961).

Klappert, B. *Die Eschatologie des Hebräerbriefs* (Munich: Chr. Kaiser Verlag, 1969).

Klemm, D. *The Hermeneutic Theory of Paul Ricoeur: A Constructive Analysis* (London: Associated University Press, 1983).

Knox, E. A. 'The Samaritans and the Epistle to the Hebrews'. *Churchman* 22 (1927) 184–93.

Koester, C. R. *The Dwelling of God: The Tabernacle in the Old Testament, Intertestamental Jewish Literature, and the New Testament.* CBQMS 22 (Washington, DC: Catholic Biblical Association of America, 1989).

— *Hebrews* (New York: Doubleday, 2001).

— *Hebrews: A New Translation with Introduction and Commentary* (New York: Doubleday, 2001).

Koester, H. 'Die Auslegung der Abraham-Verheissung in Hebräer 6'. *Studien zur Theologie der alttestamentlichen Überlieferung: Festschrift für Gerhardt von Rad.* Ed. by R. Rendtorff and K. Koch (Neukirchen: Moers, 1961).

— 'Outside the Camp'. *HTR* 55 (1962) 299–315.

Kögel, J. 'Der Begriff τελειοῦν im Hebräerbrief im Zusammenhang mit dem neutestamentlichen Sprachgebrauch'. *Theologische Studien für M. Kähler* Ed. by F. Giesebrecht (Leipzig: Deichert, 1905) 37–68.

— *Der Sohn und die Söhne: Eine exegetische Studie zu Hebräer 2,5–18.* BFCT 8, 5–6 (Gütersloh: Bertelsman, 1904).

Kosmala, H. *Hebräer–Essener–Christen* (Leiden: E. J. Brill, 1971).

Kuss, O. *Der Brief an die Hebräer* (Regensburg: Pustet, 1966).

— 'Der Verfasser des Hebräerbriefes als Seelsorger'. *TTZ* 67 (1958) 1–12.

Lane, W. L. *Hebrews 1–8* (Dallas: Word, 1991).

— *Hebrews 9–13* (Dallas: Word, 1991).

Laub, F. *Bekenntnis und Auslegung: Die paränetische Funktion der Christologie im Hebräerbrief.* Biblische Untersuchungen 15 (Regensburg: Pustet, 1980).

Lee, E. 'Words Denoting "Pattern" in the New Testament'. *NTS* 8 (1962) 167–9.

Lehne, S. *The New Covenant in Hebrews.* JSNTSS 44 (Sheffield: JSOT Press, 1990).

Lincoln, A. T. '"Paul the Visionary": The Setting and Significance of the Rapture to Paradise in II Corinthians XII.1–10'. *NTS* 25 (1979) 211–14.

Lindars, B. 'The Rhetorical Structure of Hebrews' *NTS* 35 (1989) 382–406.

— *The Theology of the Letter to the Hebrews* (Cambridge: Cambridge University Press, 1991).

Linss, W. C. 'Logical Terminology in the Epistle to the Hebrews'. *CTM* 37 (1966) 365–9.

Loader, W. R. G. *Sohn und Hoherpriester: Eine traditionsgeschichtliche Untersuchung zur Christologie des Hebräerbriefes.* WMANT 53 (Neukirchen: Neukirchener Verlag, 1981).

Löhr, H. 'Thronversammlung und preisender Tempel: Beobachtungen am himmlischen Heiligtum im Hebräerbrief und in den Sabbatopferliedern aus Qumran'. *Königsherrschaft Gottes und himmlischer Welt im Judentum, Urchristentum und in der hellenistischen Welt.* Ed. by M. Hengel and A. M. Schwemer (Tübingen: Mohr/Siebeck, 1991) 185–205.

— *Umkehr und Sünde im Hebräerbrief.* BZNW 73 (Berlin: de Gruyter, 1994).

Longenecker, R. *Biblical Exegesis in the Apostolic Period* (Grand Rapids, MI: Eerdmans, 1975).

Longman, T. *Literary Approaches to Biblical Interpretation* (Grand Rapids, MI: Zondervan, 1987).

Luck, U. 'Himmlisches und irdisches Geschehen im Hebräerbrief: Ein Beitrag zum Problem des "historischen Jesus" im Urchristentum'. *NovT* 6 (1963) 192–215.

McGrath, J. F. 'Change in Christology: New Testament Models and the Contemporary Task'. New Testament Seminar, University of Durham (Spring 1996).

McGrath, J. J. *Through Eternal Spirit: An Historical Study of the Exegesis of Hebrews 9:13–14* (Rome: Pontificia Universitas Gregoriana, 1961).

McKelvey, R. J. *The New Temple: The Church in the New Testament* (London: Oxford University Press, 1969).

McKnight, E. *The Bible and the Reader: An Introduction to Literary Criticism* (Philadelphia: Fortress Press, 1985).

MacRae, G. 'Heavenly Temple and Eschatology in the Letter to the Hebrews'. *Semeia* 12 (1978) 179–99.

Malina, B. M. *The Social World of Jesus* (New York: Routledge, 1996).

Manson, W. *The Epistle to the Hebrews: An Historical and Theological Reconsideration* (London: Hodder & Stoughton, 1951).

Martin, D. B. *The Corinthian Body* (New Haven, CT: Yale University Press, 1995).

Meier, J. P. 'Symmetry and Theology in the Old Testament Citations of Heb 1,5–14'. *Bib* 66 (1985) 504–33.

Ménégoz, E. *La théologie de l'épître aux Hébreux* (Paris: Fischbacher, 1894).

Michel, O. *Der Brief an die Hebräer.* 14th edn (Göttingen: Vandenhoeck & Ruprecht, 1984 (1936)).

— 'Die Lehre von der christlichen Vollkommenheit nach der Anschauung des Hebräerbriefes'. *TSK* 106 (1934–5) 333–55.

Mitchell, M. *Paul and the Rhetoric of Reconciliation: An Exegetical Investigation of the Language and Composition of 1 Corinthians* (Louisville, KY: Westminster/John Knox, 1991).

Moffatt, J. *The Epistle to the Hebrews* (Edinburgh: T&T Clark, 1924).

Montefiore, H. *The Epistle to the Hebrews* (London: A. & C. Black, 1964).

Moore, S. *Literary Criticism and the Gospels: The Theoretical Challenge* (New Haven, CT: Yale University Press, 1989).

Moule, C. F. D. *The Birth of the New Testament* (London: Adam & Charles Black, 1962).

Murphey-O'Connor, J. 'Qumran and the New Testament'. *The New Testament and its Modern Interpreters*. Ed. by E. J. Epp and G. W. MacRae (Atlanta: Scholars Press, 1989) 55–71.

Nairne, A. *The Epistle of Priesthood* (Edinburgh: T&T Clark, 1913).

Nauck, W. 'Zum Aufbau des Hebräerbriefes'. *Judentum, Urchristentum, Kirche: Festschrift für Joachim Jeremias*. Ed. by W. Eltester. BZNW 26 (Berlin: Alfred Töpelman, 1960) 199–206.

Nissilä, K. *Der Hohepriestmotiv in Hebräerbrief: Eine exegetische Untersuchung* (Helsinki: Oy Liitun Kirjapaino, 1979).

Nomoto, S. 'Herkunft und Struktur der Hohenpriestervorstellung im Hebräerbrief'. *NovT* 10 (1968) 10–25.

Patte, D. *What is Structural Exegesis?* (Philadelphia: Fortress Press, 1976).

Peel, M. 'Gnostic Eschatology and the New Testament'. *NovT* 12 (1970) 158.

Petersen, N. *Literary Criticism for New Testament Critics* (Philadelphia: Fortress Press, 1978).

— 'Literary Criticism in Biblical Studies'. *Orientation by Disorientation: Studies in Literary Criticism Presented in Honor of William A. Beardslee*. Ed. by R. A. Spencer. PTMS 35 (Pittsburgh: Pickwick Press, 1980).

— *Rediscovering Paul: Philemon and the Sociology of Paul's Narrative World* (Philadelphia: Fortress Press, 1985).

Peterson, D. *Hebrews and Perfection: An Examination of the Concept of Perfection in the Epistle to the Hebrews*. SNTSMS 47 (Cambridge: Cambridge University Press, 1982).

Pierce, C. A. *Conscience in the New Testament* (Chicago: Allenson, 1955).

Ploeg, J. van der. 'L'exégèse de l'Ancien Testament dans l'épître aux Hébreux'. *RB* (1947) 187–228.

Pollock, J. 'Criteria and our Knowledge of the Material World'. *PhRev* (1967) 55–60.

Powell, M. A. *What is Narrative Criticism?* (Minneapolis: Fortress Press, 1990).

Rhoads, D. and D. Michie. *Mark as Story: An Introduction to the Narrative of a Gospel* (Philadelphia: Fortress Press, 1982).

Ricoeur, P. *Interpretation Theory: Discourse and the Surplus of Meaning* (Fort Worth, TX: Christian University Press, 1976).

— 'The Narrative Function'. *Semeia* 13 (1978) 183–4.

— *The Rule of Metaphor* (London: Routledge & Kegan Paul, 1978 (Fr. 1975)).

—*Time and Narrative*. Vol. 1. Trans. by K. McLaughlin and D. Pellauer (Chicago: University of Chicago Press, 1984).

Riggenbach, E. *Der Brief an die Hebräer*. 3rd edn (Leipzig: Deichert, 1922).

Rissi, M. *Die Theologie des Hebräerbriefs*. WUNT 41 (Tübingen: Mohr/Siebeck, 1987).

Rose, C. *Die Wolke der Zeugen: Eine exegetisch-traditionsgeschichtliche Untersuchung zu Hebräer 10,32–12,3*. WUNT 60 (Tübingen: Mohr/Siebeck, 1994).

— 'Verheißung und Erfüllung: Zum Verständnis von ἐπαγγελία im Hebräerbrief'. *BZ* 33 (1989) 60–80, 178–91.

Rowland, C. *The Open Heaven: A Study of Apocalyptic in Judaism and Early Christianity* (London: SPCK, 1982).

Runia, D. T. *Philo in Early Christian Literature: A Survey.* CRINT 3 (Minneapolis: Fortress Press, 1993).

Salom, A. P. 'TA ΆΓΙΑ in the Epistle to the Hebrews'. *AUSS* 5 (1967) 59–70.

Sanders, E. P. *Paul and Palestinian Judaism: A Comparison of Patterns of Religion* (London: SCM Press, 1977).

Schenck, K. L. *A Brief Guide to Philo* (Louisville, KY: Westminster/John Knox, 2005).

— 'A Celebration of the Enthroned Son: The Catena of Hebrews 1'. *JBL* 120 (2001) 469–85.

— 'Keeping His Appointment: Creation and Enthronement in the Epistle to the Hebrews'. *JSNT* 66 (1997) 91–117.

— '*Philo and the Epistle to the Hebrews*: Ronald Williamson's Study after Thirty Years', *SPhA* 14 (2002) 112–35.

— *Understanding the Book of Hebrews: The Story behind the Sermon* (Louisville, KY: Westminster/John Knox, 2003).

Schenke, H.-M. 'Erwägungen zum Rätsel des Hebräerbriefes'. *Neues Testament und christliche Existenz: Festschrift für Herbert Braun.* Ed. by H. D. Betz and L. Schottroff (Tübingen: Mohr/Siebeck, 1973) 421–37.

Schierse, F. J. *Verheissung und Heilsvollendung: Zur theologischen Grundfrage des Hebräerbriefes*, MThS.H 9 (Munich: Zink, 1955).

Scholer, J. M. *Proleptic Priests: Priesthood in the Epistle to the Hebrews.* JSNTSS 49 (Sheffield: JSOT Press, 1991).

Schrenk, G. 'ἱερός κτλ.', *TDNT* Vol. 3. Ed. by G. Kittel. Trans. by G. W. Bromiley (Grand Rapids, MI: Eerdmans, 1965) 221–47.

Schröger, F. *Der Verfasser des Hebräerbriefes als Schriftausleger.* Biblische Untersuchungen 4 (Regensburg: Pustet, 1968).

Scobie, C. H. H. 'The Origins and Development of Samaritan Christianity' *NTS* 19 (1973) 390–414.

Seeberg, A. *Der Brief an die Hebräer* (Leipzig: Quelle & Meyer, 1912).

Silva, M. 'Perfection and Eschatology in Hebrews'. *WTJ* 39 (1976) 60–71.

Sowers, S. G. *The Hermeneutics of Philo and Hebrews* (Zürich: EVZ-Verlag, 1965).

Spicq, C. *L'épître aux Hébreux.* 2 vols. EBib (Paris: Gabalda, 1952–53).

— 'L'épître aux Hébreux, Apollos, Jean-Baptiste, les hellénistes et Qumran'. *RevQ* 1 (1959) 365–90.

Stegemann, E. W. and W. Stegemann. 'Does the Cultic Language in Hebrews Represent Sacrificial Metaphors?: Reflections on Some Basic Problems'. *Hebrews: Contemporary Methods – New Insights.* Ed. by G. Gelardini (Leiden: E. J. Brill, 2005) 13–23.

Stemberger, G. 'Review of *Der Vorhang vor dem Thron Gottes: Eine exegetisch-religionsgeschichtliche Untersuchung zu Hebräer 6,19f. und 10,19f.' Kairos* 17 (1975) 303–6.

Sterling, G. E. '*Creatio Temporalis, Aeterna, vel Continua?*: An Analysis of the Thought of Philo of Alexandria'. *SPhA* 4 (1992) 15–41.

— 'Prepositional Metaphysics in Jewish Wisdom Speculation and Early Christological Hymns'. SPhA 9 (1997) 233.

— 'Ontology versus Eschatology: Tensions between Author and Community'. *SPhA* 13 (2001) 208–10.

Stuckenbruck, L. T. *Angel Veneration and Christology: A Study in Early Judaism and the Christology of the Apocalypse of John* WUNT 70 (Tübingen: Mohr/Siebeck, 1995).

Swetnam, J. "'The Greater and More Perfect Tent.' A Contribution to the Discussion of Hebrews 9,11'. *Bib* 47 (1966) 91–106.

— *Jesus and Isaac: A Study of the Epistle to the Hebrews in the Light of the Aqedah*. AnBib 94 (Rome: Biblical Institute Press, 1981).

Synge, F. C. *Hebrews and the Scriptures* (London: SPCK, 1959).

Theiler, W. *Die Vorbereitung des Neuplatonismus* (Berlin: Weidmann, 1930).

Theissen, G. 'Review of *Der Vorhang vor dem Thron Gottes: Eine exegetisch-religiongeschichtliche Untersuchung zu Hebräer 6,19f. und 10,19f.*' *TLZ* 99 (1974) 426–28.

— *Untersuchungen zum Hebräerbrief*. SNT 2 (Gütersloh: Mohn, 1969).

Thien, F. 'Analyse de l'épître aux Hébreux'. *RB* 11 (1902) 74–86.

Thiselton, A. C. *New Horizons in Hermeneutics: The Theory and Practice of Transforming Biblical Reading* (London: Harper Collins, 1992).

— *The Two Horizons: New Testament Hermeneutics and Philosophical Description with Special Reference to Heidegger, Bultmann, Gadamer, and Wittgenstein* (Exeter: Paternoster Press, 1980).

Thompson, J. W. *The Beginnings of Christian Philosophy: The Epistle to the Hebrews*. CBQMS 13 (Washington, DC: Catholic Biblical Association of America, 1982).

— 'The Impossible, the Necessary, and the Fitting: Logical Terminology in the Epistle to the Hebrews'. Hebrews and General Epistles Group. Society of Biblical Literature (1995).

— '"That Which Abides": Some Metaphysical Assumptions in the Epistle to the Hebrews'. PhD dissertation (Vanderbilt University, 1974).

Thurén, J. *Das Lobopfer der Hebräer: Studien zum Aufbau und Anliegen von Hebräerbrief 13* (Åbo: Åbo Akademi, 1973).

Tobin, T. H. *The Creation of Man: Philo and the History of Interpretation*. CBQMS 14 (Washington, DC: Catholic Biblical Association of America, 1983).

Übelacker, W. *Der Hebräerbrief als Appell: Untersuchungen zu exordium, narratio, und postscriptum (Hebr 1–2 und 13,22–25)*. ConBNT 21 (Lund: Almquist & Wiksell, 1989).

Vaganay, L. 'Le plan de l'épître aux Hébreux'. *Memorial Lagrange*. Ed. by L.-H. Vincent (Paris: Gabalda, 1940) 269–77.

van der Woude, A. S. 'Melchisedek als himmlische Erlösergestalt in den neugefundenen eschatologischen Midraschim aus Qumran Höhle XI'. *Oudtestamentische Studiën* 14 (1965) 354–73.

Vanhoozer, K. J. *Biblical Narrative in the Philosophy of Paul Ricoeur: A Study in Hermeneutics and Theology* (Cambridge: Cambridge University Press, 1990).

Vanhoye, A. 'L'οἰκουμένη dans l'épître aux Hébreux', *Bib* 45 (1964) 248–53.

— '"Par la tent plus grande et plus parfaite . . ." (He 9,11)'. *Bib* 46 (1965) 1–28.

— *La structure littéraire de l'épître aux Hébreux*. 2nd edn. StudNeot 1 (Paris: Desclée de Brouwer, 1976).

Vögtte, Anton 'Das Neue Testament und die Zukanft des Kosmos'. *Bibleb* 10 (1969) 239–54.

von Hofmann, J. C. K. *Der Brief an die Hebräer*, HSNT 5 (Nördlingen: Beck, 1873).

von Soden, H. F. *Urchristliche Literaturgeschichte: die Schriften des Neuen Testaments* (Berlin: Alexander Duncker, 1905).

Vos, G. 'Hebrews, Epistle of the *Diathêkê*'. *PTR* 14 (1916) 587–632.

— 'The Priesthood of Christ in the Epistle to the Hebrews'. *PTR* 5 (1907) 423–47, 579–604.

— *The Teaching of the Epistle to the Hebrews*. Ed. by J. Vos (Grand Rapids, MI: Eerdmans, 1956).

Watson, D. F. *Invention, Arrangement, and Style: Rhetorical Criticism of Jude and 2 Peter*. SBLDS 104 (Atlanta: Scholars Press, 1988).

Weiss, H.-F. *Der Brief an die Hebräer* (Göttingen: Vandenhoeck & Ruprecht, 1991).

Wenschkewitz, H. 'Die Spiritualisierung der Kultusbegriffe Tempel, Priester und Opfer im N.T.' *Angelos* 4 (1932) 70–230.

Westcott, B. F. *The Epistle to the Hebrews: The Greek Text with Notes and Essays*. 3rd edn (London: Macmillan, 1903).

Williamson, R. 'The Background of the Epistle to the Hebrews'. *ExpT* 87 (1976) 232–7.

— 'The Incarnation of the Logos in Hebrews'. *ExpT* 95 (1983) 4–8.

— *Philo and the Epistle to the Hebrews*. ALGHJ 4 (Leiden, E. J. Brill, 1970).

Wilson, R. McL. *Hebrews* (Grand Rapids, MI: Eerdmans, 1987).

Wimsatt, W. and M. Beardsley. 'The Intentional Fallacy'. *On Literary Intention*. Ed. by D. Newton-deMolina (Edinburgh: Edinburgh University Press, 1976) 1–13.

Windisch, H. *Der Hebräerbrief*. 2nd edn. HNT 14 (Tübingen: Mohr, 1931).

Winston, D. 'Creation ex nihilo Revisited: A Reply to Jonathan Goldstein'. *The Ancestral Philosophy: Hellenistic Philosophy in Second Temple Judaism: Essays of David Winston*. Ed. by G. E. Sterling (Providence, RI: Brown Judaic Studies, 2001) 117–27.

— 'Theory of Eternal Creation: *Prov.* 1.6–9'. *The Ancestral Philosophy: Hellenistic Philosophy in Second Temple Judaism: Essays of David Winston*. Ed. by G. E. Sterling (Providence, RI: Brown Judaic Studies, 2001) 79–80.

Wittgenstein, L. *Philosophical Investigations* (New York: Doubleday Anchor, 1966 [1953]).

Wolfson, H., *Philo: Foundations of Religious Philosophy in Judaism, Christianity, and Islam*. Vol. 1 (Cambridge, MA: Harvard University Press, 1947).

Wright, N. T. *The New Testament and the People of God: Christian Origins and the Question of God*. Vol. 1 (London: SPCK, 1992).

Yadin, Y. 'The Dead Sea Scrolls and the Epistle to the Hebrews'. *ScrHier* 4 (1958) 36–53.

Young, N. H. 'The Gospel According to Hebrews 9'. *NTS* 27 (1981) 198–210.

— 'τοῦτ' ἐστιν τῆς σαρκὸς αὐτοῦ (Heb. X.20)'. *NTS* 20 (1973) 100–4.

INDEX OF SUBJECTS AND AUTHORS

INDEX OF ANCIENT SOURCES